Mar.

CW00369704

# Discovering
# Churches
# and Churchyards

A guide to the architecture of English parish
churches from Anglo-Saxon times to 1900

Shire Publications

*To Grace Amena*

British Library Cataloguing in Publication Data: Child, Mark. Discovering Churches and Churchyards. – (Discovering series; no. 298) 1. Church architecture – England – History. I. Title 726.5'0942. ISBN-13: 978 0 7478 0659 2.

Front cover: *Puttenham, Hertfordshire. A small village church of the Home Counties type. Except for the fourteenth-century nave, which has later figurework in its tie-beam roof, the building is almost entirely of the fifteenth century. The flint-faced chancel, the squat tower of chequered flint and stone, and the brief touches of red roofing tiles all add great charm.*

Back cover: *Dennington, Suffolk. Box pews and medieval benches with exceptionally attractive carvings on their ends, as well as their backs, are important survivals here. The side chapels are separated from the main body of the church by intricately carved parclose screens.*

ACKNOWLEDGEMENTS
The photographs are by Cadbury Lamb, with the following exceptions: pages 15, 127 (bottom), 134 (bottom), 138 and 245, by Mark Child; pages 17 (bottom), 32 (top right), 48, by Sue Ross. The line drawings are by Dennis Lack.

*Published in 2007 by Shire Publications Ltd, Cromwell House, Church Street, Princes Risborough, Buckinghamshire HP27 9AA, UK. (Website: www.shirebooks.co.uk)*
*Copyright © 2007 by Mark Child. First published 2007. Number 298 in the Discovering series. ISBN-13: 978 0 7478 0659 2.*
*Mark Child is hereby identified as the author of this work in accordance with Section 77 of the Copyright, Designs and Patents Act, 1988.*

Printed in Malta by Gutenberg Press Ltd, Gudja Road, Tarxien PLA 19, Malta.

# Contents

*Orford, Suffolk. The village clusters about its church, built on a rise, close to the ruins of an earlier chancel; the Norman tower has large diagonal buttreses; the top stage with its flushwork parapet was completed in the third quarter of the twentieth century.*

*North Leigh, Oxfordshire. The late Anglo-Saxon tower has a pair of typically round-headed openings divided by a roll-neck shaft; the pitch of the former nave can be seen on the wall.*

# Introduction

This book tells how England's churches developed. For long periods, the architecture simply evolved; occasionally, persuasive factors imposed elements of taste and fashion that had nothing to do with evolution. Old churches have retained elements of both. Yet church architecture is really about those people who put up the first buildings; those by whose usage and needs they were later expanded or rebuilt from scratch, and those who could afford to influence design, arrangement and decoration. It is about the architects, masons and builders who built according to the requirements of their local communities, incorporating their own influences, and pouring their own souls into the work. Church architecture is also about the countless generations who used the church for worship, and those liturgists who determined its form and nature.

The churches of England are the nation's heritage; they thread through the history of the land, stretching almost two thousand years from Joseph of Arimathea's wattle and daub church at Glastonbury. They played their parts in border skirmishes, at times of invasion, and during the great battles of medieval England. They were central to the break with Rome and became a melting pot for architectural taste and fashion. Their beginnings were practical; yet they became a depository of architectural flotsam in which each constructional element and decorative feature, every fixture and fitting, was influenced by some trend or innovation of the moment.

Only in their purpose were they constant: the worship of the Christian God. Some churches soared in a forest of medieval vaulting while others hardly seemed to get off the ground because it was money that mattered. The people who had money built and embellished, apparently to the glory of God, but also to their own memory. Those who did not have money simply prayed quietly and hoped the calls on their church would not be too great.

An old church can give you a unique sense of the past. You can thrust your fingers into Anglo-Saxon carvings, as the original sculptor would have done as he blew the dust from his work for the first time and cleaned out the shape he had made. You can imagine how he was dressed, what food he had with him, and what was going on around him. And you can carry on doing this through page after page of history, written into the fabric, fixtures and fittings of every church in the land. You can see the ghosts of three-quarters pagan Anglo-Saxons, on knees trembling with scepticism, and half fearing the wrath of displaced gods. You can see the Georgian squire asleep in his high-backed pew, and the bewigged rector in his three-decker pulpit, preaching hell and damnation at his congregation, well into the third turn of his hourglass. Just tuck yourself into the back of an old church and drink in its age and atmosphere, think about who built it and why, and who has been there since.

*St Peter Mancroft, Norwich. Built 1430–55, this is Perpendicular at its best; the western tower has significant corner buttresses, is richly panelled, and the flèche (spirelet) has miniature pinnacles and flying buttresses.*

# Building materials

**Introduction**

Churches were signposts in the landscape for medieval travellers, identified by their shape, size, general appearance, and the types of local stone used to build them. Even the materials used to make churchyard walls and memorials would have been familiar, for building materials, distinct styles of building and characteristics frequently relate to certain regions or localities.

The Romans left behind a legacy of bricks and brick-making in England, although the items they produced were thick, flat tiles. Square Roman bricks could be kiln-burnt or left to cure for several years before being used. The Anglo-Saxons considered it all to be too much trouble, and brick production seems not to have been kept up as an industry. The Romans used their brick tiles either as contrasting decoration in stone walls or to give extra stability in rubblestone constructions.

Before builders used stone, churches were made of wood. Large amounts of timber continued to go into the making of country churches everywhere until the fourteenth century, and it remained popular even later than this in stoneless areas. Wood could be easily and exquisitely carved, making it suitable for furnishings and interior work. Carpenters, joiners and wood-carvers were to become the most skilful and widely represented craftsmen in the churches of England. Wood continued to be used for roofing, frameworks, spires, porches, belfry stages and towers. Many belfry stages were built on low brick or stone tower bases; otherwise, some fine wooden detached belfries were constructed.

The character and colouring of churchyard walls and memorials were dominated by the availability of materials, the types used, and the degree of expertise that local masons, builders and craftsmen had attained when they tackled the jobs. Initially, the stone went to building in the immediate localities of the quarries; it was also carried short distances overland into adjacent areas and could be conveyed further afield if some of the journey was undertaken by water.

Building materials from overseas, as well as from English coastal quarries, were used elsewhere on the coast and in inland areas that could be readily reached by rivers and, later, by the canal systems of the eighteenth century. When railways were built in the nineteenth century, stone from favoured quarries was put within relatively easy reach of architects and builders.

These same three factors (the choice and availability of materials and the skill of the builders) determined the size and appearance of the church itself. Others, including the general wealth of the locality, religious influences, architectural and artistic influence at home and abroad, and the physical properties of the stone itself, affected what was done with stone in the hands of those who worked it. The way in which various stones weather determines how quickly they subsequently deteriorate.

A good general material used for church building in England was oolitic *limestone*. Limestone is composed of grains of calcium carbonate and yields blocks of different sizes that can be easily dressed, and it weathers well. The more compact types take such a high polish that they are locally termed 'marbles' and have, from time to time, been much in demand for interior furnishings and decorative and structural work.

Limestone is particularly rich in the fossilised remains of animals and plants. When polished, the shelly type from Purbeck was highly favoured by architects in the Middle Ages. True *marble* is white and composed of very fine grains of calcite. It can be polished to a waxy surface and is used in monuments and statuary to great effect. The purest form of limestone is *chalk*, softer in the southern counties than in the north. Chalk is not generally thought of as being a constructional medium, although some small downland churches have arcade pillars that are made of it. Chalk is also found between the stone ribs of vaulting, as internal dressings, and

*Reedham, Norfolk. Flushwork, comprising a framework of stone tracery infilled with black flint, is characteristic of East Anglia; it is frequently associated with tracery detailing in stone.*

sometimes as facings for internal walls.

Associated with chalk is *flint* – small pieces of lustrous crystalline silica that can be picked up from the surface of the ground. It is favoured in the stoneless eastern counties and the downland areas of south-eastern and central southern England. Flint may be black, dark brown, grey or yellowish brown; it is brittle, easy to break and cannot be carved, but it is very hard-wearing. Flint is used either by itself or in conjunction with brick or pieces of freestone, where small quantities of the latter are available. It is laid randomly or in courses. In East Anglia, flint was used as decorative flushwork. A framework of thin stone strips was filled with pieces of blue-black flint, knapped or square-chipped. This formed an attractive chequerboard patterning that sometimes contained freestone tracery, or motifs such as initials, symbols, etc.

In many areas the churches and churchyard walls are built entirely of *sandstone*, particularly in the West Country, the Midlands and the north-east. This material is composed of compacted grains of sand together with some cementing agent. The resulting textures may be fine or coarse-grained, and in a large variety of colours, from light buff to red. Sandstones with particularly large, coarse grains are called *gritstones*. Although those of the older formations produce the best building stone of its kind, it is porous, weathers poorly, and is easily discoloured in industrial areas.

Limestone and sandstone both provided *ashlar*. This is the name given to blocks of stone that are squared but not finished, in contrast to rough-hewn blocks straight from the quarries. Whether it then becomes plain, tooled, random tooled, rustic or

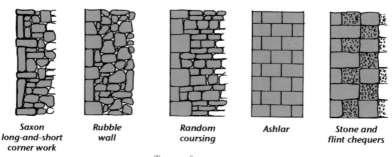

| **Saxon long-and-short corner work** | **Rubble wall** | **Random coursing** | **Ashlar** | **Stone and flint chequers** |

*Types of masonry.*

broken depends on the subsequent surface treatment it receives and the tools with which this is done. Blocks were of standard sizes that varied over the centuries and generally became larger in surface area as time went on. They were carefully and uniformly squared so that they could be laid in level, horizontal courses, with the minimum of mortar in between. Ashlar was finished on its external face, in the case of softer stone, by abrading with sand and water to remove any tooling, and to provide a plain surface. Otherwise it was sawn, and hewn with axe, bolster or chisel. The masons of each period used their tools in ways that were peculiar to them, leaving distinctive markings on their work. When ashlar was used as a surface medium for the church proper, the infilling between the skins would have been of a coarser material. While some areas had little option but to build with rough-faced stones or rubble stones, ashlar was always a considerable improvement.

*Granite* is found chiefly in the far west of England and the north-west of the country but was not quarried to any great extent until the wave of church building that swept the country in the fifteenth century. It consists of quartz, feldspar and mica: a mixture of crystals that in their natural state appear opaque, grey and flesh-coloured. The ratio of the mix gives granite an appearance that is either silver, brown, grey, grey-green or pink. The amount of quartz determines the hardness of the stone, and the feldspar is the component most likely to decay. Although granite takes a very high polish, it is difficult to carve or undercut, so it does not admit decoration in high relief. It may be very grainy, but in good-quality granite the grains are evenly distributed. Very large blocks of granite, used for walling, were known as 'moorstone'.

*Brick* was used in areas that had no good building stone of their own, as a substitute for rubble walling, and later as surface material. It was popular in the sixteenth and seventeenth centuries and came in a variety of colours, from light fawn to black, but mostly in reds and blues caused by variations in the clay beds. Bricks were hand-made until the middle of the nineteenth century.

The Tudors introduced patterns and courses into their brickwork. The length of a brick is called the 'stretcher'; the 'header' is its depth, and the joints between the bricks are called 'perpends'. *English bond* is a method of laying stretchers and headers in alternate courses, and *Flemish bond* has alternate stretchers and headers in the same course. The aim with all brickwork is to ensure that, when the bricks are joined together with mortar, no two vertical perpends lie immediately above each other; the wall is self-supporting and, where appropriate, capable of bearing a downward load. Just as blocks of stones were placed at the angles of walls to form quoins, so was this arrangement employed of bricks in their courses, to tie together walls meeting at right angles.

Straight after the Conquest, shiploads of creamy-yellow oolitic limestone came from Caen in Normandy. Large quantities of *Caen stone* were imported

*Rayleigh, Essex. The brick porch was built c.1495, at about the same time as the south chapel, during a period of rebuilding that transformed the original twelfth-century church.*

during the twelfth and thirteenth centuries, particularly for use in constructing cathedrals, abbeys and castles. Big consignments were ordered for stoneless areas where there was much work to be done. In eastern and south-eastern counties, it was used in conjunction with expensive native stone, which had to be sparingly apportioned, and usually reached its destination on barges drawn along natural waterways.

Caen stone is soft when quarried, easy to work, and hardens on exposure to the atmosphere. It is well suited to figurework, sculptured furnishing, tombs and canopies, reredoses, screens, fonts and pulpits. In areas where good building stone was hard to come by, it might be used for window tracery and frames, doorways, and stone decorative features such as gargoyles and pinnacles.

*Kentish ragstone* is a hard material, obtained from calcareous coastal Lower Greensand deposits. It can be found in churches of the south-east, where good natural building stone was scarce, and in some nineteenth-century London churches. It is either brown or bluish-grey, shelly and brittle, and gives a coarse, uneven surface to walls.

*Alabaster* is a semi-translucent sulphate of lime, which is chiefly found in central and north-eastern England. Most of the alabaster used in England was imported from the continent. It is soft, can be carved, and polishes to a pearly finish. Alabaster was a favourite medium for figurework and statuary between the fifteenth and seventeenth centuries, and during a nineteenth-century revival for polished marbles, when it was used for making fonts and pulpits. Pure white forms come from Italy.

In Anglo-Saxon times, churches were commonly roofed in *thatch*. Roofing *tiles* were widely available by the beginning of the thirteenth century. The most beautiful are of stone: brown and hand-made in the Middle Ages. The worst are garish machine-made tiles from the nineteenth century. A rash of solemn, grey Welsh *slate* spread across England, relieved here and there by the grey or blue slate from the long-established quarries of Cornwall, and the blues and greens which came from the Lake District. Other slates were quarried in the west and north-east of England. Slate is not porous; it has an even colour and surface texture and is relatively inexpensive.

*Elmley Castle, Worcestershire. The alabaster effigy of Lady Catherine Savage, who died in 1674, and her infant daughter.*

*Westleton, Suffolk. The thatched church, built in the twelfth century, is just one element in this chocolate-box village centred on its large green and duck pond.*

## Local characteristics

The overall appearance of any church built before the railway age was influenced by the form and nature of the local building stone, or of building materials that could be readily transported from elsewhere. Materials, to a degree, affected design, as did a number of other influences such as local practical considerations, the technical ability of the builder, and the style of nearby churches. All of this created regional characteristics in design and construction, frequently apparent when a church is viewed from the outside.

Local building materials do not have so obvious an effect on churchyard memorials as they do on the building. Yet what is available locally often affects the visual harmony of the whole. To some extent, it also contributed towards the treatment of, for example, monuments and their inscriptions, and churchyard walling. Each area has groups of churchyards that appear very similar, basically because their walls and memorials have all weathered in the same way.

## Materials and characteristics by county

*Bedfordshire* is an area of small churches. There is no outstanding style. The best churches, and those with fine stone spires, are in the north of the county on the limestone belt; otherwise, freestone was imported by water from neighbouring counties. The area is predominantly of clay, flint and chalk. Some green and yellow-brown sandstones provide building material, and there is a hard, brown rock called Carstone. Chalk was used on the interior of some churches, as was the soft, light, greenish-grey limestone from the Totternhoe quarry.

*Berkshire* is a county of chalk, and its churches are generally small, built in a mixture of flint, chalk, stone, tiles and bricks. Oolitic limestone and the softer Cotswold stone account for a few; and there is quite a lot of interior brickwork and a good many brick towers. The county has only a handful of spires.

*Avington, Berkshire. Widely regarded as the loveliest little twelfth-century church in the county; its rustic external appearance and large buttresses, all built in a number of materials, give no hint of the highly accomplished Norman work within.*

**Buckinghamshire** has limestone to the north, where the best churches are to be found. Chalk was used sparingly for dressings in fabrics that were often of flint and plastered rubble. Towers, porches, tracery and, in some cases, whole churches are of brick, and the county is almost spireless. There is evidence of some fine local schools of medieval masons, and what its churches lack in structural work of note is compensated for by exceptional fixtures and fittings.

*Cambridgeshire* is an important spire county. Oolitic limestone came across the waterways of the Fens in vast quantities, to supplement the local chalk and flint. The result is a comprehensive mixture of types: small, stoneless churches of flint

*Fingest, Buckinghamshire. Flint, rubble-stone and soft limestone, all heavily plastered; this church is distinguished by its single-stage Norman tower, round-headed belfry lights, and twin-gable roof.*

*St Endellion, Cornwall. The unbuttressed, three-stage tower, battlemented and with corner pinnacles, was made of Lundy Island granite in the fifteenth century; the rest of the church is of Cornish granite and local stone.*

and rubble, mixed with buildings in stone that are as impressive as any, and, overall, many which show the characteristics of adjacent regions. Chalk was used internally. The former county of Huntingdonshire, now a district of Cambridgeshire, has stone spires, in particular a profusion of broaches and numerous examples with fine spirelights. Most churches are made of brown Carstone cobbles. Although there is some natural limestone, the majority of freestone used throughout the Middle Ages was water-borne material from the quarries at Ketton and Barnack.

*Cheshire* is noted for its stout towers and reddish-brown sandstone. Its churches are made of large ashlar blocks in reds and pinks, and there is a yellowish sandstone, a grey fine-grained variety, some millstone grit and a small amount of limestone. There are some half-timbered churches, but few spires.

*Cornwall* has a distinctive local type, built largely of silver-grey, white or greenish granite, with low-pitched roofs of slate. In a wave of church building *c*.1450–1550, aisles were extended eastwards to approximately the same dimensions as the nave, without a structural chancel arch. Internally, this formed the hall-church arrangement that allowed magnificent wooden screens to be put across the entire width of the building beneath slightly pointed barrel or wagon roofs. Externally, it produced the two- or three-gable elevation without clerestory. Softer green or greenish-blue serpentine was occasionally used structurally, perhaps in conjunction with granite. The Victorians liked the way in which it could be highly polished, and so they worked it for pulpits, fonts and ornamental pillars. The county also has some Old Red Sandstone. Cornish churches are otherwise famed for their woodwork, particularly groups of fine bench-ends, and their slate headstones.

*Cumbria* has small, rough churches which lie low in the landscape, in out of the way places. In the north, there is limestone, and elsewhere both Old and New Red Sandstone, of which a light brownish-red, fine-grained variety was favoured. Above all, the county had good slate for roofing, which came in a range of natural colours, and red, reddish-brown and pink granite. However, none of this can be easily worked or carved, so most wall surfaces are rough, and the walls are coarse-textured and slaty. Locally, some of the upper stages of the towers are corbelled out from those below.

*Derbyshire* has a few grand churches. The prevailing material for church building was light brown or brownish-grey sandstone – a relatively hard, close-grained

Above left: *Tideswell, Derbyshire. An impressive cruciform building, put up in the Decorated style of c.1340–1400; its Perpendicular-style tower, added afterwards, is heavily over-pinnacled, and the church is much battlemented, but the overall effect is stunning.*

Above right: *Paignton, Devon. A large, embattled town church in red sandstone; there is a hint of Norman within, but it is mostly Early English; the tower is Perpendicular with setback buttresses to the third stage, and the porch is fourteenth-century.*

*Whitcombe, Dorset. Rough-coursed and rustic, and restored by the rector-poet William Barnes, who loved it, this is a Norman foundation with a tower dated 1596 and some medieval wall-painting inside.*

variety. Limestone quarried at Bolsover accounted for some fine stone spires. Other limestones, in black, greys and blues, were polished up and used for monumental work. Alabaster was quarried at Chellaston.

*Devon* shares with Cornwall granite and slate, hall churches and the triple nave plan. This is a region of inferior sandstones, as evidenced by the rough stonework and poorly weathered reddish or brown exteriors that many churches present today. A light cream limestone from Beer was used extensively for interior work and carvings, and veined marble from the Ashburton area took a nice polish. The county has tall towers, often with excessive stair turrets, and little external decoration. New Red Sandstone, in particular, could not be finely wrought or carved. Magnificently carved wooden rood screens are the chief glory of many interiors.

*Dorset* churches are small with wide aisles. Towers are sturdy and have stair turrets, and there are rather more clerestories and transepts than in the far west. Several churches also have wagon roofs, and there is much fifteenth-century work. Dark bluish-grey Purbeck marble – a polished, shelly limestone – was a great favourite throughout the thirteenth century, for tombs, fonts and shafts. Light brown limestone from Portland became the most important building stone of the eighteenth century.

*County Durham* has Carboniferous limestone, some sandstone and a dull millstone grit. There are a number of small Norman and Early English churches and a few nice towers, but little else until the Industrial Revolution provided the reason for a whole crop of functional churches designed by local architects.

*Essex* is a county of brick, augmented by Kentish ragstone and timber. Brick was used here in the thirteenth century, but Tudor brickwork predominates in porches, arcades and whole towers. Elsewhere, there are walls of flint, with knapped flint used as flushwork towards East Anglia. There is a distinctive type of oak-shingled spire, or blunt pyramid, and there are some detached belfries which rise in diminishing stages.

*Gloucestershire* has finely textured, creamy Cotswold stone from its portion of the oolitic limestone belt. Whether honey-coloured, golden or almost white, it has

*Fairford, Gloucestershire. A fine Cotswold 'wool' church, built in the fifteenth century, and still possessing all twenty-eight of its remarkably rich, medieval stained glass windows.*

no aesthetic equal, and it inspired medieval masons to their very best work. Most churches are small with either little bellcotes or low stone towers with corner pinnacles. There are some with set-back, broach spires. Those that benefited from the riches of the medieval wool trade are large Perpendicular buildings, some with a big window above the chancel arch. Elsewhere, the trade inspired chantry chapels or expensive additions to more modest buildings. The county has a number of good stone spires that are lofty and slender. The Cotswold type has roll mouldings at the angles.

*Hampshire* is a chalk county with only a localised amount of soft sandstone. Many of the churches have walls of flint or bricks. Some towers are of timber, most likely put up in the eighteenth century. Wood was also used for porches, shingled spires and belfries.

*Herefordshire* is a county of gems, from its group of Norman churches to its fine Georgian woodwork. Most churches are of red sandstone and are small and unprepossessing. There is a famed group of fonts, tympana and capitals with carving of Celtic influence, a lot of good fourteenth-century work, and examples of fine glass. Local peculiarities include timber towers, unbuttressed towers with corbelled-out projecting tops, and detached timber towers on stone bases. There are more spires here than in the surrounding counties. Some churches have gabled transepts at the east end, and others have circular, foiled lights above the chancel arch.

*Hertfordshire* is a county of hard chalk and flint; the latter, together with clunch and puddingstone, were the predominant materials for church walls. Bricks and tiles were made locally as early as the thirteenth century, and principally from

*Benington, Hertfordshire. A typical village church, built in the thirteenth century, with a Hertfordshire spike on the tower.*

*Nettlestead, Kent. A pretty little church, built of Kentish ragstone, with two-stage tower and pyramidal cap; it is noted for its medieval stained glass.*

the fifteenth. Good building stone came from Totternhoe (Bedfordshire) and, in consequence, there are some fine Perpendicular churches. Village churches are small and neat, and there are many pretty towers. A local characteristic is the 'Hertfordshire spike' – a slender wooden spirelet or flèche, sheathed in lead, rising above the tower.

*Kent* has flint and clunch, Kentish rag, sandstone and brick, as well as imported Caen stone for finer work. Local limestone took a high polish and was used for shafts, tombs, etc. A lot of church building took place in Kent in the thirteenth century, and generally the churches are low without clerestories. Flint walling predominated. Good clay beds facilitated large quantities of bricks, especially from Tudor times. When a chapel was erected parallel to one side (most usually to the north) or each side of the chancel, it produced a two- or three-gabled arrangement at the east end. Elsewhere, it spanned nave and aisle in one. Small towers are capped by shingled spires. An elaborately cusped, star-like form of tracery evolved in the fourteenth century and is called 'Kentish tracery'. There are many timbered porches.

*Lancashire* had comparatively few churches of note prior to the Industrial Revolution and the coming of nineteenth-century Gothic in brick. There is some white,

*Heysham, Lancashire. Of sandstone, and spectacularly overlooking Morecambe Bay, this eleventh-century church is on the site of a Saxon foundation.*

Above left: *Church Langton, Leicestershire. An ironstone church with limestone dressings; the tall tower has clasping buttresses, the nave is battlemented, and most of the building is Perpendicular.*

Above right: *Louth, Lincolnshire. The beautifully proportioned tower and slender spire are typical, if a rather grand version, of a style to be found across much of the county.*

Carboniferous limestone in the north of the county, and a number of churches were built in cream, buff or brownish freestone. Red sandstone predominates, accounting for a considerable amount of patching, enlarging and rebuilding over the centuries.

There is also a light bluish-grey, fine-grained variety, which was used in church building. There is a small group of slender spires.

*Leicestershire* has dark-cream oolitic limestone, and the lias which is quarried in the north of the county. There are some especially good churches in the east, some fine Perpendicular towers, and spires that have spirelights on the cardinal faces. Some are parapet spires with pinnacles, with flying buttresses attaching the pinnacles to the sides of the spires.

*Lincolnshire* gloried in the fourteenth century. A cream, shelly, oolitic limestone was quarried at Ancaster in the south-west. This was used all over the

*Harefield, Middlesex. The squat, low tower of brick and flint rubble is typical of the area; the church is famed for its collection of monuments and funeral hatchments.*

*Titchwell, Norfolk. A typical eleventh-century round tower of East Anglian type, here unusually topped by a thin spirelet, remained when the rest of the church was rebuilt in the fifteenth century.*

south of the county to build fine churches, tall towers and many spires. In the centre, there is an area of broach spires. The churches in the north of the county are smaller. Building stone came by water from Ketton and Barnack to the stoneless marshlands. Natural local stone included white, brownish and pinkish limestone, and a greenish-brown sandstone that was much used in church building. In the east of the county, there was only greensand and chalk, so brick was used more extensively.

*Middlesex* is a stoneless county that relied on the River Thames to carry building materials from other areas. Its churches were built of Kentish rag, rubble and clunch, rough flint and puddingstone. London Clay provided bricks, and windows and doorways were frequently made of Ketton stone. Many of the county's churches were rebuilt in the nineteenth century. Their main features are the timber bell turrets and spirelets at the west ends of naves, and battlemented towers with taller stair turrets.

*Norfolk* has chalk, clay, and flint from the fields, but no good building freestone. This came from Caen, and by river from Ancaster, Ketton, Clipsham and Barnack, to make doors, windows and quoins. Purbeck 'marble' came around the coast for fixtures and fittings. Local reeds provided a good deal of roofing thatch. The absence of stone accounts for the many round towers of rubble with flint facings – more here than in any

other county. Knapped, blue-black flints were ingeniously worked with freestone strips into 'flushwork' panelling. 'Wool' churches have dominating towers of flint, big transepts and spaces for altars. Brick was first imported from abroad into Norfolk but was made locally by the fifteenth century and used extensively. There are fine two-storey porches, some flèches and an amount of late medieval stained glass. The county is rich in good woodwork, especially screens and bench-ends.

*Northamptonshire* churches have the finest medieval masonry in the land. The county's quarries exported building stone from Saxon times and were worked extensively in the thirteenth and fourteenth centuries. There is a wealth of Anglo-Saxon remains. Standing on the oolitic

*King's Sutton, Northamptonshire. Founded in the twelfth century, the church is defined by its 198 feet (60 metres) tall spire – ribbed, crocketed, having flying buttresses to the corner pinnacles, and made of limestone.*

limestone belt, the churches are of good freestone in buff, cream, silver-grey and even reddish-brown. Elsewhere, dark brown ironstone is used; the two are sometimes put up in conjunction, to great visual effect. This is a county of spires. Clasping buttresses are also a feature.

*Northumberland* had limestone and brownish-grey or buff-coloured Carboniferous sandstone with which to build its churches. The latter, often as millstone grit, was the main material, and there is much rubblestone work. Norman work abounds, but the era of church building hereabouts was the thirteenth century.

*Nottinghamshire* has oolitic limestone and quality red sandstone, yet, with a few grand exceptions, its churches are small and of little note. Red brick is used throughout. Dormer windows are a feature. Towers tend to be low and heavy. Stone spires may have broaches or may otherwise be octagonal parapet spires. Alabaster was carved in the county.

*Oxfordshire* has oolitic limestone in the north, clay across the centre, and chalk and flint elsewhere. Churches of freestone are cream, yellow and brown, and of medium size. The county is quite rich in Norman remains and has a considerable amount of fourteenth-century work. It also has many fine monuments, particularly in its churchyards. There are numerous stone spires and a local type that has single spirelights on the lower parts.

*Rutland* is all about what the medieval masons could do with its high-quality, abundant building stone from the quarries about Ketton and Clipsham. Rutland's churches are a mix of creamy-grey limestone, honey-brown ironstone marl, and good local stone tiles. Its better church steeples – sometimes with inspirationally designed intersections between tower and spire, others with broaches and significant spirelights – are as good as the best anywhere. Otherwise, this is a county of small, towerless churches that originated before the end of the thirteenth century and have characteristic single or double bellcotes.

*Shropshire* has a little limestone in the south, but the pinkish churches everywhere are of red sandstone. The county imported 'marbles' for tombs, shafts, etc, but used local clay for bricks. The churches now presented are mostly small, and the towers are unbuttressed; some have a projecting upper stage. As one might expect in a well-wooded region, some churches are timber-framed, and there are a number of wooden belfries above the west ends of naves.

*Somerset* is all about the beauty, proportions and variety of its church towers, which are of distinctly local types. It is also a stone spire county although, with fewer than twenty, not to the extent that one might

*Cleobury Mortimer, Shropshire. The fabric of this church is famously out of true, and its octagonal wooden spire – built in the sixteenth century – has twisted over time.*

*West Bagborough, Somerset. A typical village church of the west; the Perpendicular, three-stage embattled tower has diagonal buttresses.*

think. Builders here preferred to finish their towers with highly decorated upper stages, pinnacles and decorative parapets. Magnificent churches were built in the 150 years from the end of the fourteenth century, using good local stone. To the west, there is red sandstone, and almost everywhere else there is limestone, which comes in a variety of colours from silver-grey through cream and shaded yellows to brown. The county has good porches, parapets and windows, vaulting, roofs – particularly wagon, tie-beam and king-post arrangements – screens and bench-ends. There is a considerable amount of fine figure sculpture, particularly on the exteriors of towers.

*Staffordshire* is a county of typical village churches that originated in the thirteenth and fourteenth centuries. There are also a good many that were built in the nineteenth century to cope with the increasing populations around the industrial areas. The building stone is sandstone: white, red, brownish and yellow. Local clay produced bricks that patched up a lot of sandstone exteriors or were used for rebuilding projects in the eighteenth century. There are some good stone spires. Alabaster quarries provided material for monuments, effigies, etc.

*Suffolk* is exceptionally rich in great churches, and much of what has already

*St Peter, Sudbury, Suffolk. The great south porch was once a chapel that held the shrine of a saint.*

*Dunsfold, Surrey. The thirteenth-century village church has a fifteenth-century timber belfry.*

been written about Norfolk applies here. The county has flint, chalk and clunch; its church walls are almost entirely built of the first, often as flint flushwork panelling. Wealth from the wool trade, at a time when the church porch was widely used by the people, meant that particularly large and finely decorated porches were built. Round towers are common.

*Surrey* is predominantly a stoneless county. Some local greenish-grey sandstone was used, mainly for interior structural work. Otherwise, the small churches are of hard chalk or clunch, rubble or flint. Many of its churches originated in the nineteenth century or were otherwise heavily restored by the Victorians. There are timber bell towers, some of which are of the Essex type; above them are often blunt wooden pyramids and short, shingled spires. Wooden porches are common.

*Sussex* sandstones vary in type, composition and colour: greenish, cream, buff, brown and yellow-grey. Petworth marble was used in the south-east of England, especially for fonts, and Caen stone came across the water for window tracery, quoins, etc. The latter had to be used in conjunction with the downland chalk and flint. There are some round towers, many east-west axial towers and a handful of stone spires. A special characteristic is the widespread use of low spires made of oak shingles. There are also chamfered broaches,

*Climping, Sussex. The unusual south transept tower – said to have originally been a stand-alone watch-tower – was built c.1170, and the rest of the church was added about half a century later.*

22

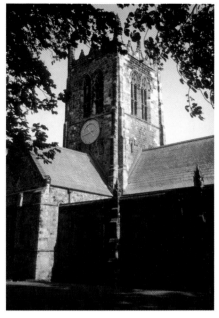

*Northallerton, Yorkshire. A sharply pinnacled, imposing church in a leafy churchyard at the end of the high street; it has a prominent, Perpendicular crossing tower with tall pairs of two-light windows on each side of the belfry stage.*

and the Sussex cap, a blunt, pyramidal top of red tiles on the tower. Timber is widely used in bellcotes and porches. Roofs tend to be in a single span over nave and aisles and, locally, they were given a heavy appearance by the use of large slabs of Horsham sandstone for roofing.

*Warwickshire* churches are almost entirely of New Red Sandstone. There is some limestone in the south-east, accounting for better masonry, and some churches of the Cotswold type. Timber was widely used and there are some good stone spires.

*Wiltshire* is a county of chalk, so the walls of many village churches include flint to a greater or lesser degree, decreasing as one travels in a north-westerly direction. The best churches are in the south, west and north of the county, adjacent to the band of limestone. The largest are to be found where there was a combination of good stone and local wealth from the wool trade. Cream or yellow-brown Chilmark or Wardour stone accounts for a few buildings, as does that from Tisbury, Corsham and Bath. There is a group of cross-planned churches of good proportions, in the centre of the county. The downland churches are small and there is much thirteenth-century work.

*Worcestershire* has a number of good towers. Some fine examples of Somerset influence were put up in the fifteenth century. Spires tend to be small, and there are a number of boarded bellcotes. Apart from those of golden limestone in the south-east of the county, Worcestershire's churches are mainly built of soft New Red Sandstone.

*Yorkshire* profited by the medieval clothing industry and a good supply of excellent building material. Builders were able to work in Carboniferous and Magnesian limestones in grey, cream and yellowish-brown, and fine-grained sandstones in a great variety of colours, but almost all with a greyish tint. A good many quarries produced stone for building and monumental work. There were also millstone grit and heavy stone slates for the flat, low roofs of the churches. The solid simplicity of those around the moors contrast in particular with the spacious churches of the south-east. The better monuments are in the north of the county. There are many good towers, some of which have open parapets and decorated buttresses and seem to be influenced by those of Somerset. Others are solid and unbuttressed. The south and west are particularly rich in fine stone spires.

23

# The Anglo-Saxon period up to 1066

**Practical beginnings**

Much church building in Britain began with the need to protect altars from the elements. Portable altars, small slabs of stone incised with crosses, came into the country under the arms of the converting saints. Those who came from Ireland to Cornwall were said to have brought small circular 'altar stones', which contrasted with the rectangular type that developed in Anglo-Saxon Britain. When standing crosses were established in the landscape, the portable altars were set up in front of them for the act of worship. When saintly relics were collected together they were often placed beneath the main altar, or interred elsewhere in the building and given their own defined area for pilgrimage and worship.

The bones of St Brannock, who brought Christianity to south Wales and Devon during the sixth century, were probably placed beneath the altar of the church he founded at Braunton (Devon). As altars developed, they were mostly made of wood. In the early days of the faith, the altar alone was consecrated, and at all times the altars of a church were afforded especial consideration during services. It was against this background, as well as under the influences of the British under Roman occupation, that church building began to develop in Britain. The Romans had left an idea of what a church might look like, a few Christian buildings and the seeds of a faith. By the end of the Anglo-Saxon era the church had an organised hierarchy, an administrative tier system and an order of precedence for its buildings. At the head, as the tenth century closed, were the cathedrals; next were the monastic and collegiate churches, and then came those churches that served defined settlements. Finally, there were all of the smaller establishments that were in some way allied to the others, and the private chapels on landowners' estates.

**New approach to old attitudes**

Before they had churches, Christians worshipped where they had done in the past, afraid to relinquish the old religions entirely. The early missionaries took a handy piece of suitable stone, inscribed a cross on it and set it up at a location dedicated to Christianity. By the eighth century these 'preaching' or 'teaching' crosses were established landmarks throughout England. The earliest permanent standing crosses were stone monoliths, put up close to pagan shrines, marking a place of former heathen worship. Some which are now in churchyards, especially in the south-west peninsula, where they

*Braunton, Devon. Distinguished by its south tower of c.1250 and its broach spire, the church also has a fine four-teenth-century screen and a large collection of sixteenth-century bench-ends.*

are also to be seen by the roadside, may have marked routes or preaching stations, or may have been put up to show the extent of land ownership.

New ideas for decoration also came with a drive for the faith, which spread from the south-east. Its art was inspired by that of the Mediterranean regions, as were those who came and those who were converted, by contact with this source. Some of the early holy men of Celtic Christianity travelled to Rome, where they were much interested and influenced by the style, ritual and usage there, and they also sourced and brought back all manner of treasures to illuminate their own foundations. It is most likely that such accumulations ultimately became objects of desire during the Viking raids centuries later.

Before any of this happened, Celtic conversion was pushed to the edges of its former territory – the north, west and south-west – and in these strongholds the crosses were kept. Anglo-Saxon work is, in some areas, evident well into the eleventh century; in others it became predominantly Anglo-Danish, such as at Hauxwell (Yorkshire) and at Prestbury (Cheshire). Indeed, the Viking involvement is curious. On the one hand, they destroyed many timber churches and plundered their treasures, and on the other, once they came to colonise and settle, not only did they embrace the faith, but their own art was quickly integrated with that of Celtic Christianity.

## New religion, new churches

Christianity is thought to have reached Britain by way of Gaul, in either the second or third century AD. It came about in a piecemeal way, introduced mainly in coastal areas by traders, travellers and soldiers who moved about the Roman Empire. In Roman Britain it had to compete against the predominant Roman religion and a number of other indigenous pagan beliefs. Third-century persecutions and martyrdoms nearly finished it off. Fourth-century tolerance of its organisation, under a series of influential British bishops, gave it a psychological prop just before the Romans withdrew.

The religion suffered heavily in the aftermath of attacks from Scotland and Ireland, and from the coming of the pagan Angles and Saxons. However, there was great potential for evangelism, as small pockets of the faith still remained within a pagan society. Meanwhile, the old British Church, as influenced by Rome, decamped for a while to the periphery and watched the advance of the pagan tide. Patrick, the son of a Roman official, who studied in Gaul, took Christianity to Ireland as a papal emissary early in the fifth century. Within a decade he founded many churches and organised the clergy. The great waves of incoming saints were the advance guard of the new Christianity, paving the way for the Celtic saints who gradually became bishops to the various Saxon kingdoms.

The earliest known Christian leader from the north was Ninian in the fourth century. He was persuaded to make a pilgrimage to Rome when papal policy was to create a hierarchy of holy men with sufficient authority to spread the word. The Celtic approach was more low-key, although no less successful, its practitioners preferring to work from quieter locations. Ninian spent some time in a monastic community in Rome; in 394, he was consecrated a bishop by Pope Siricius and sent to work among the Picts. He arrived in Galloway with a company of masons who had been supplied by St Martin of Tours, the Hungarian bishop who had served in the Roman army at the time of Constantine. About 397, Ninian's masons put up the first stone building in the area at Whithorn, the *candida casa*, and created a monastery from where he travelled the region, preaching to the Picts.

The arrival of missionaries from Ireland, beginning in the fifth century, is by far the most romantic of the Christian incursions into Britain. Among the earliest are said to have been the lady St Buryan around 465; St Kiaron, whose voyage has been dated to *c*.490; and St Piran, who arrived in 498. Fifth-century Cornwall was undoubtedly mainly pagan, despite having temporarily embraced the Christian faith in the fourth century, after the example set by more than one of its chieftains.

The slightly later spread of the faith by more formal channels, devolving on papal emissaries and single-minded bishops, was the weightier alternative. What makes the Celtic approach so much more appealing is the fact that its messengers were not saints in the sense that they had been canonised. They were not even men and women of the church. They were effectively a large body of people who had been attracted to the established centres of learning in Ireland and wanted to spread the word. Nor were they all Irish Celts. St Mullion, for example, was a Welshman. So too was St Petroc, the prince bishop who took to the faith in Ireland and established a monastery and churches in Cornwall. St Non or Nonna, whose name is preserved at Altarnun (the place of her altar), was the mother of St David of Wales.

Nor did the Irish influence stay in Britain. Celtic missionaries sailed north of Scotland and south almost to the Mediterranean. But it was with Brittany that they established the closest links, and from where many influences were derived. There are stories of Celtic missionaries becoming particularly adept at crafts, influencing trade and travelling with Breton traders. The churches in Cornwall, then, derived from the oratories they built. It is important to remember that Cornwall was isolated enough never to have become part of Anglo-Saxon Christianity and for centuries completely rejected the Roman approach.

In 563, Columba, an Irish missionary and abbot, drawing on the Irish influence, built a little church and a community of stone-sided beehive huts with dome-like thatched roofs on Iona in the Inner Hebrides. He founded a monastery there for 150 monks and preached throughout the Highlands. A product of the next generation at Iona was Aidan, dispatched to convert Northumbria at the behest of Oswald, its Christian king. Aidan established his priory off the coast at Lindisfarne in 635, and his work in Northumbria was a spectacular success. Then there was Cuthbert, who is said to have been inspired to become a monk by the death of Aidan in 651. Cuthbert eventually relocated to Lindisfarne, where he spent the rest of his life.

In 597, St Augustine and forty Benedictine monks from Rome landed at Ebbsfleet on the Isle of Thanet. They found a Christian church already at Canterbury: the chancel of the present-day church of St Martin was being used by Bertha, the queen of King Ethelbert of Kent. The missionary from the monastery of St Andrew on the

*Lindisfarne, Northumberland. St Mary's church, a Norman foundation, is said to be on the site of the original monastery that was founded by St Aidan in the seventh century; the ruins are of a later priory, destroyed at the Dissolution.*

Caelian Hill at Rome was Pope Gregory I's spearhead in his bid to stem the heathen tide following the Roman withdrawal. There would have been other Christian churches. One had probably existed for the best part of three centuries at St Albans – where the Roman soldier Alban was martyred for his faith – put up by Christians very soon after the act.

Augustine's baptism of Ethelbert on Whit Sunday in 597 was the catalyst for the wholesale conversion of Kent. He used the River Medway as his instrument of baptism. This set the Christian course for all of Saxon England. It is thought that Augustine established his own church on the site of the Kentish leader's palace, Ethelbert having withdrawn out of deference. This, the first Canterbury Cathedral, was a rectangular building after the manner of the Roman basilica, with aisles and apses. It was, to a degree, emulated in the church at Reculver (Kent), established in the same period.

Bede recorded the slow progress of conversion and baptism northwards under Paulinus. If it is true that this was the assumed name of the son of Urien, a British chief who became an expatriate in Rome at the time of the Saxon invasion, Paulinus must have returned to Anglo-Saxon England with mixed feelings and several influences. Nonetheless, he came as chaplain to Ethelwyn, daughter of Bertha and Ethelbert, who was to marry Edwin of Northumbria in 601. It was Paulinus who converted Edwin and launched Christianity throughout Northumbria, using the rivers of the land to claim his converts.

For centuries, the success of Christianity in Britain depended on how newly converted inhabitants fared in their skirmishes with territorial invaders. Personal allegiance also came into play. The wholesale conversion of Kent did not hold fast after the deaths in 616 of Ethelbert and Saebert, ruler of the Middle Saxons, based on present-day Essex. If a Christian leader was defeated or killed in battle by a heathen, such as happened in 633, when Edwin died at the hand of Penda of Mercia, the defeated region might once again turn to its old pagan gods. Paulinus's church at York was large and basilican in plan, but ultimately neither this nor his extensive missionary work throughout north-east England was enough when Edwin died in battle.

In 635, Cynegils of Wessex was baptised in the Thames at the hand of St Birinus, Pope Honorius I's missionary. Augustine had craftsmen in his own company and they were doubtless eager to show what they could do. Indeed, builders, masons and glass-workers usually accompanied the missionaries from Rome, and reinforcements of craftsmen were sometimes sent for. They were also called upon, notably from France, by the Celtic saints when building

*St Martin, Canterbury, Kent. Christian worship is said to have taken place here before St Augustine arrived in 597.*

*Bradwell-on-Sea, Essex. An Anglo-Saxon church, built on the site of a Roman fort, possibly by St Cedd c.654; only the nave remains.*

their mother churches. From the late 660s Pope Vitalian's appointee to the see of Canterbury, Theodore of Tarsus, was the force behind religious teaching throughout the country and the consolidation of dioceses. One of the products of Aidan's school at Lindisfarne was St Cedd, who set up in Saxon Essex. A building remains there today, at St Peter-on-the-Wall, Bradwell-on-Sea, put up with much reused Roman material. It has been identified as Cedd's foundation of c.654, all that remains of a one-time apsed church. Perhaps the two great names of the seventh century are St Wilfred and Benedict Biscop, who supported the movement to standardise on Roman usage. The true importance of Whitby (Yorkshire) at this time is uncertain. There was a monastery there in the mid seventh century, during the time of the beneficent Oswiu, King of Northumbria. It was the Synod of Whitby, held in 664, that accepted the authority of Rome in matters of the Christian faith and ritual. Northumbria and Mercia had become Christian and followed the Celtic tradition. The agreed deference to Rome changed all that.

Although the Celtic model for church building was to prevail, it is interesting to watch the strategies of Wilfred in particular, operating out of the Celtic heartland with an allegiance to Rome and a zeal for reform.

### A conflict of sites

Today we may come across churches very close to points of prehistoric activity. This may signify that the original intention was to use the site, but the missionaries trod rather more cautiously than their sponsors had in mind.

The early churches were not parish churches as we understand the term today. They would most likely have been allied to monasteries, for the use of monks, and in some places would have formed a cluster around the central church. We might today call these 'community churches', and as such they would have had a nucleus of local worshippers who formed the basis of the parish concept. Elsewhere, churches were founded by the missionaries, built to their specifications but operated by secular clergy at their instruction. Archbishop Theodore encouraged manorial lords to build churches on their estates, so some later foundations were in positions designated by landowners. Where this was done, the landowner would have regarded the church as his private property, part of the inventory of his estate, and a commodity to be passed to his heirs. One has the vision of numerous 'estate churches' of timber being built, their maintenance and administration being in the care of the landowner, who also held the right to appoint the priest. Between the seventh and the tenth centuries the churches of the monastic foundations were gradually acceded to by the secular clergy. From around the eighth century the whole concept of a resident priest having the charge of a secular community formed the religious basis of a parish system.

Gregory's instructions to Augustine were to leave alone the former places of heathen worship, but to purify them with holy water, destroy the old idols there and set up some tangible object of the Christian faith. This is why churches were built within the protection of ancient stone circles or next to burial mounds that are now incorporated into churchyards. Some were even built on top of barrows. There is no doubt that once the concept of building a church had been established, its physical form and nature became important considerations for the builders. A little wooden Anglo-Saxon church cannot be compared with the soaring extravagances of church architecture put up from the fourteenth century onwards; but they would still have been the largest man-made buildings around. After all, the converting missionaries had made it quite clear that they housed the power of protection.

When the Romans came, they brought with them a preference for rectangular burial grounds, and this shape continued until after the Norman Conquest. A circular churchyard, such as Wirksworth (Derbyshire), St Buryan (Cornwall) or Rudston (Yorkshire), is likely to be very old. Those which are both circular and on mounds, such as Edlesborough (Buckinghamshire) and Winwick (Northamptonshire), may well have been used in prehistoric times.

*Edlesborough, Buckinghamshire. The church was built on a chalk mound high above the village in the thirteenth century, and successive redevelopment enhanced its commanding appearance. The circular shape of the churchyard suggests that the site has prehistoric origins.*

*Knowlton, Dorset. The ruined church of flint and stone stands in the middle of a prehistoric henge monument; it has some Norman remains, and two stages of a fourteenth-century tower.*

Such high points should not be confused with churches in very flat areas that were built on artificial mounds for the purpose of keeping them above potential flood levels. The whole village of Breedon on the Hill (Leicestershire) has evolved around a hillfort, the church itself being built where once there was a Saxon monastery. The churchyards at Finchampstead (Berkshire) and Mawnan and Kilkhampton (both in Cornwall) are also enclosed by earthworks, and at other places – such as Lilbourne (Northamptonshire), Brinsop (Herefordshire), Brinklow (Warwickshire), Melling (Lancashire), Burton Overy (Leicestershire) and West Wycombe (Buckinghamshire) – they are nearby. The now ruined church at Knowlton (Dorset) was built in the middle of a henge monument. The sites of Brentor (Devon) and Coldred (Kent) are enclosed by earthworks.

Ormside (Cumbria) is on an artificial mound, and Crowhurst (Surrey) is at the top of a hill. Llandysilio (Powys) has a modern church in an ancient churchyard, one example of many ancient round churchyards in that county and elsewhere in parts of south-west England. At Berwick (Sussex) there is a Saxon barrow in the churchyard. Maxey (Cambridgeshire) is on a mound. Such churchyards have often provided evidence that an area was used before the Norman Conquest. Roman pottery was discovered at Kirby Bellars (Leicestershire) and an Anglo-Saxon cup in gold and enamel was found at Ormside (Cumbria). At Tilshead (Wiltshire) more than forty skeletons were found, supposed to be those of invading Danes, interred without coffins in hollowed-out chalk.

## Conversion by baptism

Mass baptisms had to be performed while the saint was in the area. When receptacles were used, these had to be deep enough for water to be poured over the adults who stood in them, but low enough on the ground to allow easy officiating. There was no total immersion. When the baptism service included the washing of feet, smaller receptacles were used, placed at, or below, ground level. Baptism was immediately followed by confirmation, which had to be performed under the auspices of a visiting

*Avebury, Wiltshire. A small village church of flint, local stones and ashlar; the gems are its Saxon windows and Norman font. It is located just outside the ancient stone circle.*

bishop. This cemented the idea of Christianity very firmly and made the waywardly inclined realise that there was no going back. They had taken not only a revolutionary step, but one of absolute commitment. It was particularly important to push home this message when the baptism occurred at a place previously used for heathen worship. A continuation of venue made it easier for people to accept change.

Many of the difficulties experienced by the missionaries of Christianity stemmed from their potential converts' insistence on continuing to venerate standing stones. Churches built near these, such as at Stanton Drew (Somerset) and Avebury (Wiltshire), were probably an attempt to compromise on the part of the missionaries. Occasionally, as at Pewsey (Wiltshire), huge sarsen stones form part of the foundations or may be built into churchyard walls. Often, ancient standing stones that were pressed into the service of Christianity were inscribed with sun symbols. An example of this is the wheel-head symbol, comprising a circle enclosing a cross, which continued to be worshipped as both a Christian motif and part of a fertility ritual.

### Standing crosses: early signs of the faith

Points of the new faith were never more tangibly or vigorously represented than by the great stone crosses which spread across the north in the wake of Celtic teaching. The idea of vine-scroll decoration was taken from the Mediterranean regions, and animals and birds from Germanic origins were adopted and adapted into the beautifully executed vine scrolls. Into these were interwoven a riot of decorative motifs, both natural and fantastic. Cumbria has fine examples of Norse, Danish and Celtic art in its churchyards. Scrolls, two-, three- and four-strand plaiting, interlace and knotwork provided the earliest decoration. The figurework of Christ, the Virgin Mary, saints and biblical tableaux, which were features of Northumbrian work from the seventh century, persisted as favourite decoration for churchyard crosses for the next nine hundred years.

The best cross shafts for Norse and Christian themes are at Bewcastle, Gosforth and Irton in Cumbria and at Ruthwell in Dumfries and Galloway. The appearance of beasts on crosses is of Scandinavian origin, and most are to be found in the north. At Kirkby Stephen (Cumbria) the fragment remaining has figurework and interlacing. The same is true of Burton-in-Kendal (Cumbria), where there is also scrollwork. Other interesting late pre-Conquest crosses or remains can be found in the north at Eyam and Hope (Derbyshire), Leek and Checkley (Staffordshire), Dacre (Cumbria),

*Far left:* Eyam, Derbyshire. *The eighth-century preaching cross decorated with scrolls, plants and biblical figures, in a churchyard packed with the graves of plague victims.*

*Left:* Halton, Lancashire. *The restored eleventh-century cross, one of several in this churchyard; made of sandstone, it has a shaft on four sections and with carvings that include the Evangelists.*

Heysham, Whalley and Halton (Lancashire) and Winwick (Cheshire).

There are three Anglo-Saxon cross shafts at Ilkley (Yorkshire). The churchyard at Creeton (Lincolnshire) has two, one with interlace and the other including incised crosses. Although they are now inside the church, there are two joined fragments of a

shaft, c.1000, at Nunburnholme (Yorkshire). Anglo-Saxon work is present in the churchyard shafts at Alstonefield (Staffordshire) and in the three at nearby Checkley. There are both figures and animals at Masham (Yorkshire).

To date accurately a cross that has no inscription, one needs to know the artistic influences at work in the area, who brought them and for how long they were there. As they were overtaken in turn, different areas admitted a succession of designs on their crosses, and there were regional characteristics. Whorls, scrolls, other geometric patterns, plaiting, interlacing, vine scrolls, human heads, leaf motifs, animals and figurework appeared variously on both the heads and shafts, and much of it was stylised.

The standard shape for the early crosses, outside the south-west, consisted of a tall shaft with a comparatively small head. The inscribed and wheel crosses of Cornwall attest to the resurgence of Christianity from Wales and Ireland in the fifth and sixth centuries. In the south-west, the shafts were often dumpy in appearance and crudely incised, as for example at St Dennis (Cornwall). The tallest of the Cornish type is in Mylor churchyard. There

*Bradbourne, Derbyshire. The remains of an Anglo-Saxon preaching cross, dated AD 800, which includes a scene of the Crucifixion.*

are several in the churchyard at St Levan.

Elsewhere, churchyard crosses might be circular in cross-section, as at Masham (Yorkshire), Brailsford (Derbyshire) and Wolverhampton (Staffordshire), or rectangular. Occasionally they were constructed with both circular and rectangular sections in the same shaft, as at Ilam (Staffordshire) and at Beckermet St Bridget and Gosforth, both in Cumbria. The cross at Wolverhampton is of the ninth century and that at Brailsford is of the eleventh. The tapering shaft at Stapleford (Nottinghamshire) is also decorated in sections and has divided banding; it includes interlacing and a face. The tenth-century example at Sproxton (Leicestershire) has interlacing and a beast. A fusion of both these designs can be seen in the fragments of two crosses at Sandbach (Cheshire). The ninth-century stump at Bakewell (Derbyshire) also has vine scroll and animals, as well as human figures.

Many crosses in Cornish churchyards may have interlace or plait decoration and inscriptions in Roman transitional or Hiberno-Saxon characters. A comprehensive listing includes Cardinham, Feock, Lamorran, Lanhydrock, Lanivet, Lanteglos-by-Fowey, Launceston, Lostwithiel, Mawgan-in-Meneage, Mylor, Padstow, Par, Phillack, Porthilly, Roche, St Allen, St Clement, St Dennis, St Ives, St Juliot, St Neot, St Teath, Sancreed and Wendron. There are pillar stones in the churchyards of Gulval, Lanivet, Lanteglos-by-Camelford, Lewannick, Phillack and South Hill, and coped stones at Lanivet, Phillack, St Buryan and St Tudy. At St Buryan the eighth-century cross head shows the Crucifixion, and at Zennor there are two which are even older. There is a very rustic example at Roche, two at St Juliot, another of the sixth century at Altarnun, and five at Sancreed. Others of interest are at Phillack and Lanivet. Cornwall, like the north-west of England and the west coast of Wales, has a predominance of the wheel-head type.

A ninth-century example can be seen at Rolleston (Staffordshire); there is another at Dearham (Cumbria), and a tenth-century example at Gosforth in the same county.

*St Teath, Cornwall. The Anglo-Saxon wheel-head cross is 13 feet (4 metres) tall, and is decorated with interlace and leaf scrolls.*

Most were done in local stone, and some of the finest examples extant were carved in the granite of the far west. The exception to this is the Hiberno-Saxon preaching cross at Breage (Cornwall), which is the only sandstone wheel cross in the county. The best survival in Devon is at Colyton. Another fine tenth-century Celtic cross is in the churchyard at Nevern (Pembrokeshire). On later pre-Conquest crosses there was a gradual decline in the old style; vigorous and barbaric decoration moved towards more extensive figurework, especially in the head.

The cross became the spot around which followers of the faith were buried by choice, after a precedent set by the saint who was their teacher and minister. In 752, the Pope granted St Cuthbert permission to establish churchyards around churches. This formed the graveyard concept and the idea flourished. The ground was consecrated by a bishop, its cardinal points being marked by wooden crosses. If the graveyard included the grave of the missionary at whose cross the preaching took place, so much the better.

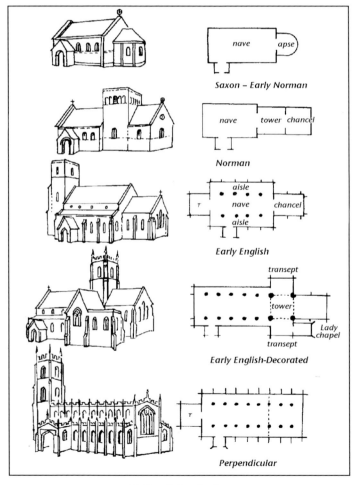

*Medieval church plans.*

## Location and design

Churches were built to the north of any preaching cross. At first, the area of the churchyard was undefined in extent. It was not enclosed and had no legal standing. The priests considered burial therein to be their prerogative but the people wanted to be given the same rights, thereby initiating a gradual acceptance of the laity into the same ground. Whether or not the physical area of the first churchyards seemed adequate was hardly an important issue. The bishop made a roughly circular tour of consecration and that, more or less, set the boundary.

Before the Conquest, people fled to their church in times of trouble and filled the churchyard with their animals and possessions when they were threatened. In Anglo-Saxon times the churchyard was used as a place for taking oaths and dealing with disputes. Justice was meted out around the churchyard cross, the symbol of both the faith and the community obligation to it, and the consecrated area around the church was considered to be inviolate from the earliest times.

## Design influences

Anglo-Saxon work has its origins in the building styles which swept up from the Mediterranean regions, through Europe and into Scandinavia. Churchmen travelled abroad, bringing back ideas and icons, while picking up geographical variations and local styles. These in turn were influenced by the availability of different building materials. The earliest churches in England were built of wood and roofed with thatch, by people who were used to working predominantly in those materials.

The design and appearance of a church also depended on the availability of skilled builders, and the abilities of those in areas where good building stone was available. There were quarries of fine stone lying roughly north-eastwards out of Northamptonshire, so it is no accident that, even today, Anglo-Saxon fabric is comparatively well represented in that area. Men like Benedict Biscop, the seventh-century founder of the monasteries at Jarrow and Wearmouth, provided the focus for received influences in church building and design. It was he who brought ideas from Rome and stonemasons from the continent, and who widened the use of glazed

*Jarrow, Durham. Adjacent to monastic ruins, the church has a Saxon chancel and there are windows of the period; the Saxon nave was destroyed, and replaced in Georgian and Victorian times.*

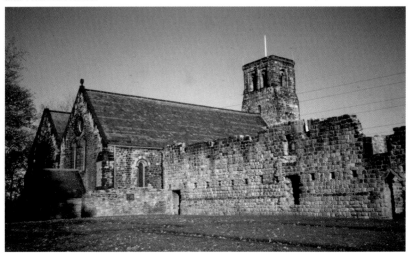

windows in churches.

The first influence on the design of churches in England was the Roman *basilica* plan. This was the name the Romans gave to the buildings that housed their public halls, law courts and exchanges. Here was a two-celled, rectangular ground plan in which the body of the building was separated from side aisles by rows of pillars. There was a semicircular apse at the west end with an altar, behind which sat judges or officials in a similar position to that adopted by the priests at the early altar tombs.

This design housed and protected the altar and gave it prominence within its own area. It provided a separate compartment for worshippers. Even so, exactly why this style was adopted is uncertain. While Britain belonged to the Roman Empire, all of its earliest churches were built in a contracted basilica form. In the southern areas, where the influence of Rome remained strong, this style of building was favoured for a long time afterwards. The ground plan was similar to those being built on a much larger scale abroad. By the end of the seventh century only the larger and more important buildings were of this type, and most of these were in southern England.

The Roman basilica style was fully developed when it arrived in Britain and did not subsequently progress, as was the case with the preferred Celtic plan. Apsidal sanctuaries were either semicircular or polygonal on plan, and apses were sometimes put up at the ends of aisles. It is unclear exactly why chancels came to be built to the east of naves, but that is the style which was widely adopted by the beginning of the seventh century.

The early eastern apses housed a stone altar built on mosaic or coloured tiles to enhance its visual importance. The cruciform ground plan of the church came about when transepts were built between – and at right angles to – the nave and the sanctuary apse, forming a cross shape. The two cells were sometimes separated by a small arcade. Saxon transepts were unusual, and surviving evidence, as at Hadstock (Essex), is extremely rare.

### The Celtic plan

The Roman basilica style of church building remained popular in the south and south-east of England, while the Celtic plan took hold elsewhere. It began with the small single cells that were the early Celtic sanctuaries or private chapels, of the

*Breamore, Hampshire. The round-headed Anglo-Saxon arch at the entry into the south porticus is composed of 3 feet (90 cm) thick voussoirs with big impost blocks bearing cable moulding. The inscription has been translated as: 'Here is made plain the word to thee.'*

*Greensted, Essex. The nave wall, built of oak trees split in half, has been variously dated between c.845 and c.1100, and the brick chancel is Tudor.*

type that can still be seen in Cornwall. As the converting missionaries and saints spread out of Ireland into the north and west of England, so too did this style. By the seventh century it consisted of two cells: a rectangular nave with a smaller, square-ended, rectangular chancel to the east. There was no dividing arcade between the two cells. The Anglo-Saxons may have favoured the square end simply because they had difficulties describing and constructing an alternative. The nave wall at Greensted (Essex) shows how, in the mid ninth century, walls were built of wood by splitting tree trunks along their length and positioning them with their flat surfaces inwards. The tops of these trunks

Above: *Wing, Buckinghamshire. The polygonal Anglo-Saxon apse has pilaster strips that carry the round arches of a shallow ornamental arcade.*

*St Lawrence, Bradford-on-Avon, Wiltshire. The north porch of this eleventh-century church has a series of short pilasters, occasionally reeded, and a typical Anglo-Saxon doorway.*

were shaped so that they could be secured to a plank by wooden pegs, and the bases were let into a horizontal member. Only occasionally did the Celtic meet the Roman, producing a rectangular nave with an apsidal ending. The Saxon builders gave a rare polygonal apse to the sanctuary at Wing (Buckinghamshire). The north porch at St Lawrence, Bradford-on-Avon (Wiltshire), is given as evidence of a kind of early transeptual arrangement that probably enclosed an altar and was used as a side chapel. A move, *c*.1000, towards the separate transept arrangement can be seen at Breamore (Hampshire).

## The essential crypt

Another part of early church building in England that had its origins in the Roman basilica was the crypt. This was a cell or chapel built beneath the body of the church. The concept derived from the Roman *confessio*, the vault behind and beneath the altar area of the basilica. Crypts were reached via a spiral stone staircase leading from the nave or a transept. They were usually to the east, below the main altar and constructed within the limits of the chancel. The walls were thick, the ceilings vaulted in stone, and the central space was sometimes divided by an arcade from a surrounding walkway, called an ambulatory. Repton (Derbyshire) is a particularly fine example. There is another Saxon crypt at Wing (Buckinghamshire).

In most crypts, pillars were either square or cylindrical, but short. Bases and abaci were made of roughly cut square blocks of undecorated stone. Sometimes the interior of the crypt could be viewed from the nave, through a hagioscope or squint. Crypts were used for a variety of purposes. The bodies or disinterred bones of saints were laid to rest there, in which instance the crypt might become a place of pilgrimage and worship. When the early travelling monks and missionaries returned from their fact-finding journeys, or pilgrims came home, they used church crypts as convenient store rooms for their accumulation of religious artefacts. The crypt at Hythe (Kent) is reputed to contain the skulls of thousands of warriors slain during a battle between Britons and Saxons in 456.

## Building the first churches

Saints, missionaries and monks all built churches, initially influenced by the one-room oratories, Celtic cells and beehive-shaped huts that may still be seen in Ireland and Scotland. People lived in little huts made of wattle and daub, a kind of basketwork of interwoven reeds held together and covered by a thick application of mud. It is likely that the cells which first protected the altars were constructed

*Monkwearmouth, Durham. A Saxon foundation, but of the original church only the west porch, west wall, tower, an inner doorway and some carvings survive; much of the rest was subjected to restoration and rebuilding in 1875.*

*St Lawrence, Bradford-on-Avon, Wiltshire. This is the blueprint for Anglo-Saxon church building, tall in relation to the width, and with external flat pilasters and string courses, round-headed arcading, and narrow doorways.*

in this way. Worshippers stayed outside, until it occurred to them that they could be protected from bad weather if they built a larger room adjoining the one that housed the altar. The negative side of this was that, a secular precedent having been established for building their shelter, the upkeep of that part of the church would remain the people's responsibility.

During the eighth century church building suffered in areas under the influence of Mercian kings, when religious and moral decline subverted the faith. Then came the period of Danish invasions. Church buildings were lost, but vigorous Viking art was acquired, finding its way into carved stonework. Canute rebuilt many of the churches that had been destroyed and consolidated the Anglo-Saxon and Danish elements. Anglo-Saxon church building did not just continue for five hundred years and then stop; the same labour force carried on after the Conquest, working under their accumulated pre-Conquest influences, and in some places probably accepting Norman styles very slowly. By the seventh century stonemasons were being imported from France.

Anglo-Saxon churches had many distinguishing features. Chancels were small in ground area, and naves were very high in comparison with their width. There was no particular need to erect a hall that would accommodate everyone, for there was no legal requirement to attend worship. The nave at Monkwearmouth (Durham) is a supreme example of typical Anglo-Saxon dimensions, and that at St Lawrence, Bradford-on-Avon (Wiltshire), is as high as it is long. Typical proportions can also be seen at Bratton (Wiltshire), Brixworth (Northamptonshire), Wareham (Dorset) and Escomb (Durham).

*Bredon, Worcestershire. Lightly inscribed mass dials on the church wall.*

### Telling the time

It has always been important to know the times of church services. The concept of the sundial originated in the ancient world, but its principle was easily and universally grasped. People understood that the shadow cast by a stationary object moved at the same speed each day as the relative position of the sun changed. Hence the shadow from the gnomon, an intervening metal pin or rod fixed into the church wall, fell along the same plane each day at the same time. The particular interest was in noon and the times of the important church services, mass and vespers (evensong). These were sometimes indicated by incised lines radiating from the central pin, that denoting mass at nine o'clock in the morning being more deeply cut than the others.

Some form of sundial has been used, associated with the church, since the Anglo-Saxons incised scratch, or mass, dials on stone slabs attached to the south-facing exteriors of their churches. Dials may be static or portable. At Kirkdale (Yorkshire) the signed, late Anglo-Saxon (*c*.1060) dial has a long explanatory inscription in heavy carving on slabs. Hands are sculpted around the dial at North Stoke (Oxfordshire) and that at Bishopstone (Sussex) includes a cross. There is an Anglo-Saxon mass dial at Saintbury (Gloucestershire).

Anglo-Saxon dials gave only a rough approximation of the time between sunrise and sunset. Some were quartered into three-hour 'tides', which equated with the lengths of the old Roman watches. This meant in practice that, while the quarters each side of midday remained constant, the length of the other two depended on the season of the year. Others divided daytime into anything up to twelve sections on the vertical face of the slab. Sunrise and sunset were indicated as halves of the same horizontal base line, and midday was shown by a vertical incision at right angles which joined the base line midway along its length. The figure was usually bisected by intermediate lines at 45 degrees.

### Anglo-Saxon church building

Very few reasonably complete Anglo-Saxon churches remain and some have been partly or wholly incorporated into later buildings. The little church of St Lawrence at Bradford-on-Avon (Wiltshire) is the most complete example. Only the nave survives

*Deerhurst, Gloucestershire. The west tower is Anglo-Saxon, with windows inserted in the fourteenth century; there is a Saxon chapel here, and important pre-Conquest work throughout the building.*

at St Peter, Bradwell-on-Sea (Essex). At Kirk Hammerton (Yorkshire) is a mid-eleventh-century tower survival with twin bell openings, former nave, south doorway and chancel arch. The basilica-inspired church at Wing (Buckinghamshire) and those of St Martin, Wareham (Dorset), Breamore, Boarhunt and Corhampton in Hampshire, and Deerhurst with Odda's Chapel (Gloucestershire) all have extensive Saxon building and individual features.

The main examples of Anglo-Saxon arched openings extant show that they were small and narrow, yet tall in relation to their width. Good examples are the chancel arches at Waterperry (Oxfordshire) and Boarhunt (Hampshire). They were frequently cut straight through the wall and constructed of stones covering the whole of its depth. *Imposts* (the top part of a column from which the arch springs) were either large, square blocks, sometimes moulded or

*Worth, Sussex. Wider than many Anglo-Saxon arches in relation to its height, this chancel arch is said to be the largest of its kind in England.*

41

Above: *Little Missenden, Buckinghamshire. Thin Roman bricks have been reused in the abacus of the Anglo-Saxon chancel arch.*

Left: *Great Dunham, Norfolk. The triangular-headed Anglo-Saxon doorway at the west end of the nave.*

chamfered, or formed by stepping a number of flat projecting stones, one on top of the other, above the jambs. The arches themselves were round-headed or triangular and were sometimes faced with dressed stones or turned with Roman bricks. There was rarely any moulding, and where imposts were used these were frequently no more than a plain stone, in some instances chamfered, projecting from the wall. Occasionally, a shallow, flat hood moulding projected from the surface of the wall, all around the opening. Although many jambs were constructed using large blocks of stone, some included baluster shafts. Good examples of typical Anglo-Saxon doorways are at Colchester (Essex), Somerford Keynes (Gloucestershire), Bradford-on-Avon and Britford (Wiltshire), Worth and Bolney (Sussex) and Escomb (Durham).

Doorways were first put up as portals through the west wall of a cell or into the ground-floor enclosure of a tower, where this was used as a chapel. Bricked up, but visible, is the portal at Stoke D'Abernon (Surrey). Later, the single western portal gave way to doorways in the north and south walls near the west end of the nave, sometimes admitting into portici or side chapels. Less often they might pierce the walls at the east end of the nave in the position where transepts developed. The doorway in the tower at Earls Barton (Northamptonshire) is a virtual template for those of its time.

### Materials and shapes

Anglo-Saxon builders often used bricks, tiles and masonry from the old Roman buildings. Otherwise they built of rubble and ragstone, flint, clunch and other pieces of chalk, undressed limestone and sandstone. The Anglo-Saxon mason used an axe to dress his stone. He laid his stones in horizontal courses and, before quoining was introduced, turned his angles in an irregular manner. *Herringbone work* was a characteristically early style of walling used from the time of the Roman occupation until well after the Norman Conquest. It involved placing horizontal or vertical courses of stones, bricks or reused Roman tiles, slanted in rows that were alternately inclined to the left and right.

*Marton, Lincolnshire. The eleventh-century tower, with its Anglo-Saxon windows, is built of limestone rubble and includes courses of herringbone masonry.*

It was commonly thought that by not bedding in flat a wall could be strengthened and the weight above better supported. Practically, it meant that where irregularly shaped stones were used the workman could achieve a more level finish between courses by laying stones of different shapes and sizes diagonally. Sometimes there was a vertical course of thin masonry between each row. Herringbone work also had a clear decorative value, and there is no doubt that it was used in this way in non-constructional situations. This feature is mostly found in the lower part of church walls, as in the tower at Bampton (Oxfordshire), and in field walls, in which applications it was also used for several centuries to effect repairs.

Perhaps the most obvious feature of Anglo-Saxon church walls is quoining, in particular the style known as long-and-short work. *Quoins* are stones placed one upon the other along the external angles of the building where two wall surfaces meet. Their purpose was to strengthen the whole structure before the use of buttresses.

Early on, when they were frequently rough, unhewn and irregular, quoins gave stability to weak walls such as those made of flint or rubble. In early work, large stones of different sizes were simply placed one on top of the other; each piece rarely squared with its neighbours.

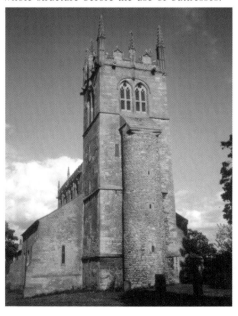

Another method involved placing rectangular blocks alternately lengthways and end-on to form the angle. Megalithic quoins were sometimes as tall as several courses of walling and may be randomly laid using stones of varying sizes. When blocks with the same area of cross-section were placed horizontally and vertically it resulted in the *long-and-short work* so characteristic of Anglo-Saxon towers.

*Hough-on-the-Hill, Lincolnshire. Three stages of the tower are Anglo-Saxon and have a rare semicircular stair projection of the period.*

*Barton-upon-Humber, Lincolnshire. A tenth-century tower built on eighth-century foundations; the lower stage has light pilaster strips, and a round-headed arcade beneath a triangular-headed arcade, and the pairs of windows reflect these.*

## The multi-purpose towers

Church towers made their first appearance in the seventh century. The greater number of remaining Anglo-Saxon towers are in a band running north from East Anglia through Lincolnshire, in which they are particularly well represented, Durham and Northumberland. Most are western towers, built on a square, rectangular or circular base plan, but not all towers of this period were put up to the west: Barton-upon-Humber (Lincolnshire) and Langford and North Leigh (Oxfordshire) (both central), were not originally so. Central towers made their appearance at this time, put up between the nave and the chancel. The whole ethos behind tower building, design and placement has never been satisfactorily understood. We know how some of them may have developed from existing building or architectural features; we know all about watch-towers and the like; we understand 'building upwards to the glory of God', and we know 'bigger and better' became a matter of honour between

*Breamore, Hampshire. A tenth- or early eleventh-century church, with long-and-short work, pilaster strips, and double-splayed Anglo-Saxon windows, making this a blueprint for the period.*

*Earls Barton, Northamptonshire. The mid-tenth-century tower, built of stone and rubble, with typical long-and-short quoins, pilaster strips, diamond-shaped and semicircular arcading, little round-headed and triangular-headed lights, and baluster shafts.*

settlements. Yet with tower building there remains a small but key element that is still just outside our grasp. Even the Roman basilica plan, in which the altar was brought forward of the apse, provided for the idea of an interim space that could be developed. Then there was the presence of a porticus, built across the juncture where nave met sanctuary, and gained through doorways in the internal walls. These were, in effect, apse chapels and should not be confused with the porch porticus, which gave entry into the church from the outside. These, too, were sometimes used as side chapels and had their own altars. When they were positioned between nave and sanctuary, however, the result was an embryonic cross plan. Having gone thus far, it was an obvious step to insert another segment between nave and apse and, for whatever reason, raise the walls at that point, forming a tower. An excellent example of how the evolution of cruciform developed almost to completion can be seen at Breamore (Hampshire), where the church conforms to all Saxon criteria. A late example of a wholly cruciform Saxon church is at Tintagel (Cornwall), of *c*.1080.

It is likely that pre-Conquest towers were finished with a blunt, four-sided pyramidal cap. The gabled west tower of Sompting (Sussex) – the so-called Rhenish helm – appears still to have its original style of cap. By the tenth century, towers were commonplace, primarily intended to house bells, but also used as places of refuge, as lookouts and landmarks. Where appropriately situated, they were landmarks from the sea and signposts for travellers on their journeys. The pre-eminent extant Saxon tower is surely that at Earls Barton (Northamptonshire). While the church at Langford (Oxfordshire) is important for its Saxon survivals generally, the tower itself is completely Saxon and also has pilaster strips. Anglo-Saxon towers rarely had window openings in their lower stages, and their doorways were comparatively small, suggesting that they had an important role to play in protecting the community in times of trouble. Single belfry windows were sometimes put in, but most commonly they were the double type.

The early builders could not build great crossing towers above piers and arches, so they either worked from ground level or extended existing one- or two-storey porches upwards. This arrangement of porch towers existed at, for example, Corbridge (Northumberland), Bardsey (Yorkshire) and Monkwearmouth (Durham). There is a Saxon porch at Titchfield (Hampshire) that was built up into a tower. Some towers were built of a piece, others in several stages divided by string courses. They either tapered towards the top or were built up in a series of successively narrower stages. The variation used depended, to some extent, on the materials available.

Many stone towers were externally decorated, in whole or part, by pilaster-style stripwork. This was an effective way of breaking up flat areas and making them more pleasing to the eye. Pilasters were shallow rectangular stone battens of square

45

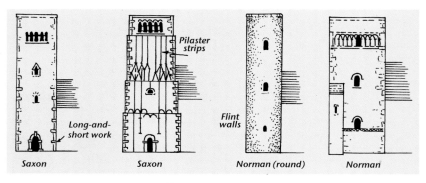

Saxon · Saxon · Norman (round) · Norman

Pilaster strips

Long-and-short work

Flint walls

*Romanesque towers.*

section, protruding just a few inches from the surface of the wall. They imitated the struts and beams used in the construction of wooden buildings and were occasionally used as structural supports. Some pilasters ran the whole height of the tower, while others terminated at a horizontal string course, frequently that which separated the second and third stages. In this case, the pilaster decoration on the two lower stages might be done of a piece, enclosing the ground-floor doorway and the little external window openings in the stage above.

Within this framework there was sometimes long-and-short work, the shorter lengths arranged to make pointed or round arch figures between the vertical strips. The arches were occasionally made as 'Y' or 'V' shapes connecting the vertical strips, or the strips were effectively turned into little shafts with the inclusion of flat 'capitals' at the points of spring and similar bases at the foot. These features were quite plain, in contrast to those on the classical Greek and Roman pilasters.

Sometimes the tower was used as a chapel at ground level, with accommodation for the priest on the floor above and an opening for him to see into the nave. Each stage probably had a wooden floor, and the tower could be progressed by means of wooden ladders. There were usually either little single lights or pairs of openings to illuminate each stage, and there was always a much larger opening through the east wall of the tower into the nave, as at Deerhurst (Gloucestershire) and Monkwearmouth (Durham), or the fine triple arrangement at Brixworth (Northamptonshire). The greater number of openings usually pierced the belfry stage. Barton-upon-Humber (Lincolnshire) has an exceptional Saxon tower, with a western narthex, or porch, attached to it.

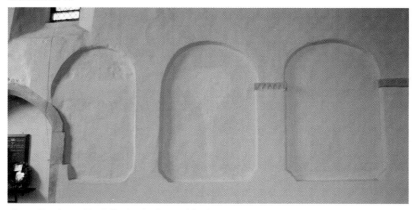

*Great Dunham, Norfolk. Anglo-Saxon blind arcading in the nave.*

*Thursley, Surrey. The deep splays of the Anglo-Saxon windows in the north wall of the chancel are decorated, and the openings still have their original timber frames to which covers would have been attached.*

## Windows

The Anglo-Saxon emphasis on height rather than breadth and the fact that the walls of the church were rarely pierced with windows created a false impression of strength. They appear to be solid but are comparatively thin. The whole structure was held together using a strong mortar, which sometimes included crushed Roman bricks, and was often plastered externally with a mixture of sand and lime. Arches above window openings were sometimes constructed of reused Roman tiles. The openings themselves were small, which meant that the interior of the church was dark at all times.

Builders did not have the knowledge to construct large windows. Glass was available from abroad and could be made in England using imported foreign labour. However, it was thin, easily broken and expensive; more practical was a smaller, unglazed or shuttered opening to keep out the elements. Oiled linen, parchment and animal skins were also used to block up window openings when light was not required. Avebury (Wiltshire) is a good example of where window openings might be placed in the nave walls of an Anglo-Saxon church.

Most windows of this period were straight-sided and passed through the whole thickness of the wall without any kind of recess. If there was no decent building stone to be had in the district, the jambs were constructed of rubble and, where they had

semicircular heads, these were also turned using larger, thinner pieces of rubblestone. At Escomb (Durham) there are small Saxon windows high in the walls. There are triangular-headed windows of this period at Bosham (Sussex) and in the twin openings of the impressive Saxon tower at Holy Trinity, Colchester

*Holy Trinity, Colchester, Essex. Anglo-Saxon, built of stone and reused Roman bricks, the tower has typically narrow and round-headed windows of the period.*

(Essex), which is partly built of Roman bricks. Some openings, as at Avebury (Wiltshire), were circular and were each made from a single piece of stone. Splays were important, as the greater the internal surface the more direct light would be allowed through and the larger the area of available reflected light.

Window jambs frequently inclined towards the top, giving a wider splay at the base. The earliest openings of this type were built more or less flush with the external walls. They had a single internal splay, which gave a much larger internal opening, sometimes twice that of the window area. Later in the eleventh century the double splay came about, whereby the opening was placed back from the line of the outside wall (in which case the external jamb might simply be chamfered) or placed centrally.

The sides of Anglo-Saxon windows were rarely moulded. Double or triple lights were constructed by cutting semicircular-headed, straight-sided holes through the wall and then dividing them with the appropriate number of straight shafts or balusters. Balusters usually bulged at the centre, but were sometimes straight-sided, and were built between flat, squared stones, one of which formed the impost between the arches on either side, and the other was the base. Both the impost – and in some cases a capital – and the base were sometimes corbelled away from the surface of the wall.

## Hogbacks and other sculpture

Although the years of Danish invasion had a limiting influence on church building, especially in those areas most vulnerable to attack and occupation, some northern churchyards have fine examples of Anglo-Danish art. These are tombstones of a particular type known as hogbacks. They are low in relation to their height, have a curved upper surface with a gable at either end and are highly decorated throughout. The general shape is reminiscent of the Viking House of the Dead, and the inward-looking animal carvings at the ends may have some significance in warding off evil spirits.

At the top there is usually a frieze of some minor decorative motif, repeated in continuous order and following the curve of the stone. Beneath may be either vertical or horizontal bands of knotwork, plaiting or running spirals, or there may be scenes depicting Scandinavian mythology. There are examples at Brompton-in-Allerton

*Heysham, Lancashire. The fine tenth-century Viking hogback tombstone that includes carved symbols of Christianity, characters of Norse legend, and carvings of animals and foliage.*

(Yorkshire), Lowther, Aspatria, Gosforth and Penrith (Cumbria) and Heysham (Lancashire). Elsewhere, there are coffin-shaped or hogback coped stones to be found in whole or part, notably in the far west at St Buryan, St Tudy, Lanivet and Phillack in Cornwall. Muncaster (Cumbria) has Saxon and Viking stones. Indeed, there is a Viking cross in the chancel at Hovingham (Yorkshire).

The Anglo-Saxon sculptors, working with hammer and chisel, enjoyed creating animals, birds, leaves, vines and biblical characters. The acanthus leaf, which in Classical art appeared widely on Corinthian and Composite capitals, made its first appearance in England in the tenth century.

A doorway at Britford (Wiltshire) shows how interlacing and vine scrolls looked in the ninth century, and there are connecting slabs with interlace, knotwork and floral motifs. There are other Anglo-Saxon gems in the same county, notably an exceptional ninth-century cross shaft at Codford St Peter that appears to show a rustic reveller at his happiest, and a fragment of similar date at Colerne that has knotwork and intertwined dragons. At Knook there is a fine tympanum of rustic beasts and scrollwork, of sufficiently indefinable date to be ascribed as Saxo-Norman overlap. The two roods at Langford (Oxfordshire) are of national importance; one is of a headless Christ with outstretched arms and is ascribed to *c*.1000, while an unspecific, later date, although still of the Saxon period, has been suggested for a drooping Christ suffering on the cross. While these illustrate the advance of carving techniques and the relative talents of the carvers, the former bears comparison with that of *c*.1100 at Romsey Abbey (Hampshire), which is more natural in form and has the hand of God emerging from a cloud above. The latter rood at Langford might be compared with the style of that at Breamore (Hampshire), where the Christ is also suffering. Of similar date is the remarkable flying angel at Winterbourne Steepleton (Dorset), which appears to be kicking up his heels in some form of ecstasy. If, as has been suggested, he may also be holding a skull, perhaps we have here some symbolic depiction of celestial happiness over a saved soul. It is nothing like the two Saxon angels who float in low relief above the chancel arch at St Lawrence, Bradford-on-Avon (Wiltshire).

*Little Langford, Wiltshire. The Norman south doorway is full of decorative motifs of the period, including waves of zigzag, and the tympanum includes the likenesses of a bishop and the tree of life with three birds.*

*Breedon on the Hill, Leicestershire. There are many eighth- and ninth-century carvings of friezes and architectural figurework relocated in this church; these are part of a set stretching across the wall behind the altar.*

They are almost classically robed and are kicking up their legs in a quite different way, perhaps as an aid to flight. At Breedon on the Hill (Leicestershire) there is an eighth-century carving showing obscure cat-like creatures with large tails. They are walking in single file but appear to be interacting with each other.

Meanwhile early Christian art was arriving from Gaul, adding to that which had come from Rome, and local craftsmen were developing their own styles. Carvings were made of wood, church plate was introduced, and altar hangings, embroidered altar cloths and vestments all contributed to the richness of the developing church. By the tenth century the workshops in English monasteries were turning out bells and carvings with the assistance of secular labour. Artists and draughtsmen were producing fine paintings and manuscripts. There was some trade in ex-stock church fittings, as there was to be later, in the thirteenth century, when there was a vogue for polished marble.

Workshops made aumbries to hold the church's ornaments and sacred vessels, and piscinas – the internal drains for the disposal of the water in which the priest washed the vessels or his own hands. By the tenth century English masons generally had mastered the principles of church building in stone.

*Breedon on the Hill, Leicestershire. The gem of the church's collection of Anglo-Saxon sculpture, the so-called 'Breedon Angel', shows Byzantine influence and was probably undertaken by sculptors from Greece. This modern replica can be seen in the south aisle; the original is in the ringing chamber.*

*Deerhurst, Gloucestershire. Late ninth-century cylindrical font carved with double Celtic trumpet spiral and a border of vine scroll. The pillar it stands on is thought to be part of a Saxon cross.*

## Baptism and fonts

Infants were first baptised in fonts in the second century AD, and even at such an early date there were fonts in some churches. By the sixth century baptism had become general, and the baptism of infants became compulsory in England in 816. The ceremony and the fonts that facilitated it were at first in the open air. In Cornwall baptism was sometimes associated with springs and nearby chapels. The early fonts were small, shallow pools, hardly more than ankle deep in water and with steps at each end. Although fonts in Britain developed from an approximately round shape, the earliest in other areas were known to have been square.

It is likely that the majority of pre-Conquest fonts were made of wood, although none has survived from this period. Of extant examples made of stone, most are either circular or tub-shaped. They follow the design of the wooden barrels that were used to hold the baptismal water in early wooden churches, the barrels themselves being a continental innovation. Stone tub fonts became popular as an increasing number of churches were built in stone. What ended the popularity of this design was neither the Conquest itself nor the imposition of a new art, since the Romanesque was common to both, but the

ability to improve on standard designs and a consequent intolerance of all that was plain or crudely fashioned.

It has always been extremely difficult to date Saxon fonts accurately, especially those which are of plain, unmoulded stone. Some can be recognised by the infrequent and crude carvings. A certain amount of early interlacing, which was fairly common on the shafts of Celtic crosses, was to be developed into a standard pattern on Norman work. However, some font bowls have been assigned to the Anglo-Saxon period on the evidence of their decorative carving. Others can be dated by an inscription. The bucket-shaped bowl at Potterne (Wiltshire), which was found buried beneath a later font during restoration in 1872, is inscribed around the rim. The early ninth-century font at Deerhurst (Gloucestershire) is the best-preserved of its kind. The bowl rests on a pillar which is thought to be part of what was once a Saxon cross.

The light interlacing of Celtic influence similarly dates the roughly circular font at Washaway (Cornwall). At Morwenstow, at the north-east tip of the same county, there is a real oddity which invites considerable *Potterne, Wiltshire. A plain, bucket-shaped Anglo-Saxon bowl with the first verse of Psalm 42 inscribed in Latin around the rim.*

Far left: *Thursley, Surrey.*
*The Anglo-Saxon font has a*
*small, tapering bowl with a*
*band of chevron around the*
*top, and a roll moulding part*
*the way down.*

Left: *Melbury Bubb, Dorset.*
*The tapering tub font, thought*
*to have originally been*
*part of the base of a pre-*
*Conquest shaft, is carved*
*with intertwined creatures*
*wrestling upside down.*

conjecture about its age, but the bias is towards Anglo-Saxon. Here is an unmounted, egg-shaped container barely 24 inches (61 cm) high, with bowl and stem hewn from a single block of stone. It is misshapen, with a central band of cable moulding, a form of decoration developed as a primary motif after the Conquest. Other font bowls believed to be Anglo-Saxon include those at Kimbolton (Cambridgeshire), Ford, Poling, Selham and North Stoke (West Sussex), Thursley (Surrey), Hinton Parva (Oxfordshire) and St Martin, Canterbury (Kent).

An Anglo-Saxon cross-shaft socket, with ornamentation of Roman influence, would have made a square font for later baptisms or might have been used, in part, to support a later bowl. One may come across a font which is a hollowed-out capital or pillar base from an early church or, as at Wroxeter (Shropshire), the reused base of a Roman column. The fonts at Melbury Bubb (Dorset) and Wilne (Derbyshire) have both been carved out of the circular section from pre-Conquest cross shafts and set upside down. At Dolton (Devon) two blocks from an Anglo-Saxon cross stand one on top of the other, a squared block supporting a tapering, hollowed-out bowl. Generally, the amount and standard of carving that the Anglo-Saxons achieved on their crosses was not maintained in the interior of the new stone churches or their fixtures. In England very few fonts now ascribed to this period are known to have been embellished with anything other than an inscription, a plain moulding or cable decoration.

### Coffins and inscriptions

The Anglo-Saxons sometimes buried their dead in wooden coffins, but it was not until early in the seventeenth century that wooden coffins made of flat boards came into general use. Some churches have examples of pre-Conquest coffin panels, slabs or lids: St Tudy (Cornwall), Wirksworth (Derbyshire), Dearham (Cumbria) and St Minver (Cornwall). There are Saxon grave covers at Kirkoswald (Cumbria). In this connection, we might mention the tablets inscribed in ogham script. This was an early style of writing used from about the fourth century, mainly in southern Ireland, where there are some three hundred examples extant. Most of those remaining in Britain have been dated to between the fifth and seventh centuries and are memorial inscriptions of some kind. The style devolved on the arrangement of short lines in groups to form letters and, ultimately, words. In its simplest form, the individual letters each comprise vertical or sloping lines of the same dimensions, and there are about twenty in the alphabet. The letter was also determined by the length of the lines in a group. The best-known example is probably the inscribed piece of granite, most likely a grave marker, at St Kew (Cornwall). There are also stones bearing ogham script in the churches at Lewannick and St Clement, in the same county.

# Norman
# 1066-1160

**Builders of the large churches**

The Saxo-Norman overlap accounted for some new village churches, as at Hales (Norfolk) and Stow (Lincolnshire). William I confiscated Anglo-Saxon held lands, and many estates, often with church buildings on them, passed into the hands of Norman favourites. Vacancies among the clergy were regularly filled by churchmen from across the Channel. There were usually builders and craftsmen in their company who were anxious to impress with an improved style of architecture that enabled them to build wider and bigger arches. The result was the establishment of Norman Romanesque and its rapid development to a point where its quality exceeded that which had been achieved in France. At the time of the Conquest most parishes in England had a church, and it has been estimated that during the century that followed as many as seven thousand were built.

William re-established the teachings according to Rome, made Lanfranc head of the Church at Canterbury in 1070 and brought both doctrine and architecture very much in line with continental Europe. Under Lanfranc's leadership monasteries were reformed and rebuilt and a new period of church building came about. At first the buildings were solid-looking and solemn, with little sculptural decoration or colour. They were as functional as their predecessors, although they must have appeared to be on a far grander scale. Every village was to have a church.

After the Conquest a number of hard-working builder bishops set their hands to dramatically reconstructing the fabric of their cathedrals, as well as laying the foundations of ecclesiastical reform. Concurrently, the new abbots set about rebuilding their monasteries. Both bishops and abbots went for size and splendour. Occasionally practical building skills did not quite meet the vision and the whole lot came tumbling down, or disastrous fires destroyed years of construction. The promoters simply set about raising more finances and building even bigger and better. The point of all this was that it continued to send unequivocal messages to the people about the strength and ascendancy of the Christian religion, psychologically urging them to emulate the works in their own way. Practical work being carried out on the great churches provided the inspiration for the movement that rebuilt so many of England's smaller churches, as well as setting the parameters of their style, form and decoration.

New town churches were built particularly to serve monastic interests, occasionally by monasteries that wished to retain the nave of their abbey church for their own use. There was a third approach to monastic endowments. In moves reminiscent of those to come at the Dissolution, the accumulated wealth of many small churches was appropriated for their use. This trend was to be resolved early in the twelfth century when an edict prevented monasteries from appropriating parish churches without specific episcopal approval.

William II (1087–1100) made unreasonable demands on the church. He took abbeys either for himself or to rent and continued to exact pecuniary advantage between the time of the death of Lanfranc in 1089 and his belated appointing of Anselm as the unwilling but obvious successor in 1093. By the reign of Henry I (1100–35) the Norman style had fully asserted itself in the construction of village churches. The thatched timber structures that had been put up before the Conquest, and that had survived the ravages of the elements and the later period of human neglect, were now in need of replacement. They were to be swept away and replaced in a fervour

*Iffley, Oxfordshire. The west front, built 1170–80, is a tour de force of late Norman decorative work in perfect symmetry.*

of religious zeal and stone church building throughout the first half of the twelfth century.

By Stephen's time (1135–54) the church was all-powerful, and the ensuing period of civil strife had little effect on the church's influence or on church building. Over 150 monasteries were to be established, and the great period of parish church building ended only at about the same time as Stephen's reign. Examples of church building from the reign of Henry II (1154–89) are the parish churches at Iffley (Oxfordshire), Kilpeck (Herefordshire), Pittington (Durham) and Stewkley (Buckinghamshire).

### Norman small church plans

Norman walls are distinguished by their apparently solid appearance. In reality, an infill of rubble hardcore was faced with dressed ashlar blocks, on which masons worked diagonally with an axe to produce deep, uneven surface cuts. Otherwise, cut stone was used which had not been dressed. The stone blocks were wide-jointed and held together by copious amounts of thin mortar. As the period progressed, less mortar was needed and the building stones were more closely abutted. Although buttresses proper were introduced during this period, most walls were not supported in this way.

Churches continued to be built as two cells: a larger nave and a smaller apsidal sanctuary, their lengths usually in a ratio of 2:1, each of equal width and height. For a while the apsidal ending was revived in south-eastern and eastern counties. Soon the sanctuary grew narrower than the nave, and the two-celled arrangement gave way to a three-celled plan, admitting a central choir. When a tower was added, this was usually done axially above the choir when the church had a square east end, and to the west of the nave when the east end was apsidal. Churches continued to be built along these lines until the population outgrew them. For the first time in England it became important to accommodate everyone within the church, so transepts were

*East Meon, Hampshire. The Norman crossing tower of c.1150 has richly decorated, round-headed bell openings with circular openings above, and a pretty lead-covered broach spire.*

added to the north and south of the choir, from which they were separated by arched openings. Transepts were simply extra rooms put up in convenient positions, and they created the first real cruciform churches. Towers built above them became crossing towers. Arches around the crossing offered considerable scope for decoration, and the ways in which they were so treated are well worth study today. It was usually the one into the chancel that received the greatest amount of embellishment, followed by that between the nave and the crossing, and then the other interior arches. Sometimes small apsidal chapels were built out of the east walls of the transepts, and it is not difficult to envisage how this became, in the later medieval period, a useful position for chantry chapels.

Throughout the twelfth century church builders continued to put up aisleless naves in new churches. Aisles were first added to the north side, then to the south out of necessity. Only occasionally were they planned and executed together. Building on to Anglo-Saxon dimensions caused considerable problems because the naves were so long, narrow and ill-lit. Aisles were usually built parallel to the entire length of the nave and about half of its width, the two areas being separated by an arcade of several bays. This in itself would have left most of the nave very gloomy indeed, so the problem was solved by creating a clerestory. The walls were raised above the new arcade and pierced with larger lights than previously.

*Stillingfleet, Yorkshire. The twelfth-century door is made of five vertical sections; it is adorned with two decorated C-shaped hinge straps and the representations of a Viking ship, male and female figures, interlocking crosses, and a tree.*

## Porches and towers

Towers ceased to be the main entrance to the church, even though very few porches were built before the thirteenth century. Those still in use as nave towers continued to play a part in the church services, but otherwise they became the support for belfries. In many cases the Normans extended upward the Anglo-Saxon west porches, thickening the walls where necessary. They had also mastered the technique of raising a central tower above piers placed at the internal angles. This proved to be the most important advance in the design of towers for it admitted masonry bulk, much appreciated by the Normans. It meant that crossing towers became a standard feature of twelfth-century church building. The cruciform arrangement was always most satisfying when built in conjunction with a central tower, because such a structure unified the whole building in a way that was not possible in the case of a western tower. Externally, there were two other factors that helped to enhance the visual unity in the case of towers that appear to grow from the body of the church: the treatment of the western face of the church as a façade, and the way in which blind arcading, lights and sound holes, there and on the towers, were decoratively treated as of a piece. The idea of this can be seen in an embryonic stage at Stewkley (Buckinghamshire), and at Iffley (Oxfordshire) there is a supreme example.

Although wooden spires with up to six sides were not unknown, most Norman spires were low, pyramidal caps. They were covered either in stone or, more commonly, in wooden roofing tiles. Few had parapets and some had saddleback or double saddleback roofs. This style, which was popular in northern Europe, occurred when two opposite walls of the tower were gabled, and the apex was formed by the roof ridge. The stages were climbed by means of a new innovation: the circular

*Stewkley, Buckinghamshire. This church is a riot of Norman zigzag decoration, as exemplified in the triple-arch arrangement around the west door.*

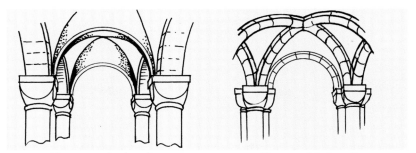

*Norman groined vault.*                    *Norman ribbed vault.*

or octagonal exterior stair turret. Built from the ground up to just below the belfry stage, where they were usually angled into the wall, external stair turrets spoiled the line of the tower. Of the rare Norman hexagonal towers extant, two of note are Ozleworth and Swindon, both in Gloucestershire.

## Construction and vaulting

Forest oaks were felled to make the trussed rafters and heavy tie beams of the new steep-pitched roofs. The tie beams were set close together above both nave and chancel and sometimes had the flat boarding of a ceiling battened on to them. Until this time roofs had been held up by angled timbers joined together at the apex, and repeated at regular intervals along the length of the building. Stability was given to the structure by adding a horizontal beam that connected pairs of rafters at some point along their length. The Normans knew how to construct a simple barrel vault in stone – and also how to intersect them effectively – but they did not have enough confidence in the strength of their walls to do so over large areas. Experimental vaulting was carried out above porches and crypts, where the side walls were low and the span relatively small. It was extended to aisles, which were longer but narrow, and finally to small chancels. By intersecting two barrel vaults at right angles, the groined vault was formed. It was an obvious decorative step to make a ribbed feature of the intersections, then turn them into definite mouldings and add bosses at the points of spring. By the mid twelfth century, quadripartite vaults were appearing, divided into four sections of equal size by transverse diagonal ribs that crossed in the centre. Sexpartite vaults were similarly sectioned but included an additional rib that divided the vault into six unequal parts.

*Bredon, Worcestershire. The simply vaulted Norman porch with heavy moulded ribs and zigzag around the doorways.*

57

*Stewkley, Buckinghamshire. The Norman string course of lozenge shapes is continued around the head of the arches and along the walls of the nave.*

The Normans understood the principles of conducting lateral thrusts and put up plain, rectangular, single-stage buttresses with their upper surfaces sloping into cornices or the eaves of roofs. In order to retain accepted decorative continuity, they were built along external walls, where they marked the division of bays. They were also put up at the angles of walls, for the first time, in the twelfth century, extending a short equal distance along the walls from where they both met. These are known as clasping buttresses. Later examples of Norman buttresses had thin shafts let into their outer angles. The builders ran horizontal string courses between the buttresses, beneath or up to windows, or along lengths of open wall. Occasionally the string course ran above the head of a window arch, in effect forming an integrated hood moulding or dripstone. Early string courses were generally heavily done and were square in cross-section, but chamfered below into the wall. Later, both upper and lower angles might be chamfered with a quarter round forming a leading edge. In some cases the chamfered upper edge became a fillet, which developed a roll on the underside. String courses ran right around the building – often both inside and out – tying it together visually. Sometimes they were enriched by decorative motifs of the period. The other type of string course, in theory at least, is the corbel table. Although it has a more practical purpose, in that it is a run of small stone projections that help to support a roof, parapet or cornice, it is nonetheless another means of providing visual unity.

### Windows, arched openings and decorative work

Typical Norman window openings were relatively small and narrow in the

*Climping, Sussex. The late Norman round-headed west doorway, c.1170, of the south transept tower is decorated with zigzag and dog-tooth motifs, and the inner order has a trefoil-shaped arch.*

*Malmesbury, Wiltshire. The south doorway has eight orders, and each is richly carved; three comprise panels of biblical scenes and the others have patterns of interlaced foliage.*

nave and chancel, where they were placed high in the wall, but generally they were larger in the clerestory. They were placed flush with the surface on the outside and deeply splayed internally. Most were single lights, although they were sometimes grouped in three behind the altar, rather more for appearance than any practical purpose. As arch ordering – imposing one arch upon another – became popular around doorways and arches within the church, so too was it used to great effect around Norman windows. There might be two or three orders around the window, with the inner arch sometimes moulded from cill to cill, with the characteristic zigzag, or chevron, of the period, continued around the sides and the head. Beads, pellets, diamonds and other minor decorative motifs were used in conjunction with the main moulding. Where a hood moulding was included, this might also have a diaper pattern worked into it. Sometimes the sides of the openings were adorned with decorated shafts, caps and bases. Circular windows were widely introduced into towers – as at Old Shoreham (Sussex).

Norman sculptors produced a vast number of different surface motifs that were used to greatest effect around arched openings: arcades, windows and doorways, and the pillars, capitals and mouldings associated with them. The mouldings themselves tended to be either chamfered (where the straight edge was cut off at an angle), rounded or quarter rounded with shallow hollows. Twelfth-century decorative work was frequently bound by twisted, cord-like *cable moulding*. This came in a whole range of sizes, thicknesses and densities.

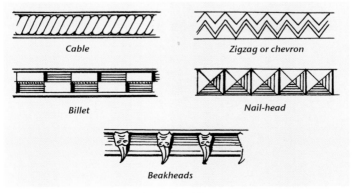

*Carved mouldings.*

*Elstow, Bedfordshire. The twelfth-century tympanum depicts Christ in Majesty bestowing a blessing, in the company of St Peter and St Paul.*

Such decoration was put up in single or double rows, although the amazing multi-ordered chancel arch at Tickencote (Rutland) is one of the exceptions to this. It is not possible to define exactly all of the motifs one may encounter from this period, although several were used overwhelmingly and have been given names. *Chevron*, or zigzag, for example, is the most instantly recognised of all Norman ornamentation. This is the characteristic V-shaped moulding which first appeared early in the twelfth century. Where this 'V' shape was carved out of a similarly shaped background, the result is *indented* moulding. *Billet* consists of short, raised rectangles that are either square or semicircular in cross-section and look as if they have all been cut from a length of plain stone rope. Put up to alternate in more than one row, it is then called *alternate billet*. Many of the regular surface motifs are used in association with rows of plain spheres, known as *bead*, or *pellet* in its larger form.

Sometimes rows of quite large spheres are in themselves the main decoration. *Lozenge* is a diamond shape, usually wider horizontally than vertically. *Double cone* is a rounded, diamond shape, conoid at the leading edge and blunt at the point of contact with its neighbour. *Nail-head* is a continuous line of four-sided pyramids, set square. It is similar to *star* ornamentation, which is cut away on each side, forming points at the angles.

Sometimes decorative mouldings were more obvious. The raised outline of castle battlements was depicted in *embattled* moulding, a name also used to describe triangular shapes with chamfered leading edges. *Medallion* is

*Compton, Surrey. The double sanctuary has a vaulted lower chamber that is approached through a decorated round arch; the gallery chapel above is separated from the chancel by a wooden rail of the Norman period.*

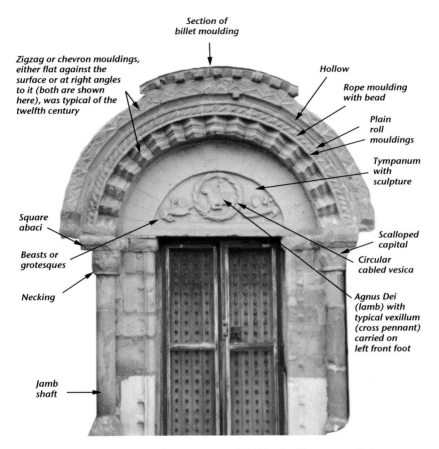

**Section of billet moulding**

**Zigzag or chevron mouldings, either flat against the surface or at right angles to it (both are shown here), was typical of the twelfth century**

**Hollow**

**Rope moulding with bead**

**Plain roll mouldings**

**Tympanum with sculpture**

**Square abaci**

**Beasts or grotesques**

**Necking**

**Scalloped capital**

**Circular cabled vesica**

**Agnus Dei (lamb) with typical vexillum (cross pennant) carried on left front foot**

**Jamb shaft**

*Features of a twelfth-century doorway, exemplified in the Norman north doorway at Upleadon, Gloucestershire.*

a basic oval, often formed by a bead or pellet, enclosing a recognisable likeness of a bird or beast, which occasionally also strays out of the centre. *Beakheads* take the form of long beaks or pointed chins, extending over a convex moulding to the roll below. Here were birds, animals, dragons and grotesques, sometimes whole rows painstakingly sculpted to be as identical as possible. At Wroughton (Wiltshire) the crocodiles which terminate the mouldings around the south door are really nothing more than the beakhead design applied to the corbel concept. It is a motif that encompasses many different shapes, but all with a single purpose. These creatures represent the servants of the devil, ready to capture the souls of those who go lightly to church. Sculptors also carved birds, fishes and animals as they saw them, or in ways which had symbolic Christian significance. They sculpted likenesses of their friends or people in the community, and everyday things in their lives – the tools of various trades, shells, flowers, foliage, fruit, nuts and seeds.

Both chancel arches and doorways were very lavishly sculpted, the former usually on the west face only, and the latter on the outside. These arches were sometimes of

*Petersfield, Hampshire. The chancel arch, of c.1120, has billet and chevron decoration, and forms a remarkable group with the slightly later round-headed and multi-shafted windows above.*

several orders, each of which might be similarly decorated or differing from order to order. When zigzag was used, it was deeply cut and ran either along the surface of the wall or at right angles to it. Occasionally the visual appearance, and thus the importance, of a chancel arch was enhanced by blind arcading on either side. Most arches used in the Norman church before the middle of the twelfth century were semicircular. Rarely was a stilted arch used, in which the jambs continued briefly above the impost to a higher point of spring. The horseshoe shape was also occasionally used. In Norman arches the huge blocks of stone which had formed the width of the jambs in a single length gave way to smaller pieces of cut stone on the surface, with an infilling of rubble. Arches were higher and wider but, since the height of a round arch could not safely be more than half of the distance across, many simply did not withstand the weights imposed on them from above. If the weight was too great, they collapsed; at the very least, it is the reason why they dropped over time, pushing the imposts outwards as the downward thrust changed direction. It is also the reason why most Norman semicircular chancel arches have survived in the best condition in small country churches, where there was always less masonry above. This point is often illustrated by whole nave arcades which now lean out of true.

### Norman constructional arches and arcading

Nave arcades are rows of arches supported by *pillars* – the name given to the structure from ground level to the point at which the arch springs. Sometimes they are called *piers*. Architecturally, pillars comprised – from the top – *abacus*, *capital*,

*Ickleton, Cambridge-shire. The round arches of the nave have com-pletely flat soffits and spring from flat cushion capitals above plain cylindrical pillars.*

*Malmesbury, Wiltshire. The Decorated 'watching chamber' over the nave was a later insertion into the Norman triforium.*

*shaft*, *base* and *plinth*. There was little structural necessity for any of this, but builders were moving away from the purely practical, basic load-bearing devices. What went on beneath the point of spring assumed various shapes on plan, and the contours of those shapes were to be followed by a variety of mouldings and decoration. These developments happened slowly at first. The Norman abacus, the topmost element of the whole pillar, was flat and square, following the general concept of the plain, flat stone used in Saxon times. The under edge came to be either chamfered or rounded, and sometimes carried a plain moulding. As time went on, the vertical surfaces of the abacus were given a number of mouldings and some minor decoration.

Most early Norman capitals are plain. It was easy to take a squared block of stone and round off the lower part to meet the shaft below, thus forming a simple *cushion capital*. Step two was to scallop the sides, scribing a series of cone shapes on the lower part of the square block. Scallops and fluted and trumpet motifs began a general move towards decorating the underside of the capitals, as at Melbourne (Derbyshire). Meanwhile a leafy form of the *volute* – the decorative spiral scroll – made the transition from classical architecture to the corners of some Norman capitals. Sculptors began to squeeze in leaves and beads between the scallops, and suddenly there was a rush of sometimes semi-barbaric, often fantastic and occasionally innovative decoration all over the capital. A cluster of columns, forming a compound pier, gave later Norman builders a wonderful opportunity to construct interesting, frequently moulded abacus shapes and to produce some spectacularly decorated capitals beneath them. Birds and animals appeared, as did running vines and numerous types of foliage.

A narrow roll moulding, or *fillet*, usually separated the shaft from the abacus and

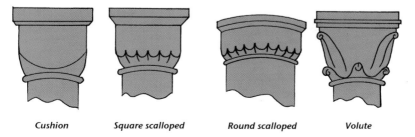

| Cushion | Square scalloped | Round scalloped | Volute |

*Norman capitals.*

*Kirkby Lonsdale, Cumbria. A 'green man' is illustrated on the capital of a Norman pillar in the north aisle.*

*Studland, Dorset. The engaged shafts are early Norman work, with variously decorated scalloped capitals and plain abaci.*

capital. Single shafts were cylindrical, octagonal or square. Shafts of greater girth tend to be earlier; the more slender and the compound piers came later in the period. Quite often, a heavy square central pillar might have narrow shafts at each of its angles. In smaller churches, one frequently comes across Norman arcades in which cylindrical and square shafts alternate, or else the north arcade is of one type and

*Studland, Dorset. The shafts of the Norman piers have decorative spurs at their base.*

Above left: *Dunstable, Bedfordshire. The Norman arches are unusually tall and narrow for the period; the shafts are slender and have scalloped capitals.*

Above right: *Long Sutton, Lincolnshire. The pillars of the nave arcade, c.1180, are either circular or octagonal; the arches are chamfered; the capitals are scalloped, and the abaci have nicked corners.*

the south arcade of another. Most were plain, although a few – perhaps the taller or better-proportioned shafts – were decorated. Some appear to be spirals, others are covered in a net, such was the blossoming ingenuity of the designers. Some have horizontal bands of moulding along their length, frequently a cable or roll, and others have not escaped the ubiquitous zigzag. Shafts on either side of doorways, and those associated with chancel arches, came to be lavishly decorated. So too did some of the pillars in structural positions elsewhere in Norman churches.

The base, the lower part of a pillar below the shaft, was frequently a flat fillet above a bold roll moulding. In cross-section, the latter might be round or quarter round and, where one stood on top of another, there could be a shallow hollow between. All of this stood on a plinth, sometimes referred to as a sub-base, which rested on the floor. The plinth was either circular or square and was made out of a plain, unmoulded block of stone. Many of the square ones had chamfered corners, and some, in which the base and plinth were more integral, were treated to mirror-inverted cushion capitals. Plinths were occasionally decorated with a tongue, a spur or some type of decorative foliage that curved outwards towards the corners.

## Wall markings and masons' marks

Long before the Conquest, certain church rituals encompassed the whole build-ing. Throughout the Middle Ages, when bishops consecrated churches, they marked twelve crosses with oil, on both the inside and the outside – one for each article in the Creed. Internally, these were painted, but those on the outside walls were later incised or affixed in metal. Otherwise, the outline might be picked out in stone, for example in hard flint in a freestone wall. Every church is dedicated to God, with a subordinate dedication to either a saint or one of the inexplicable divine forms known as a mystery. The service of consecration, which took place before allowing in the laity, gave it the secondary name into whose owner's care were henceforth entrusted the souls of those who worshipped there.

Masons' marks appear on individual features within the church, and may still be found on internal and exterior walls of ashlar that have not subsequently been scraped or rendered. Before the appearance of named architects and the emergence of architecture as a profession, the master mason was effectively both the architect and the builder of the church. The idea of a mason or master mason putting his own mark on his work is thought to date from the Romans, and the practice became common in Britain after the Conquest. The mason had an individual mark that he put on to the dressed stone before it was used. These marks tended to be basic geometrical shapes, stylised initials, lines and angles, with an additional stroke or figure to make them individual. Some had the definite outline of birds or animals, often those with symbolic or religious significance. This trademark or signature was sometimes passed on to a mason's descendants in the same trade, who simply added a further figure: another branch to the same pedigree, identifying a mason's personal work and the extent of his output. Many of the marks assumed quite complicated designs. Today we can use them to check on the standards of workmanship and the area over which a particular mason or his descendants worked. They may also be a useful guide to the length of time taken to build a church that is all of the same period. Masons' marks should not be confused with votive or pilgrims' crosses, which are small and can easily be overlooked. These were scratched or incised, often around the entrance, by travellers, or others such as knights or crusaders. They were usually evidence of a vow that had been made.

## Piscina and sedilia

It was the Normans who gave status to the piscina, which for the preceding three centuries had simply taken the form of a hole in the floor. With the Normans came the floor-mounted model with a vertical bore through the shaft – the pillar piscina – and the wall-mounted alternative, which allowed the piscina to become not so much a drain but a feature with a drain in it. The last type also entailed providing a channel through the wall. The piscina was set up in the chancel, where close proximity to the altar conferred additional status on it. There are early examples, although none in Britain before the mid twelfth century, in which the drain is in a kind of basin, protruding from the wall, with an arched alcove built into the masonry immediately above it. The clean vessel was placed on the floor of the alcove. The logical step was to make a scalloped or dish-shaped indent with a drain hole in the floor of the alcove, and then begin to decorate the head of the arch and the sides, using the common treatments of the day for arches. Once this took place, the piscina became a feature which was an integral part of the wall.

The piscina was frequently incorporated into the design of sedilia. These were recessed seats, up to four in number, usually built into the south wall of the chancel, on which the officiating priest and his assistants rested themselves during the long services. Early examples are not stepped, and the recesses of those built in the Norman period frequently had characteristic round arches.

## Norman fonts, their evolution and designs

The workmanship of Norman fonts was decisive, the designs were varied and the ornamentation pleased succeeding generations of worshippers. Permanent materials were used; lead was an innovative constructional material for a small number of fonts, and it lined those made of porous stones. The earliest fonts made in stone after the Conquest, often to replace existing ones, were unmounted, fairly plain tubs. This basic design was followed by cubical and cylindrical bowls, mounted on pedestals. The cylindrical bowl remained the most popular form, unmounted, mounted on a cylindrical stem, or mounted on a central stem with several other supports, which might be decorative or functional. In came square bowls, often on thick corner colonnettes and sometimes with a central stem. Cup or chalice shapes appeared,

Above: *King's Sutton, Northamptonshire. An early twelfth-century font, roughly octagonal and shaped like a cushion capital, set on a cylindrical shaft that tapers downwards.*

Above: *Stewkley, Buckinghamshire. The plain, tapering Norman tub font.*

mounted, unmounted or octagonal. In the twelfth century font bowls were most commonly made from a single block of stone, hewn to shape inside and out.

The design of Norman fonts was influenced by the locality, the ease with which stone from local quarries could be worked, and the expertise of the mason. A large number of regional styles were evolved. The West Country is particularly rich in Norman fonts. There are some sixty in Cornwall; Somerset and Devon have nearly 150 each, and there are about sixty in Gloucestershire. In Buckinghamshire there is a group of richly decorated hemispherical bowls at Aylesbury, Bledlow, Buckland, Chenies, Great Kimble, Great Missenden, Little Missenden, Pitstone, Monks Risborough, Saunderton, Wing and Weston Turville. These contrast with the 'Herefordshire group' of Castle Frome and Eardisley (Herefordshire) and Chaddesley Corbett (Worcestershire). Although this group completes the work of an obvious school or workshop, a similar influence can be seen at Stottesdon (Shropshire).

In the Norman period an almost infinite variety of decoration developed. It began with a small amount of crude carving, and the design that followed reflected, in relief, the cushion capitals and shafts of the period. From the end of the eleventh century blind arcading became the standard decoration on font bowls. Sometimes it was plain and clumsy, as at Walsgrave (Warwickshire), or intersected in slight relief, as on the square bowl of Crambe (Yorkshire), or boldly carved as at Hendon (London). It

*Little Missenden, Buckinghamshire. A Norman chalice font of the Aylesbury type, with a decorative band, a fluted underside, and a base that takes the shape of an inverted cushion capital.*

is impossible to name, in architectural terms, or to describe accurately, every decorative motif or feature one may encounter on Norman fonts, or even to explain it all comprehensively.

Most Norman fonts had at least one band of continuous moulding. These were usually at the top, as string mouldings, or as base mouldings at the foot of the piece. The most common were of interlacing or plaited cables of varying thicknesses and widths, or otherwise single plain rolls that tended to be much thinner than the cables. The thickness of the base mouldings varied considerably and was not always in proportion to the bowls. Most frequently the base mouldings were two heavy plain rolls set either one on top of the other or with a hollow between them. In some instances there were three rolls, in which case the lowest was often exaggerated. Arcading, and therefore capitals, shafts and base mouldings, was used extensively as decoration on Norman fonts.

Three basic designs of capital were represented on Norman font bowls: cushion capitals, scalloped capitals, and the leaf forms. The cushion capitals were the earliest type of the period. These have a square upper section but are rounded into an ornamental convex shape to meet the top of the shaft below. The flat face on each side of the cushion is known as a lunette. This was, however, the easiest to carve and is the most common type. Then came scalloped capitals. These have the same type of cubed upper section but have the lower angles carved into a series of vertical cone shapes, similarly rounded individually towards the lower edge. Where the capitals are scalloped, lack of space dictated that there were rarely more than two scallops on the leading edge. Finally came the leaf forms, notably the volutes, used in later Norman work, forerunner of the plantain leaf and waterleaf caps. The volute is the spiral twist of Ionic descent at the ends of a divided leaf where they bend upwards and around the angles of the capital. On some fonts the volute shape is not actually carved but is indicated by a kind of horned upper member to each capital in plain relief. Otherwise, more discerning makers scored a three-lobed leaf to indicate that they had in mind some kind of foliated capital. With the exception of the capitals and bases on the font supports, and some large angle shafts, there was not enough space on these font capitals to include much in the way of decoration. Nor was it possible to reproduce the vertical mouldings that sometimes occupied the spaces between the scallops of structured capitals.

Most of the shafts that decorated Norman fonts were semicircular and plain, although one occasionally comes across shafts that were in some way incised. The single diagonal line, running from top right to bottom left, was a popular decoration; sometimes close parallel lines and upward-pointing arrows were used. Supporting pillars at this time were usually cylindrical and plain, except for an occasional annulet. This was a small, narrow string placed around the shaft somewhere along its length, although usually at an aesthetically pleasing distance from the capital or base moulding. The designs

*Minstead, Hampshire. There are galleries here, box pews, and this plainly panelled, three-decker pulpit; the font – square and tapering, with figurework, animals and eagles – is from the 1100s.*

*Combeinteignhead, Devon. The circular Norman bowl has an upper band of saltire crosses, a line of palmette decoration, and a thick roll connecting with the plain stem.*

on the supporting shafts were very similar to those of the font bowls, but there was a greater area on which to work. Where more than one shaft supported the bowl, they were not always of the same thickness, nor were there always similar shapes to the shafts or similar designs on them. Bead decoration was frequently used between lines, giving the shafts a twisted appearance.

Font plinths were usually thick and could be square, round or octagonal. Mostly they were plain, although some have sparsely incised decoration along their upper faces, with the occasional leaf carved out. An innovation of the period, which lasted for about one hundred years from the middle of the twelfth century, was the spur projection. This was a raised, claw-like protrusion from the base moulding of the font and its plinth. There was usually one at each corner, thick at the base, then curved and tapering outwards and downwards. Often these spurs had one or two lines carved into their upper surfaces, and in some instances the whole feature was a defined leaf shape. As time went on, these became more common. Spurs were also used quite extensively at the time between the base mouldings and plinths on structural piers within the church.

The font bowl was the carrier for a whole range of decorative motifs which together epitomise the Norman style. A favourite among these was the tree of life. Sometimes it was suggested by little more than a vertical vine but later on it achieved a realistic plant-like appearance in its more sophisticated forms. These 'trees' might be flanked by saints, Adam and Eve, or guarded by beasts. Heads of humans, animals and mythical beasts appeared on fonts, often at the corners; wolves and cats were popular, and birds abounded. Frequently they were carved on their sides, or even upside down. There are some instances in which whole scenes were cut at 90 degrees to the rest of the embellishment, simply because the maker had more surface space to work on that way round.

Almost any small decorative feature the mason could think of, and which could be repeated, appeared on font bowls during the eleventh and twelfth centuries. The billet – a line of short, raised rectangles, squares or cylinders with spaces between – is a good example. This decoration was sometimes used in conjunction with, or sandwiched between, rows of diamond-shaped lozenges. Other diamond shapes were formed by the open latticework and raised pyramidal shapes of nail-head. Rectangular decoration came in the form of shingle and fret, joined and combined rectangular shapes repeated in a band as the Classical key pattern. Several Classical motifs found their way on to Norman fonts, especially the later ones. These included the fleshy-leafed acanthus, which derived from the Corinthian capital, the palmette, honeysuckle and fan-shaped anthemion. These fan-like or foliate shapes were sometimes done above a narrow border of swirls. The pearl, bead, pellet and stud – varying sizes of spheres, often with a hole in the centre – were very common. They were frequently used as additional decoration on some other feature, such as the centre of flowers, along lines of scrollwork, around arches and as general infilling. When bead is pierced, it is said to contain a drill hole. This was often used together with a guilloche, a ribbon-like decoration that was placed extensively in borders. The two may appear as separate bands of decoration, beginning in parallel, then dipping

*Hambleden, Buckinghamshire. The straight-sided, cylindrical tub font has fleur-de-lis style cross motifs in triangular panels.*

and swirling, interposed with leaves, beads and other minor decoration. When the ribbon includes spheres along its length, it is said to be a beaded guilloche. Strangely, zigzag or chevron – the continuous V-shaped moulding that was so characteristic of the period and widely used around arches – was not a favourite on font bowls.

Another feature, especially used as an edging at the base or rim of the font bowl, is the sunk star. This takes the form of a raised, open 'X' shape, which is sometimes separated from its fellows by alternating vertical members. Less common was the closed, four-pointed star. Many variations of circular decoration, called medallions or paterae, were used on the bowl, commonly flat circular, oval or medal-shaped mouldings. Occasionally they were huge and the only feature on one surface of the font. By contrast, they might also be made out of, or include, a variety of other motifs. For example, rosettes or rose-shaped paterae might be a cluster of petal shapes in rose-like formation with a central bead, surrounded by an oval – or even octagonal – outer circle. Some were quite complex, having outer whorls, beads and petals. The circles were made up of one-, two- or three-strap banding, or strapwork with heads or foliage as the main theme. When strapwork was used inside the circle, it sometimes also enveloped it. One characteristic ornament of the period, which seems to be a link between the independent medallion and the repeated border shapes, is the shell. Here the back of a rather fleshy, fan-shaped shell was encircled above its shoulders, but the base spreads out on either side to meet its neighbours. In some cases, the whole of the underside of a circular font bowl was given a shell-like appearance, being scalloped or fluted, and moulded to meet the stem.

Various kinds of leaves and petal shapes – notably the fleshy acanthus leaf – were widely used as border decoration on Norman fonts. This was often done in conjunction with running vines, scrolls or rinceaux. The running vine was generally an undulating leaf trail with leaf forms carved horizontally and alternately above and below the undulations. Occasionally bunches of grapes hung from them. Sometimes the shell or scallop was used in this way, although they were not attached to the vine, as were the leaves. The leafy scrolls or rinceaux basically look like partly rolled pieces of paper in cross-section. In some places they were emitted from the mouths of human faces or beasts. Vine foliage was usually two- or three-lobed. In some examples the scroll became a serpent, snake or mythical beast and was often interlaced. Strands are said to be interlaced when they intertwine both with themselves and with one another. In the twelfth century this feature was very effectively done and included a wide range of small motifs, floral embellishments and even animals and birds.

Semicircular arches were widely used to decorate Norman font bowls. They gave a spacious framing to figurework beneath, even if the makers showed a wry sense of proportion. In some instances extant, the arch is scarcely more than the shaped underside of a decorative frieze at the rim of the bowl, made out of cable, scrollwork or knotting. There was no standard representation of the arches. They might be thin and shallow with flat, squared edges; otherwise they could be bulbous and top-heavy for the badly proportioned pillars. Some of these misshapen arches unwittingly looked like blunt, three-centred types, and the horseshoe arch was rarely intentionally used on font decoration. What did evolve around the font bowl was a fine, stilted type of

*East Meon, Hampshire. The square font of black Tournai marble, c.1130–40, has scenes from the story of Adam and Eve, arcading, and trails of animals, birds and foliage.*

arch in which the semicircular head was raised high above supporting imposts on tall pillars with proportionally little space between. Figurework was not aesthetically possible in such narrow spaces but was occasionally attempted.

Circular fonts were very successfully done during this period. Masons rarely made square, hexagonal or octagonal shapes, and surviving unmounted polygonal fonts are very few. The pre-Conquest style of pedestal font mostly developed into round, cup- or chalice-shaped bowls. They were both mounted (the most common form throughout the whole of the period) and unmounted. The former rested on a central pedestal or stem, or on a number of legs or shafts – sometimes both. The single shaft support was sometimes an inverted earlier bowl, shaft or capital. Those made wholly in the twelfth century were often formed as mounted, coniferous capitals. They rested on a squat shaft with a plinth. To this was added four thinner corner supports, so the bowl stood on five legs. These were often little more than decorative embellishment, with no structural significance, and were themselves ornamented or carved. However, a similar design was also used to support larger, square bowls of the period, in which the component parts might be more functional. Structurally useless, purely decorative legs were sometimes added to an existing, unmounted font.

## Cornish fonts

There is a type of font common to Cornwall, where a peculiar local style evolved during the three centuries following the Conquest. The basic shape is a short central stem supporting a cup-shaped bowl with a decorative leg at each corner. The best example is at Bodmin, and others of this type can be found at Roche, St Austell, Cuby, Crantock and St Columb Minor. Cornwall was remote enough from what was going on elsewhere to create unique font bowls out of local materials. The work was mainly done in granite, but serpentine, greenstone and sandstone, catacleuse, Pentewan and Polyphant stone were also used. Very close to the idea of using angels' heads as capitals on font bowls was that of putting carved heads (usually bearded) at the corners. In many cases the space between was filled by a six-lobed flower within a circle, the whole ringed by a serpent or snake with a head at each end. Examples of these are at Altarnun, Lawhitton and Launceston in Cornwall, and Bratton Clovelly (Devon). Another group is represented at Feock, Fowey, Ladock, Lanlivery and St Mewan. These are circular bowls, made of catacleuse stone, and include diagonal crosses, circles, rosettes, zigzag and the common tree of life theme.

## Square and rectangular fonts

The best square bowls can be found in Norfolk, in a group comprising Breccles, Burnham Deepdale, Castle Rising, Shernborne, Sculthorpe and Toftrees. The last two are very intricately carved. A strange, if restrained, combination of the Norfolk designs

*Fyfield, Essex. The square late twelfth-century font, made of Purbeck marble, has leaf forms and fleurs-de-lis, and is mounted on an octagonal stem.*

can be found at Preston (Suffolk). In Suffolk the fine square bowl at Great Bricett is worth noting and contrasting with the square, late twelfth-century font of Purbeck marble at Fyfield (Essex). Figurework is scarce on square fonts; sculptors preferred barbaric designs, knotwork and interlacing. Notable examples include Fincham and Breccles (Norfolk), Ashby Folville (Leicestershire), Lifton and Marystow (Devon), Bridekirk (Cumbria), West Haddon (Northamptonshire), Lenton (Nottinghamshire) and Locking (Somerset).

## Cylindrical tub fonts

There were few plain tub or drum-shaped font bowls of the period. Some of the very best figurework was done on the continuous surfaces that these fonts provided and, except that they were of stone and usually unmounted, there was little uniformity in treatment. Also, there are a number of Norman fonts which are classified as round but which are shallow tubs, mounted on a stem. Some tubs extant are large; some are squat. There are straight-sided bowls with the same base and rim dimensions, called 'vertical tubs'. There are others with concave sides which look as if they are being pulled in at the middle by a very tight string course. And there are barrel-shaped

Right: *Puddletown, Dorset. The Norman tapering, beaker-shaped font has an all-over palmette pattern, and a plain, ribbed Jacobean font cover with ball finial.*

Below: *Avebury, Wiltshire. The early twelfth-century font has an intersecting arcade with cushion capitals, and crude figurework showing the trampling of dragons.*

bowls which bulge outwards at the same place. The majority of cylindrical tubs extant are bucket-shaped – narrower at the base than at the rim. When the circumference of the base exceeds that of the rim, the shape is said to be an 'inverted bucket'. Cylindrical Norman tubs can be found at Cassington (Oxfordshire), Little Billing (Northamptonshire), Lewknor (Oxfordshire), Morville (Shropshire) and Alphington (Devon). There is a beautiful united stem and tub-shaped bowl at Stoke Abbot (Dorset). That county has an oddity in the narrow tub-shaped – defined as a 'beaker' – font at Puddletown.

## Figurework on fonts

There are a number of mid-twelfth-century tubs which include beautiful figurework. Generally, figures were placed beneath arches, and sculptors found they had sufficient space around the average-sized bowl to accommodate the apostles or a good number of bishops. Single figures were by far the most popular, although it was possible to represent whole scenes or stories that could be woven around the central figure. Cowlam (Yorkshire) is an example of this.

The age of figurework throughout the Norman period can be determined by its size, style and detail. Of course, figurework by itself is by no means infallible evidence of age. Work by a good early school, or done in a more important or better populated area during the eleventh and early twelfth centuries, might be better than later efforts in a poorer or more rural area. Age is usually judged by the architectural features that are reproduced in miniature on the font. Even so, much of the early figurework is often flat and crudely done. Faces are either expressionless or maintain perpetual fear through round, buttonhole mouths and eyes. Figures usually filled the spaces, even to the extent of pushing pillars and arches out of shape. They were frequently poorly proportioned, both within themselves and also in juxtaposition with their surroundings. Many were spindly and skeletal with very little decoration. Limbs were shown in awkward positions, often at impossible angles. As time went on,

*Luppitt, Devon. The barbaric Norman font is square with masks on the corners; the scenes include centaurs with spears, men fighting, and fearsome beasts attacking each other.*

73

*Brookland, Kent. The twelfth-century circular lead font includes two tiers of ornamental arcading depicting signs of the zodiac and corresponding occupations of the month.*

arms tended to point straight downwards as if the figures had come to attention. Otherwise a hand might be raised in benediction or salute. With few exceptions, the earlier figures faced straight outwards from the font, and this was always the favourite way of showing biblical characters. The makers portrayed their contemporaries or colleagues wandering sideways-on around the bowl, usually engaged in some rural pursuit. Christ is usually shown seated, although most other figures on Norman fonts at any time are standing. Gradually more attention was paid to detail: faces and expressions, hands and feet, the folds of clothes. Fingers and toes, for example, might be very delicately done on the best examples. Hands, which had been idle for most of the period on the stone fonts, began to include items of office, tools and weapons. Scenes from the life of Christ were very popular, particularly the baptism.

Less frequently, one will also come across Old Testament figures. Perhaps inevitably, since their sin made necessary the whole rite of baptism, Adam and Eve are favourites. Saints, bishops and apostles abound, often included in famous scenes from their lives, and an amount of personification occurs. Fonts which have particularly good figurework can be found at Orleton (Herefordshire), Avington (Berkshire), Kirkby (Lancashire), Stanton Fitzwarren (Wiltshire) and Southrop (Gloucestershire).

*Lady St Mary, Wareham, Dorset. The late Norman lead font is hexagonal and has two statuettes on each face, beneath arches. The pedestal is thirteenth-century work.*

# Transitional
# 1150–1200

**The catalysts of change**

The second half of the twelfth century was characterised by the use of the pointed arch as a constructional feature. There have been a number of suggestions as to how this came about: for example, that Romanesque non-constructional decorative shapes may have been responsible. In surface interlacing on Norman fonts there is a pointed arch scribed between each pair of columns. Others affirm that western knights who fought in the Crusades from 1096 were influenced by the architecture of the east and may have been the catalysts of change. It is more likely that eastern architectural influences became more widespread because of increased trade with the Near East. Another likely explanation is that builders who were looking to vault rectangular areas realised they could solve certain practical and aesthetic problems by using pointed arches. By 1190 the pointed arch was commonplace.

**The pointed arch**

Imagine a room that is not square but is to be vaulted. The obvious solution to achieving uniformity at the point of spring is to raise the sides of the lower arches so that the crowns are in all cases level. That solved one problem for the twelfth-century builder of vaults but created another. Whereas the larger arches remained curved throughout, the lower part of the smaller arches on each side now became vertical. It meant that the lines of the groins – the angles of masonry where the vaults intersected (usually left plain and not ribbed at this early period) – were distorted. None of this occurred if pointed arches were used. Their heads and points

of spring could be constructed on the same levels throughout, facilitating groining without distortion. When this proved to be successful, it occurred to the architects that here was a way of constructing taller buildings. What it was really all about was a sense of verticality – of building upwards in a way that the stronger, force-resistant pointed arch allowed.

*St Margaret, King's Lynn, Norfolk. The twelfth-century south-west tower of this twin-towered façade has decorative shafting, alternately thick and thin, on its wide buttresses.*

For a while, round-headed and pointed arches were built side by side at the same time. This may sometimes be seen where a chancel arch is round but the nave arcade next to it is in the new style. There are instances where one type was imposed upon the other. Round belfry openings, for example, might be contained within pointed arches. Or a clerestory of round-headed lights might be put up above an arcade of pointed arches. Very late Transitional interiors are at Castle Hedingham (Essex), where round arches were retained, and at Little Dunmow, in the same county. The two are perhaps no more than a decade apart, yet, in the latter, the transition to pointed arches on Early English pillars is almost complete. Just to confuse the issue, the magnificent church at Iffley (Oxfordshire), which was built mid-period (1170–80), is overtly a Romanesque *tour de force*.

## Mouldings of the period

During these fifty years or so, round arches were put up with deep, hollow mouldings. By using chisels, the masons were able to chamfer and thus soften the sharp edges of squared blocks, as well as around successive orders of arches. Some had heavy roll mouldings and other characteristic Norman decoration, but this was more cleanly and deeply cut. The zigzag moulding on the arcade at Wimborne Minster (Dorset) shows this very effectively. Old-style scalloped capitals continued to be popular, associated with pointed arches. Elsewhere, such as at Castle Hedingham, round arches were raised above capitals with stiff-leaf forms. Similar decoration, in essence, occurs in the north aisle of Whitchurch Canonicorum (Dorset). All sorts of leaves began to creep in, as naturalistic motifs succeeded the barbaric and geometrical. There was the waterleaf, a squashy affair that curved upwards and outwards from the centre of each side of a capital, before ending with inward flourishes at the angles. Also during this period, the plantain leaf emerged as a decorative device. This was a chunky piece of foliage, flat, broad and in sections.

## General changes into the thirteenth century

Generally, the height of churches increased, as did the height of towers, and new walls became slightly thinner. The masonry was more finely jointed, and improved

*Studland, Dorset. The Norman corbel table that runs around the outside of the north and south walls has human heads, the likenesses of animals, and other decorative motifs.*

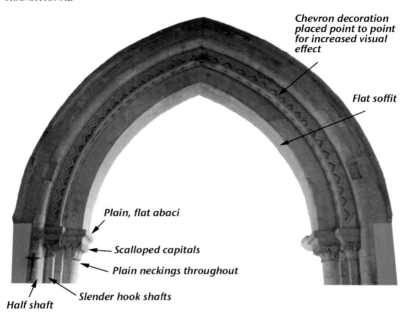

**Chevron decoration placed point to point for increased visual effect**

**Flat soffit**

**Plain, flat abaci**

**Scalloped capitals**

**Plain neckings throughout**

**Slender hook shafts**

**Half shaft**

*Features of a twelfth-century arch of three orders, exemplified in the pointed tower arch at Bredon, Worcestershire. Two of the orders spring above scalloped capitals.*

masonry tools enabled the individual stones to be better worked. Inside the church, pillars became more slender, and occasionally round and octagonal forms alternated within the same arcade. Single-light windows were made more effective by increasing their size and number, and deepening their splays. Purbeck marble, which was to become a great favourite in the following years, made its appearance, often used as shafts between windows. And these sometimes reflected three eras – Romanesque in decoration, Transitional in their pointed heads, and Early English in the use of the new marble.

*Peasenhall, Suffolk. The late twelfth-century bowl has large hemispherical mouldings against the flat sides, which are decorated with pointed arches in light relief, and the heavy cylindrical stem has engaged shafts at the corners. There is a lobed base below.*

# Early English
# 1200–1300

**Developing first pointed**

Gothic church architecture was beginning to take shape by about 1190. The Early English period was the first in which church building and church design came together as a marriage of equals. Although the population was still small, it had almost doubled in one hundred and fifty years since the Conquest. Human coverage of the countryside was sparse and sporadic, but many of those settlements that already had church buildings were finding that these were too small to meet the needs of the community. A programme of great church building and refurbishment began, and, as it gathered momentum, the whole concept filtered down to the country parishes. There was also a considerable improvement in quality, and distinct local styles emerged. Schools of masons set up in rural areas, particularly where there was good building stone to be had from local quarries. In some areas the emerging wool trade, which was to have a huge effect on church building over the next three centuries, was already helping to finance the schools of masons. It also contributed towards improved designs in church architecture and the construction of individual features.

**Building the roof**

Thirteenth-century church roofs were made of wood and were pitched higher at the beginning of the period than latterly. The point of the beamwork was to create a stable framework that would support the stone tiles, slates and lead that were variously used to cover it and at the same time transfer the heavy weights imposed by all of this material. Even those roofs that did not have stone vaulting were still capable of pushing the walls beneath out of shape, which meant they might spread outwards. Carpentry was an important trade, both for making the roof timbers and setting them up, and in centring arches. General roof construction involved a ridge piece at the top, running the length of the roof's apex, and wall plates at the base of the roof, on either side, on top of the vertical walls. Between the two, also running the length of the roof, were purlins, which helped to brace the sides. The whole structure was connected on either side by vertical principal rafters

*Didling, Sussex. The nave of this plain church, with the most rustic of stalls, and tie beams connecting the walls, is still lit by candles.*

set at intervals, with supporting common rafters placed between the purlins, the wall plates and the ridge piece. The wall plates took the weight on the principal rafters and transferred it to the walls of the building. The favoured arrangement across the span of the roof at this time was the solid tie beam that ran from wall to wall. This usually continued past the wall plate on either side, and rested on

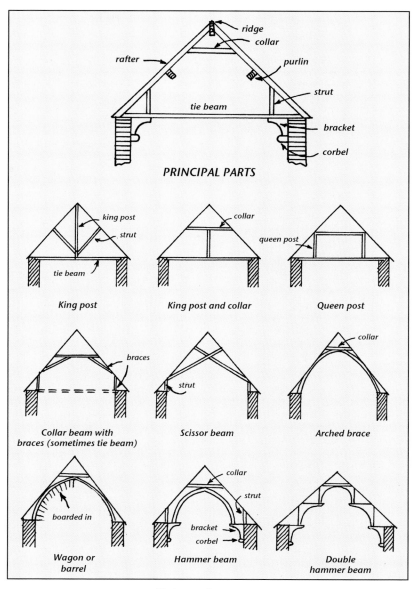

*Timber roof structures.*

79

the wall behind. A tie beam was often carved with minor motifs of the day or might have had an embattled upper surface.

The roof was sometimes given extra support by means of a *king post*, a piece of timber built vertically between the ridge piece and a tie beam. The king post was often chamfered or worked into an octagon and was usually carved in some way that made it stand out from the other timbers. Even more stability might be given to the roof by building two shorter timbers between the tie beam and the principal rafters at a point equidistant from the centre of the span. Sometimes these uprights were connected by means of a horizontal member, to form a square within a triangle. The two vertical pieces are called *queen posts*, and the piece of timber connecting them is a *collar beam*. Diagonal braces might be set up almost anywhere within the framework, for example wedged between the bases of the queen posts and radiating upwards and outwards to some corresponding point along principal rafters. The collar beam was usually used in support of a more sophisticated framework, but occasionally one was set closer to the apex of the roof and supported by diagonal braces tied into the principal rafters. This is called a *collar beam roof*. For extra strength, more than one collar might be inserted. A rare form of roof construction, which sometimes included a collar beam and braces, was the *scissor beam roof*. This, as its name implies, consisted of cross-beams between the principal rafters on either side. Certainly, as the period progressed, roofs became less steeply pitched and the tie beam went out of favour, except in the case of lean-to roofs, leaving an arrangement of trussed rafters. The lean-to came into fairly common use. In this construction, the roof connected a principal wall of a building to a lower one built some distance from it, by means of a single slope. Small tie beams can still be seen where they were used to span aisles that were built with lean-to roofs. Occasionally, thirteenth-century roofs were flat-boarded, but the beamwork was more usually left exposed.

## The thirteenth-century plan and internal arrangement

New churches put up in the thirteenth century were either rectangular or cruciform in ground plan. In the case of the latter, the choir that had occupied the space beneath the tower now found itself removed towards the east, and the crossing was left empty. If an existing building already had an apsidal east end, the chances were that this would be remodelled as a square-ended chancel. Later, chantry chapels were conveniently placed in the angles between chancel and transepts. Suddenly there were various segregations going on within a church building, the design of which was being manipulated to encourage and accommodate them. Looked at objectively, it was all about power and money, and nothing epitomised the former more than the screen, so placed to separate the east end of the nave from the choir or chancel. Indeed, the word 'chancel' is derived from the Latin *cancellus*, meaning 'screen'. It drew a positive line of demarcation across the church and gave a strong and unmistakable message to the laity: 'You stay in your place, and we will intercede with God from ours and look after your spiritual welfare.'

By its presence, a screen also suggested that it might not be permissible for the laity to observe every facet of the rites being enacted on their behalf beyond it. This was coupled with a general lengthening of chancels in order to give the clergy more space in which to manoeuvre. In larger churches square-ended Lady chapels were added, built parallel to the chancel and dedicated to the Virgin Mary, in churches where this was not the main dedication, or sometimes the Holy Trinity. Transepts continued to be a cost-effective solution to the problem of the increasing numbers of worshippers.

## Developing the pointed arch

When builders began to understand the theory of thrusts and the effects of loads and strains, they were able to devise better means of effectively dealing with them. The pointed arch came about as a result of improvements in the way vaulting was

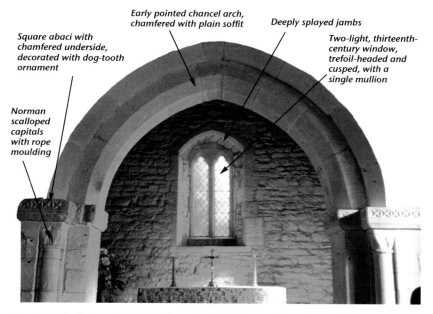

**Early pointed chancel arch, chamfered with plain soffit**

**Deeply splayed jambs**

**Square abaci with chamfered underside, decorated with dog-tooth ornament**

**Two-light, thirteenth-century window, trefoil-headed and cusped, with a single mullion**

**Norman scalloped capitals with rope moulding**

*Features of a thirteenth-century chancel arch. This example, at Alstone, Gloucestershire, is pointed and double-chamfered, and there is dog-tooth decoration on the capitals.*

applied. Imagine a rectangular room with round-headed arches around its perimeter, and the diagonal ribs extending in height beyond that of the wall ribs. The next step would be to make the ribs of equal height. At the same time, the builders realised that the thrust from a vaulted roof was concentrated at the corners, and that supports placed at these points would resist the outward thrust. The combination of the pointed arch and strategically placed buttresses produced a much stronger structure.

The establishment of the pointed arch gave rise to a whole range of features that have since been defined. The face of an arch, when shown in elevation, is called the *front*, and the separate blocks of stone that make up the actual shape of the arch are *voussoirs* – with the exception of the central, V-shaped block at the *crown* (the highest point at the top), which is the *keystone*. The underside of an arch is known as the *soffit* or *intrados*; the opposite surface of the curve, measured around the top of the voussoirs, being the *extrados*. The first stone on each side, at the point where the arch begins above the *impost* (the topmost moulding of a capital), column or out of the wall, is called the *springer*. The position on the arch as it scribes up and away from the upper edge of the springer is the *point of spring*. The horizontal distance across the opening, between the two points of spring, is the *springing line*, and that between the two lower edges of each springer is the *span*.

The *centre* of the arch is a point below the springing line, which could be connected by an imaginary vertical line with the centre of the keystone. The centre of the arch is important in determining both the shape of the arch and the position and quantity of the wedge-shaped blocks of stone of which it is formed. The latter are placed along lines known as *radiating joints*, which converge from points at equal intervals along the arch to the centre. The radius of the arch, as of a circle, is usually inscribed from the centre to the curve of the arch, through the joints between the voussoirs. These joints are usually straight, but occasionally, when greater strength was needed, they might be stepped or rebated. This is the basis on which an arch remains standing: the correct balance of mutual pressure withstanding the weight of downward thrust.

Several types of arch predominated throughout the Early English period. The simple segmental arch was given a slightly pointed treatment. The pointed horseshoe is not often seen but is in essence a stilted arch: one which has a point of spring above the level of any real or imaginary impost, giving the appearance of being raised, as it were, on legs. This probably derived from eastern architecture, in which the horseshoe may be as great as two-thirds of a circle, and is formed from a centre above the line of spring. The second, the lancet shape, is much more familiar as a prevailing feature of Early English style. This arch is formed on an acute-angled triangle from its base line of spring. Its cousin, the drop lancet, was formed on an obtuse-angled triangle from its base line of spring. The lancet continued into the fourteenth century, but very rarely later, until the nineteenth-century revival. The drop arch is formed on an obtuse-angled triangle where the span of the arch is greater than the radius. It was used in the Early English period and throughout the Decorated period that followed. The other common arch of the thirteenth century was the equilateral pointed arch, formed by two segments of circles, the radii and the width of the arch being equal. More decorative, or used in secondary positions that were not particularly load-bearing, were trefoil-headed arches (round or pointed), which mirrored a favourite decorative motif of this period. Cinquefoil arches began to take their place later on.

Arches are often constructed with a number of recesses and these could be quite numerous and highly ornamented. In Gothic architecture these recesses or divisions are called 'orders', of which the generally low arches of thirteenth-century arcades had no more than two or three. A common decorative practice at the time, and one that masons frequently applied to chancel arches and to a lesser degree to responds (the half pillars that usually die into the walls at the ends of arcades), was to carry the arch of the inner order on to corbels. They often inserted a shaft with a foliated capital and moulded base between the arch and the corbel, and in most cases the

*Breedon on the Hill, Leicestershire. A typical Early English arrangement of triple lancet windows at the east end of the chancel, flanked by aisles with single lancets.*

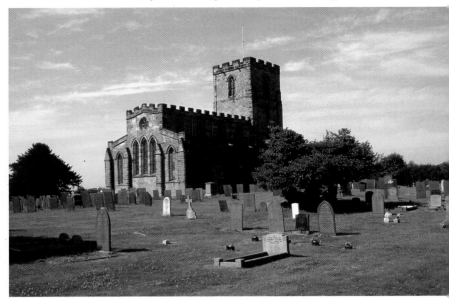

other mouldings were carried right down to the ground. As regards decoration, arches were treated quite separately to the piers below them.

Once the pointed arch became established, stone vaulting was given a similar treatment. In the larger churches, aisles, naves and chancels were vaulted. Masons continued to experiment, even if the result never quite developed its subsequent complexity. They especially favoured chancels with sexpartite (divided into six parts) and quadripartite (divided into four parts) vaulting. Where intersecting vaults met, they had curved edges (groins) and these were usually ribbed. The ribs were generally narrower than previously, moulded on their undersides, and each formed from a longer block of stone. A common arrangement included diagonal ribs running from corner to corner across the bay of the vault, a longitudinal ridge rib at the apex of the main vault and transverse ridge ribs intersecting the figure. More complex arrangements resulted in an increased number of smaller cells between the ribs. At first these were filled with rubble, but later by blocks of ashlar. Subsidiary pairs of shorter, intermediate ribs, called *tiercerons*, began at the same outer points as the diagonals and met the transverse ridge rib at an angle. They did not cross through the centre of the vault. Tiercerons were put up abutting, and in conjunction with, transverse ribs set at right angles to the axis of the vault and the longitudinal ridge rib. All were given the basic moulding of the period. As the thirteenth century progressed, bosses were put up to disguise the points of intersection, and carved with stiff leaf or more naturalistic forms.

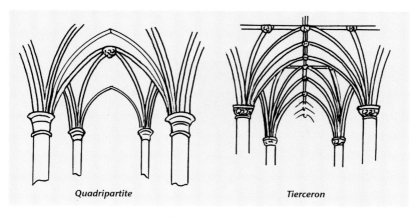

Quadripartite          Tierceron

*Early English vaulted ceilings.*

### Early English decorative motifs and mouldings

The chamfer, a paring away of masonry across the arris at the right angle where two wall surfaces met, became a feature of the Early English period. Chamfers might be flat or slightly hollowed. The latter presented better opportunities for decoration because a concave moulding needs, ultimately, to be carved back into the wall at either end in a kind of scallop. Whereas the flat thirteenth-century chamfer might have been terminated with simple rolls and hollows, possibly with a fillet, or brought to a sharp edge along the centre of a roll, the sculptors could deal much more freely with a pointed scallop. What they produced are known as chamfer stops, delightful ornamental flourishes that nestle into the ends of the chamfers. A favourite motif was the stiff leaf, or at least a curly, three-lobed version. Occasionally the decoration on the chamfer stops was separated from the rest of the chamfer by a small horizontal roll. Often the chamfer stop at the head of the feature differed from that at the foot,

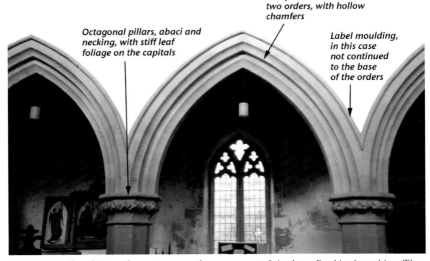

Low pointed arches of two orders, with hollow chamfers

Octagonal pillars, abaci and necking, with stiff leaf foliage on the capitals

Label moulding, in this case not continued to the base of the orders

*Features of a thirteenth-century arcade, as seen at Ivinghoe, Buckinghamshire. The pointed Early English arches of the nave spring above octagonal capitals with a fleshy form of stiff leaf clinging to their bells (so called from a supposed resemblance of the capital to an upturned bell).*

particularly if a vertical chamfer was involved. These motifs could be quite inventive.

Pointed arches went up higher and higher, letting in more light. Complex building arrangements and heavy motifs were no longer fashionable. In their place came simplicity and purity, and the use of light and shade, in a way that had not previously been possible, to pick out decorative features. Among these were the early Gothic mouldings that were sometimes undercut to such an extent that they were structurally unsound. Their creators wanted to accentuate every detail in sharp relief, against the shadows in the hollows, and the deeper these were cut, the more effective was the contrast. Their base feature was the prevalent *roll moulding*.

*Eaton Bray, Bedfordshire. The nave arcade of c.1240 has a cluster of eight shafts to each pier, and corresponding capitals with stiff leaf.*

By slightly arching the roll, and leaving the sharp edge of the block (the arris) uncut, they achieved the pointed *bowtell*, the forerunner of all Gothic mouldings. First the bowtell, pointed and round, took a narrow, square-shaped fillet along its centre. This created a single leading edge. To this, two further fillets were added, one each on the upper side and the lower surface, set equidistant from each other. The fillets were widened, and they developed from the square-edge form to those that were semicircular in cross-section. Later in the period, masons produced the *scroll moulding*. This was achieved by cutting a quarter round, and one edge of a square fillet, and then continuing a semicircle from that point rather than completing the fillet. When complex arrangements were made of these forms, as on bases and capitals, the results could be quite stunning.

### Pillars, arcades and aisles

Aisles were low and narrow until *c*.1250, when they were widened and heightened. In larger churches, they were separated from the nave by taller pillars and pointed arches. Apart from that, it was a matter of heightening, widening and extending laterally, using new techniques and features. In keeping with the new lightness of touch, the piers in country churches were slimmed down. The blocks of stone were more skilfully cut, were worked to a better finish by improved tools and techniques, and fitted more tightly together.

In new buildings, and where funds were available, clusters of pillars began to take shape. These comprised a central pillar with either a number of detached shafts against it, or a cluster of attached columns. Sometimes the whole pier was formed of a cluster of engaged columns sharing a single, central core, in which thicker shafts occasionally alternated with more slender ones. Detached shafts made of polished

*Pershore Abbey, Worcestershire. The multi-ordered Early English arches of the nave are dated c.1120–30.*

85

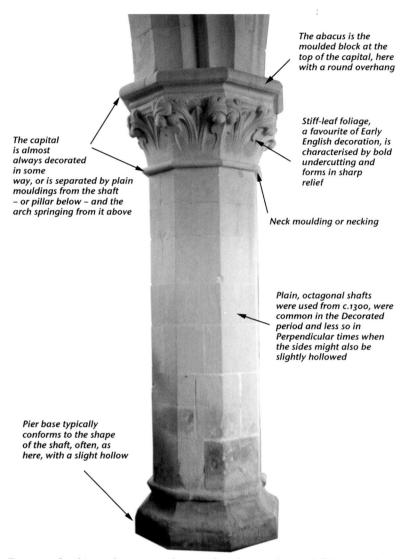

The abacus is the moulded block at the top of the capital, here with a round overhang

Stiff-leaf foliage, a favourite of Early English decoration, is characterised by bold undercutting and forms in sharp relief

The capital is almost always decorated in some way, or is separated by plain mouldings from the shaft – or pillar below – and the arch springing from it above

Neck moulding or necking

Plain, octagonal shafts were used from c.1300, were common in the Decorated period and less so in Perpendicular times when the sides might also be slightly hollowed

Pier base typically conforms to the shape of the shaft, often, as here, with a slight hollow

*Features of a thirteenth-century column with its base and capital. This example is at Ivinghoe, Buckinghamshire, where the five-bay arcade has octagonal columns, and capitals with sharply cut stiff leaf.*

stone or forms of marble were fashionable between 1160 and 1300. It was not unusual for masons to embellish otherwise plain shafts by encircling them with a shallow, plain fillet or one of carved ornament, called an annulet, which was sometimes arranged in connection with other mouldings.

Taking in turn the individual elements of the thirteenth-century pillar from ground level, we begin with the plinth: it became octagonal on plan, before developing similar circular characteristics to everything that was going on above. Bases were pulled

*Melton Mowbray, Leicestershire. The church of St Mary is noted for its double-aisled transepts.*

back so that they seemed less massive, and were circular on plan. Decorative roll mouldings decreased in size, and from the mid twelfth century to the mid thirteenth, pairs of them were worked together, admitting a deep hollow between what was known as a *water-hold*. The feature began to lose its popularity after about 1240 when the size of the roll mouldings increased, and the water-hold space between them was made much smaller, and sometimes filled by a smaller roll. The double or triple roll base, in which the lower member was sometimes elliptical rather than circular, was widely used throughout the period.

Above the shaft, many Early English capitals were basically circular, moulded, and frequently shaped like an upturned bell. The earlier ones were plain, except for rounds and hollows, but very soon a stylised suggestion of *stiff leaf* began to take shape, followed by that very characteristic motif in all its forms. Stiff leaf was the tangible representation of the naturalistic trend of the age. To begin with, it was not of any particular type and took its name rather more from the erect nature of the stalk than from the style of the actual leaf. Stiff leaf generally splays upwards and outwards on a number of stalks that are often anchored at their base, or die into the feature below. The motif itself started out very conservatively: perhaps individually a three-lobed leaf on a long, stiff stalk. Early examples hugged the bell of the capital and were widely spaced, with deep hollows between, but they were large and not particularly well executed. Then they were sculpted in pairs, with both leaves growing from one stalk. Soon, masons mastered the technique and saw all this foliation as a great expression of joyfulness. The leaves acquired five lobes, even seven, and became attached to leafy scrolls. They were bent and curled, and appeared to grow freely. The leaves never left the plane of the capital but wound their way around it in a way that became so sculptural and all-enveloping that the capital appeared to be a secondary feature, hidden beneath.

Above the capital was the abacus, the link between it and the point of spring of an increasingly moulded arch. The thirteenth century was to bring a change from the square abacus to a circular type. It was sometimes cut out of true to admit the contours of any decoration beneath on the capital, or the shape in cross-section of any clasping shafts. The abacus was given a rounded upper edge and, although the mouldings were light, they tended to be deeply undercut if that was also a feature of the base. This form continued until *c*.1360.

## Development of windows

Arch shapes were also a feature of windows. In France, glass appears to have been used in churches as early as the eleventh century, and it was French glassmakers whose work was applied to larger churches in England during the latter part of the twelfth century. Where there was no glass, there might be a cross-banding of lead that acted as a windbreak. The great benefit of glass was always that it allowed windows to be larger and so let more natural light into the church, without admitting the elements. It also meant that more window lights could be constructed, and they could, in theory, be placed anywhere, without discomfiting clergy or worshippers. Unsurprisingly, when funds were available, the smaller country churches bought more glass: a thick, greyish type that was sometimes embellished by monochromatic, predominantly grey, patterned grisaille.

The lancet window, which made its appearance in the thirteenth century, was beautifully proportioned, aesthetically pleasing, and designed to take glass. So called because its shape resembles the narrow blade and tapering tip of a surgeon's knife, it evolved as a mirror of the pointed arches going up within the church. Early lancets were less pleasing: broad, low and of roughly the same proportions as the preceding round-headed styles. Initially they were put in as single lights, flush with the exterior wall but having a deep internal splay. They were widely spaced in the wall of the church, which must have made very little difference in terms of light value. Gradually they increased in height and width, builders having, for the first time, a shape with which they could preserve desirable proportions. The point at the top suggested upwards movement, which in turn suggested that lights could be of different heights. Once that had been established, it was clear that lights of varying heights could be grouped together, creating an interesting pattern in itself and producing irregular, but symmetrical, points of infill.

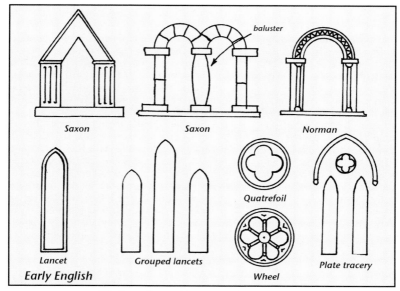

*Windows: Saxon, Norman and Early English.*

*Little Missenden, Buckinghamshire. The three-dimensional aspect of the east window triple lancet arrangement in the Early English chancel is picked out by the forward arcade and the double shafting.*

As the single lancets increased in size, so the amount of solid wall between them decreased. The next step was to bring the lancets together, in either pairs or threes, but usually of the same dimensions. The north and south walls of aisles and the east and west walls of transepts were favoured for this treatment. Grouping single windows together admitted a greater concentration of light. This so reduced the area of wall between that, in essence, mullions (defined as the internal vertical divisions

*Tilty, Essex. A very early type of Early English lancet arrangement: single lights, set in deep splays.*

*Ivinghoe, Buckinghamshire. The north window of the north transept, dated c.1300, is of three lights with pointed trefoils in the head.*

between the lights of a window) were created. Then the potential of lancets in groups was fully realised. They were built in clusters of threes, fives and even sevens, with the larger collections occupying end walls such as the north face of north transepts, the south face of south transepts and the east wall of chancels, above and behind the altar. When an uneven number of lights was put up in a group, they were usually stepped upwards towards the centre light, which was sometimes increased in width. Alternatively, they might be progressively increased in width and height, in pairs, from the outside.

The walls of most churches were still thick, so the internal splays were deep and wide. In the case of single lancets, the width of the splay might be five times that of the opening, in order to make the most of the light coming through the window. The internal appearance of groups gave an optical illusion of greater unity than was evident from the outside, and the sculptors capitalised on this. Pointed hood mouldings were put up around the head of the splay, and slender shafts with little caps and bases on each side. The shafts were often detached, made of a different stone to the rest of the window, and polished. Here was, in effect, the mullion concept as decoration.

At first, each lancet had its own individual dripstone or external hood moulding. In the Early English period, these tended to be quite slender, although with a deep hollow on the underside. They closely followed the contours of the head, keeping close to the wall, and terminated with foliate stops at the points of spring. In the case of a group, the stops were replaced by short, horizontal string courses of similar construction to the dripstones that were linked together by this means. The position of the strings for the whole group was usually determined by the points of spring at the heads of the outside lights. Since these were the shortest, it follows that the remaining lights were stilted in relation to the strings, and the dripstones became progressively longer towards the centre of the feature. As the lights became taller, and the distance between them diminished, a single dripstone was raised above the

*Bledlow, Buckinghamshire. Predominantly a thirteenth-century church; the pointed, inserted window shows how cusping and tracery were developing into the Decorated period.*

group. This device linked them all together and created the basic window shape of several lights, needing only to be completed with infill tracery.

The first step towards this occurred when a circular opening was cut through the wall, beneath a circumscribing arched dripstone above the heads of two lancets of equal height. The solid tracery that resulted from apparently piercing a flat surface is called *plate tracery*. Again, this was an earlier innovation inasmuch as any window opening cut through a flat plate of stone is plate tracery, and this was certainly being done by the mid twelfth century. When groups of lancets were treated in this way, the wall above might be pierced with circles, ovals, trefoils and lozenge shapes. The lancets themselves had little pointed trefoils in their heads, offering the potential for even more interesting shapes in the spaces between.

The vertical divisions between the lights became very narrow and were continued upwards. This formed a framework in stone, of real mullions, and divided into smaller lights what had developed into the head of the window. The result of this is known as *bar tracery*, which began *c*.1245, using simple geometric curves constructed of separate pieces of stone. The earliest types consisted only of foliated circles, although as the period progressed, trefoils and quatrefoils came into fashion. The lancet lights took this treatment well, and the bar tracery was often *cusped*, that is given the projecting points or featherings that are characteristic of Gothic tracery. Early cusps came from the flat underside of the arch, were neither chamfered nor connected with any other mouldings, and were sometimes decorated with a leaf. They were cut out of solid stone in the lower lights, but individually inserted in hollows in the sides of circles, where they stayed in place by mutual pressure.

### String courses

String courses were associated with almost every part of the church fabric. These were narrow, elegant bands of projecting mouldings that ran either horizontally or vertically, separating sections of the church from each other, helping to highlight certain features, and tying everything in together. A string course could run around a wall and, upon encountering a stepped cluster of windows, might become a hood moulding or dripstone that both closely followed the line of their heads and ran horizontally across the spaces between. It would then continue seamlessly around the wall. The simplest string courses commonly ran just below the windows, separating them from the solid wall below. If a buttress was encountered, the string course was invariably continued around it. In this way, it either became a decorative motif that broke up a flat surface or had a practical use by separating the buttress into vertical sections of different depths. Thirteenth-century string courses differed from those of the previous period, as they tended to stop whenever they came across a projecting feature or obstacle which crossed their path. Less frequently were corresponding strings carried around the inside of the church.

### Crockets and other decoration

Perhaps the most enduring and versatile piece of decoration to make its appearance in the thirteenth century was the *crocket*. It is said to have taken its form from the volutes found on classical capitals overseas, and its name from the French word for a hook. Crockets were widely used to decorate the vertical ribs and angles of spires and pinnacles, the sloping edges of gables, canopies, flying buttresses, and occasionally around hood mouldings. Early English examples are crisply carved, being formed of long stalks curving outwards into fairly tight leaves. Later in the period these stalks became flatter, ending in bunches of leaves – occasionally triple-lobed – that were much more loose in execution. Crockets were placed at regular intervals along their chosen host feature and in some instances afforded handholds or footholds for builders.

A favourite decorative motif of the period was the *dog-tooth*. This was a square or four-leaved 'flower', which might be quite flat but was more usually raised into a pyramid, set diagonally to its neighbour and repeated the required length along the hollow between two raised mouldings. The outside quarters touched each other in most cases, the space between forming a diamond shape; but there are also examples where the motifs are separated from each other. Each quarter or 'tooth' of the pyramid offered the potential for further embellishment, and these were occasionally cut as actual leaves.

### Towers, spires and bellcotes

Many churches in the thirteenth century were small and towerless. This was not an ideal state of affairs for a village, at a time of increasing religious feeling and emerging one-upmanship in church design. One of the solutions was to put up a *bellcote*, or a gable for bells, at the west end. Some had two openings beneath a single gable, to hold a pair of bells; others had double gables, which considerably increased the weight. The bellcote was supported by a system of struts, braces and supports that might continue to the

*Bredon, Worcestershire. The restored fourteenth-century Easter sepulchre with crockets along the canopy edge. Permanent, stone-built and elaborately decorated examples replaced earlier wooden representations of Christ's tomb.*

*Frampton, Lincolnshire. The tower, which was built about 1350, has clasping buttresses, and the short spire with broaches and three tiers of spirelights is typical of the area.*

ground; the average roof at this time had not been constructed to withstand the weight of bells. Nor had the walls of the nave. It was likely that the additional load would push the west wall of the nave outwards, so a buttress was put up against the centre of the west face in order to contain the thrust. A similar, but smaller, bellcote was sometimes put up on the east gable of the nave between the nave and the chancel. The small bell inside it was rung by means of a rope inside the church. Western bellcotes and the cradle for the sanctus bell were both treated similarly; they were usually gabled and, as crockets became fashionable, were decorated. Others were topped by little spirelets that might also have crockets.

The proportions of Early English towers were similar to those of the Norman period. The prevailing ground plan of the thirteenth-century tower was square, although some of them were octagonal, and very occasionally the top stage of a square structure was built as an octagon. Usually the towers were fairly squat and of two or three stages separated by moulded string courses. The upper stage was invariably topped by a parapet and, less frequently, with angle pinnacles.

Window openings increased in size, particularly in the topmost stage, where they were frequently just holes in the masonry. The most obvious difference from the preceding period was the use of pointed arcading instead of round-headed arches on the belfry stage. This arcading might be quite ornate, for the most part emulating blind arcading within the church, with moulded, pointed arches on slender columns with little capitals and bases. As the period progressed, paired belfry lights came into favour, contained within a single arch. Their pointed heads changed to trefoils, and a simple geometrical motif was placed in the spandrel between each coupling.

*St Enodoc, Cornwall. A Norman church with a spire, unusual in this county, which was built in the thirteenth century. Until the 1860s, the building was submerged beneath sand.*

Relatively few Early English towers were buttressed.

From this time onwards tower design and decoration developed almost as a separate entity. At one end of the scale, thirteenth-century village builders were erecting incredibly plain towers, as at Brookthorpe (Gloucestershire), which also has a saddleback roof, and, at the other end, there was the sophisticated design-school detached tower of West Walton (Norfolk).

The natural, vertical extension of the tower was the spire, and schools of spire builders soon became established in areas where there was a good supply of local building stone. An upward precedent had been set by the low pyramidal cap. Up went octagonal spires in wood or stone, their intersection with the tower hidden by castellated parapets. Where tower and spire were to go up together, they were designed of a piece, usually without a parapet. When spires were built on top of square towers, with no parapet between, it left a space at each of the angles. The triangular figures that covered these were half-pyramids, inclined from each right angle on the base to a point along each diagonal side of the octagon. These devices, called *broaches*, were of no standard height and were individually built to suit the spire, and supported internally by corner arches called *squinches*. The whole structures on which broaches were used were named broach spires. A third type of spire occurred at this time, favoured where lead or wooden shingles were used as the covering material. In these, the base of the spire met the four cardinal sides of the tower, while the slope was raised to meet the octagon, well above the line of intersection with the tower. Whatever the criteria for raising a spire in the first instance,

*Chesterfield, Derbyshire. A large, cruciform church, built in the fourteenth century. It is distinguished by a twisted spire, still on the move, for which unseasoned timber has been blamed.*

94

in construction it was always no more than an elongated roof. Like other roofs, many were given eaves in the form of an overhang that rested on a corbel table. In early examples, the spire hardly projected from the walls and, in consequence, was not corbelled out in any significant way. In such instances, little more than string courses or minor mouldings sufficed, sometimes embellished with a frieze of trefoils or quatrefoils.

Thirteenth-century spires were treated in many ways, and might have any combination of several features. Many were ribbed vertically and most were given a finial. On the base of the cardinal sides (the alternate faces to those having the broach, where such a figure was present) the builders frequently put up a large spirelight. This was a pointed or trefoil-headed opening placed between perpendicular jambs, beneath a steep and often ornamented gable that sometimes carried a finial. On taller spires, similar but smaller spirelights were sometimes constructed at regular intervals in graduated tiers along its length.

### Thirteenth-century buttresses

Many Early English buttresses were straight-sided and achieved their full height without decreasing in projection, although they were usually narrower than before. This type was quite likely to have vertical, chamfered edges or slender shafts at the right angles. However, the characteristic thirteenth-century buttress rose in stages. Where the depth remained the same, those stages might be picked out by moulded string courses that sometimes continued along adjacent walls, thus tying together the whole external fabric of the building. Otherwise,

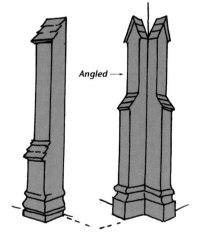

Angled —

*Early English buttresses.*

*Porlock, Somerset. The thirteenth-century church has a squat stone tower with angled buttresses, and a wooden spire covered with oak shingles that was truncated in 1703.*

each stage of the buttress tended to be narrower than the one below, inclined by means of a slope in the masonry or by covered set-offs – the horizontal surfaces left when a piece of masonry is cut back in order successively to reduce its thickness. The lower edges of the set-offs projected, or were given a moulded drip that would direct water clear of the masonry. The quantity of set-offs might differ at any given stage of the same buttress; they might be a single tier cut out of one block of stone, or as many as seven tiers; more usual are two or three at each stage. On multi-tiered buttresses, the angles of inclination of the set-offs were usually more acute as they ascended. Thirteenth-century builders finished their buttresses either by sloping the upper stage into the cornice of the building, or by giving it a triangular elevation topped by a gable. The vast majority of buttresses of this period are plain, except for the occasional string course or dedicated moulding, or a collection of mouldings above the plinth. A shallow, horizontal moulding was sometimes placed as extra decoration beneath the dripstone. More ornate are those buttresses that were given blind arches on their leading edges, possibly with cusping, or had similar decoration associated with their gabled heads.

### Porches and their uses

In the thirteenth century, and indeed for centuries afterwards, the church porch was at the heart of village life. It is why porches today still have their notice boards with an eclectic mix of religious and secular information pinned to them. It was a meeting place where transactions took place and where promises were given and accepted on holy ground. The first part of the marriage celebration was carried out there, and they were also linked with the service of baptism.

Most village church porches of the period were necessarily small but were deep in comparison to their width, and high-pitched and gabled. They were usually built on the south side of the church, to protect the main entrance. However, where landowning families approached the church by a pathway from their residence in

the opposite direction, a reasonable porch might also have been put up over a more convenient north door. Outer openings on to the churchyard usually had a dripstone or hood moulding which terminated on either side above a corbel. Otherwise it ended in a stop, which was either a human head or some floral motif that lent itself to a circular or oval design. Most of the decoration occurred around the opening and on the inside walls and was typically of square or lozenge diaper work. In the early years of the thirteenth century porch builders simply adapted the Norman idea of making their porch doorways out of several recessed arches. Some of them placed cylindrical, detached shafts in each nook of the jambs. By now, circular capitals and bases were taking over from the cushion and scalloped capitals of recent years, and the bases were no longer formed of heavy blocks, nor part of the fabric of

*Bledlow, Buckinghamshire. The fourteenth-century south porch built, like the rest of the exterior, of flint and clunch with limestone dressings.*

the lower wall. The interior of the porch might be ornamented with a colonnade of slender columns, set on little round bases with plain mouldings, arched at the heads, with stiff-leaf capitals and bands of diaper work such as dog-tooth above. More usually, however, the interior walls were plain. These led to plainly moulded doorways into the nave that were either pointed or trefoiled.

There were some other interesting features of thirteenth-century porch design. Two occurred in larger churches: the double-opening doorway, in which a slender shaft was used to divide the entrance into two, and the double-arched doorway. The latter comprised two separate arches, built one behind the other at the main entrance, which were treated quite independently as regards decoration. They were positioned to accommodate a wide intervening jamb space on either side, which might be quite lavishly decorated with a blind arcade of pointed arches and typical arch mouldings of the period.

The Early English period also brought an increase in the number of porches with at least one upper room or chamber. Access might be from inside the porch or from within the nave. There is little doubt that rooms were built above church porches between the twelfth and the fifteenth centuries for several different reasons, and during their existence most will have been used for purposes other than the original. Almost every suggestion for their origin is likely: library, accounts room, weapons store, depository for documents, general store room for commodities against times of want, and meeting room, were all just possible. Some have fireplaces, and little openings through which any occupant could see into the church, and in others there is evidence of an altar. It is possible that village priests may have inhabited the upper rooms at some time during the day. The other suggestion is that they were living quarters for hermits or anchorites. On the balance of probabilities, the human element has much in favour of it.

## Vaulting and buttresses

Builders learnt that weights tended to concentrate more at the corners of the buildings, and that the outer thrusts of the arches of a vault meant that the weight of the heavy masonry shifted laterally rather than vertically. They were experimenting with more sophisticated styles of vaulting, while at the same time building thinner walls. They realised how, and why, walls were being pushed outwards and initially devised a solution that involved constructing buttresses to meet each other exactly at right angles where two walls met. These are called *angle buttresses*, and they preceded those that actually enclosed the angle, known as *clasping buttresses*.

*Stebbing, Essex. Built of flint, clunch, tiles and limestone in the thirteenth century; a crouching gargoyle and gable cross outside, and a fine stone rood screen within.*

97

Buttresses were also involved in the means of admitting more light into the church. One of the ways of achieving this was to raise a clerestory above the nave and pierce it with windows. Many more clerestories went up in the thirteenth century, thus increasing the height of the nave walls and necessitating a series of external buttresses along their length to combat the possibility of an outward masonry shift. In practice, there was little need for buttresses where a clerestory (and in larger churches, a triforium or blind arcade beneath it) was raised over the nave arcade. This is because the thrust from any vault, in such instances, was mostly carried down the arches to the ground. This was not the case where churches had particularly tall aisles and correspondingly high nave walls. The *flying buttress* was developed and infrequently used during the thirteenth century. Imagine a conventional buttress ascending the outside wall of an aisle but continuing above it to a point where it meets a horizontal bar of masonry that is attached at its other end to the clerestory wall. That is a flying buttress – usually straight along its upper surface and either chamfered or curved along the underside. Its purpose was to relieve the potential outward thrust from a high vaulted roof, and finding the correct position for the relieving bar was a matter of trial and error.

## On the roof

At this time it became fashionable to erect a *gable cross* in the position of a finial on the roof at the east end of the nave. The thirteenth-century gable cross characteristically took the form of a Greek cross (in which the arms are of equal length), usually enclosed in a decorated circle. Less often a Latin cross was used, in which the upright is longer than the arms. Some crosses were not placed immediately on the apex of the roof, but on their own tiny gable, built at right angles to the roof line, with the cross itself facing east. The three-lobed leaf, which might also be surrounded by other swirling leaf forms, lent itself well to the ends of the arms of a gable cross and as the ornamentation for any circle that enclosed it. In the case of Latin crosses, the lower parts of the uprights might be formed into little bases and plinths.

The other interesting thirteenth-century embellishments to the outside of the church were *gargoyles*. Water collected behind the stone masonry of parapets and therefore had to be transferred to the ground. This was done by piercing holes through the stonework and inserting lead spouts that projected outwards. In the thirteenth century the masonry associated with these spouts was either left plain or carved with fairly conservative mythical beasts, birds or grotesques. The water was conveyed either through their open mouths or by means of a spout protruding below the body of the creature. Early English gargoyles differ from later ones in projecting further from the wall.

## Thirteenth-century fonts

Fewer fonts were made in the thirteenth century than at any other time. Early English fonts were generally smaller, shallower and more slender than their predecessors. In some instances a Norman font, or part of it, was incorporated into a new design, and occasionally the tub shape was retained. Hughenden (Buckinghamshire) is an example of such an alliance. One of the earliest remaining examples of this period is at Charlton-on-Otmoor (Oxfordshire). At Broadwell, in the same county, there is another font from the beginning of the thirteenth century.

Octagonal bowls began to be developed late in the twelfth century, and the square shapes continued; both were to be standard designs for the next two hundred years. Thirteenth-century fonts were made of freestone, various local shell marbles or Purbeck 'marble', which polished to produce a texture that was much in demand, and which is to be found in areas that were easily accessible by water. Although these marbles could take a high polish and thereby made up in lustre what they lacked by way of decoration, their popularity was relatively short-lived. Ornamentation on them was generally conservative. The fashion was for continuous bands of shallow arcading, with nothing more to detract from its beauty.

Above left: *Eaton Bray, Bedfordshire. Thirteenth-century, convex, cup-style font with central stem, four corner shafts, moulded bases, and freely carved foliation on the capitals.*

Above right: *Preshute, Wiltshire. One of only seven fonts in the country made of black marble; material for this was from the Tournai quarry in Belgium. It has a diameter of 3½ feet (107 cm).*

The roll moulding on thirteenth-century fonts was delicately done. Many had semicircular string courses that separated a main band of ornamentation from a frieze above or below. A few bowls, such as the one at South Kilworth (Leicestershire), took the shape of a pier capital with angled edges, foliated or with leaf shapes. Generally, however, there was great restraint in foliated ornamentation, although the bowl at Eaton Bray (Bedfordshire) is an oddity to disprove that statement. More than ever before, shafts were used to support the edges of bowls, rather than simply abutting them as wholly aesthetic decoration. They had deeply moulded capitals and bases, reflecting those on the piers of the period. An example of this is at Leighton Buzzard (Bedfordshire), where the overall design is otherwise similar to Eaton Bray.

The bowls of the marble fonts were either octagonal or square. Usually they had a shallow arcade of slender, but uniform, semicircular, pointed or trefoiled arches, but they were sometimes quite plain. Occasionally cusping was introduced into the design. There were up to seven arches in single or double continuous order on each face of the square or octagonal fonts, whether they were made of freestone or marble. The bowls might rest on a central stem and have up to eight supporting shafts, which became more slender and better proportioned as the period progressed. Sometimes, the arches were a rustic horseshoe shape, as at Nassington (Northamptonshire). At Coleby (Lincolnshire) is a refined form of the Romanesque style with intersecting arches: narrow openings between slender columns with Early English bases. At Lakenheath (Suffolk) there is a beautiful exception to the customary thirteenth-century font bowl. Stiff-leaf foliage appears on fonts in friezes, at the intersection of arches, and forms the capitals of support shafts, as at Gatton (Surrey). In some instances – as at Hadleigh (Essex), where the supports are very similar to those at Eaton Bray – stiff leaf is used as the main decoration on the outside of the bowl.

Most thirteenth-century fonts were mounted, sometimes on massive pedestals, and raised from the floor of the church on stepped platforms that enhanced their importance. There is a good example of this at Battle (Sussex). However, in marked contrast, the early Gothic period also produced a very beautiful shallow cup design, whose shafts were at first detached and later engaged. Good examples of cup bowls are at Shere (Surrey), which has a very plain design, and at Michelmersh (Hampshire), which is much more ornate.

Stone fonts of the thirteenth century carried rather more ornamentation than their marble counterparts: fleurs-de-lis, vine scrolls, stiff leaf, shells and flowers were among the favourite motifs. In essence, the design of shafts on the font closely followed the evolution of the pier. Their capitals were sometimes foliated, and the shafts themselves might have a vertical fillet. The bases and plinths of the stone fonts might be circular or square and followed the shape of each other. Circular bases sometimes included a water-hold moulding.

## Piscina and sedilia

The pointed or trefoil-headed piscina and sedilia became very popular and were often designed as a single feature and built side by side in the wall of the chancel. Piscinas were also put into the eastern ends of aisles, where they may now indicate the former position of an altar, and, more occasionally, on the inside wall of the porch or in the nave. The drain might be a simple indentation, a neatly scalloped bowl, or one formed of several scallops like the petals of a flower radiating from the drain hole. Double piscinas became common following the papal announcement that the sacred vessels, such as the chalice, and the priest's hands should not be washed in the same basin. Some of them included a credence shelf of wood or stone above the basin, on which the sacred vessels were placed prior to use and immediately afterwards. The seats of sedilia were either built on the same level, or were stepped downwards towards the west. Once again, they were separated externally by slender shafts with characteristic capitals and bases, and little roll mouldings, or might be decorated with stiff leaf or more naturalistic foliage. A shallow string course, running around the walls of the chancel, might be continued as a hood moulding above and between the arched heads of the piscina and sedilia.

*Bredon, Worcestershire. Early English stepped sedilia of three bays, trefoiled and cusped, and (left) a trefoil-headed piscina.*

# Decorated
# 1300–1377

### The favoured style

There is a fine early Decorated church at Hunstanton (Norfolk), and one that is slightly later at Trumpington (Cambridgeshire). Great Bardfield and Stebbing, both in Essex, each have remarkable interiors that were entirely built later in the period. In architectural terms, the church at Boston (Lincolnshire) spans the whole of the Decorated era. It was a time when many great guilds came into being, and an increasing number of craft workers organised themselves into groups that were frequently associated with the church. Work on and about the church required the expertise of several trades: masons, carpenters, painters, glaziers, rope makers, candle makers, and a good many itinerant labourers. In the matter of stone alone, there would be financial reward for quarry owners, business people who leased small pockets of quarry land, workers who dug the stone, carriers who transported it overland or by water, people who built the transport by which this was achieved, and makers of the handling equipment. Then there were toolmakers, and a range of tradesmen who actually worked the stone. Timber also had to be felled and transported before it could be cut as required in church building. In large towns, there would have been sufficient ongoing work for the practitioners to organise themselves into semi-permanent groups.

Church porches that were put up then were fairly plain, with high-pitched roofs and exterior openings that were very similar to the interior doorways. Occasionally they had parapets and might also be decorated with heraldry, typically over the doorway or in the spandrels. Some of the porches that were built of stone were given an upper room in which parish records and other documents were placed in church depositories for safe keeping. Here, too, parish meetings took place. During this period a number of openwork timber porches were erected, built on stone or timber bases, and occasionally on little low walls. The porches were usually gabled with arch braces and had bargeboards that were frequently carved. Doorways might be moulded and pointed with openwork sides which included designs of geometrical tracery. One of the most fascinating mid-fourteenth-century examples of this type is at Aldham (Essex). In the same county there are fourteenth-century porches at Great Bardfield and Stebbing.

The dressed blocks of stone that made up the external fabric of the

*Harberton, Devon. The two-storey south porch, buttressed and pinnacled, with stair turret. The church has a wagon roof of 1436 with eighty different carved bosses.*

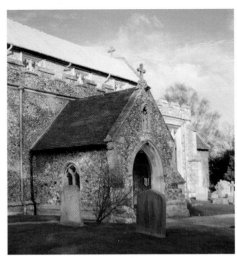

*Great Bardfield, Essex. The porch, with its pretty side light, and almost all of the church are fourteenth-century; it has a spectacular stone chancel screen of the period.*

buildings were generally larger, and longer in relation to their height. Tooling was finely done, and the stones fitted very tightly together. Whitbourne (Herefordshire) is typical. A major thread that linked new and old buildings was the use of heraldic devices and coats of arms, which epitomised the splendour of the age. The Decorated style was never to be fully developed in England, even though a massive programme of church building began to take shape from about 1330. It was destined, however, to exemplify English church building at two extremes of competence.

### Fourteenth-century development

As applied to the humble village church, the term 'Decorated' was always fairly ambiguous. Nowhere in England did the style achieve its full potential, and there

*Warfield, Berkshire. The distinguishing features of this mid-fourteenth-century chancel are the gently flowing tracery of the east window, and the quality of the carving of the reredos and around the sedilia and piscina.*

*Pershore Abbey, Worcestershire. The Decorated upper stages of the lantern tower, built c.1330–40, are supported on the high arches of the Norman church of c.1100.*

are few village churches that aspire to the kind of embellishment that is conjured up by the word. There was no great advance, no innovative principle or particular turning point that heralded the Decorated period. On the ground, churches increased in size but retained their basic plan of chancel, aisled nave, western tower, and north and south porches. Chancels were rarely given aisles, although they were frequently built large enough to accommodate them. There is a fine chancel at Stanton St John (Oxfordshire), built just as Early English progressed into Decorated, and one of slightly later date at Warfield (Berkshire). The chancel at Lawford (Essex) is a *tour de force* of some innovative master mason's art, and very much a vehicle for his tracery pattern book. Patrington (Yorkshire) is another example of a chancel that has a range of beautiful traceried windows. In some instances, windows of unprecedented size were put into the chancels.

Naves and sanctuaries were lengthened; transepts and chapels were added. New aisles were built parallel to existing naves and, where transepts were already in place, such aisles were often erected only as far as the west walls of the latter. Whenever this occurred, it provided a blank interior wall that could not be pierced for a window but proved to be a logical position for a side altar and, ultimately, a small chapel. Where larger transepts existed, the opportunity was sometimes taken to create aisles within them.

Western towers continued to be favoured: square on plan, typically larger in base area than at any previous time, and rising in two, three or four stages. Despite the success of Uffington (Oxfordshire) and Doulting (Somerset), octagonal towers were very infrequently built. They are at their best above the crossing, where they appear as a more homogenous part of the church. There is a western octagonal tower of the fourteenth century at Standlake (Oxfordshire). Occasionally square towers were erected, plain and unbuttressed during the Decorated period, and they were sometimes made to look older, as at Whitbourne (Herefordshire), by the use of mixed stonework in uneven courses.

Stair turrets were considered as an aesthetic and integral part of tower design. They were typically octagonal with deep base mouldings and strings, and frequently ascended beyond the belfry lights. In all, they were better proportioned than previously, and many were given surface panelling. Where fairly large lights existed in

*Shottesbrooke, Berkshire. Built c.1375, the ribbed spire is a triumph, and the curvilinear windows are on the cusp of the development into Decorated.*

the upper stages of a tower, adjustments might be made to their arrangement on one face, in order to accommodate a successful stair turret. Turret lights were usually tall and narrow. At the beginning of the period they were mostly elongated lancets, but the development of tracery was soon to be applied, even here. The lancet became a depressed ogee head; ornamentation, tracery and cusping were all added. Similarly, belfry openings, although they remained unglazed, were either single two-light windows with traceried heads in each face of the tower, or pairs of two-lights with a quatrefoil between them. An arrangement of small holes pierced through the solid masonry was another innovation of the fourteenth century. These so-called *sound holes* obviously enabled the sound of the bells to be heard more clearly, but they were also a means of allowing ventilation into the ringing lofts.

There was a move towards building steeples, and the octagonal tower was not altogether dismissed in this regard; it might be put up between the top of a square tower and the base of an octagonal spire. Spires were taller, more acute, and slender, particularly so where they were built in stone. They were sometimes given a slight entasis so that the sides would not appear to be concave. Notably in the south-east

of England, spires were covered in oak, lead or timber shingles. The broach became smaller and eventually went out of fashion, being occasionally replaced by square or octagonal pinnacles at the angles. The parapet spire took over, although there occasionally were combinations of broach, parapet and pinnacles being put up throughout the period. By far the most common form of spire was one that had neither broach nor pinnacle but was raised behind a fairly plain parapet. This was sometimes relieved by vertical ribs or ridges, which might also have ballflower or crockets along their length. Horizontal banding was rarely used because this detracted from the impression of height. Sometimes, however,

*Ashbourne, Derbyshire. The tower was added to this Early English church in the early fourteenth century, and the 212 feet (65 metres) ribbed and crocketed spire with spirelights was put up c.1350.*

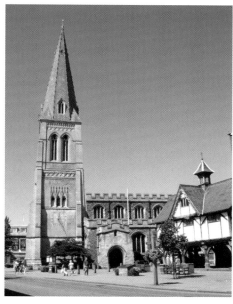

*Market Harborough, Leicestershire. The fourteenth-century tower has angle buttresses and a recessed spire with broaches; the church is otherwise mostly Perpendicular.*

wide bands of panelled trefoils or quatrefoils in relief actually turned these into something of a feature. Spirelights continued to be put in; they were most usually placed on the cardinal sides, but were placed alternately where they appeared on both cardinal and diagonal surfaces.

This was the period when angle buttresses, and those placed on the diagonal, continued as pinnacles beyond the parapet. Some of these were virtually spirelets. This gave additional height to the structure and, when they were ornamented, a pleasing appearance against the skyline. Where pinnacles rose above the level of the parapet, the two might be connected by a diagonal, flying buttress, with a straight moulding ornamented on its angled underside. There is a fantastic arrangement of buttresses, pinnacles and stylised broaches on the steeple at Heckington (Lincolnshire). Even buttresses that eventually died into the tower tended to rise at least to the full height of the walls. This enhanced the feeling of strength, overall mass and solidarity.

Fourteenth-century doorways varied in size and in some instances, in larger churches, were divided into two. Usually the doorways were pointed and had their jambs chamfered at an angle of 45 degrees. These were more shallowly recessed than during the preceding period. Although detached shafts were gradually being abandoned throughout the church, they still often occurred in the jambs of doorways. In their general manner of usage, early fourteenth-century shafts and mouldings appeared little advanced from the Early English style. Gradually, however, they became narrower and a more intrinsic part of the overall arrangement of vertical mouldings. The arch mouldings were either carried on the same plane as engaged shafts or were continued down the jambs without caps. In many instances, bases became dispensable. This enabled the arch mouldings to carry on down to plinths that were themselves chamfered out on the lowest projecting block of stone. Small doorways of the period, and even larger ones with no great weight above them and more than a single order of arches surrounding the opening, might have been given more decorative arch styles. These are often found associated with a pointed inner arch and might comprise a non-structural, trefoil-headed opening, sometimes an ogee trefoil, or a wholly ogee-shaped arch. Occasionally, the mouldings that formed the jambs of a small doorway were combined with those of an outer arch, entirely independent at the head, yet both progressing to the same base or plinth. In any event such doorways were frequently afforded a degree of enrichment that was out of character with their size. The head of the arch might itself be cusped. Where one arch rose above another, the space between was sometimes filled by decoration along the head of the lower arch. This terminated in a foliated or crocketed pinnacle. The doorway surround might be even more lavishly decorated if it was beneath a straight-sided or ogee-shaped hood moulding in the form of a canopy. Certainly these might sometimes be plain, but in most cases they were at least enriched with crockets. The hood moulding on either side of the doorway might terminate with the heads

of monarchs and their consorts, or with armorial bearings. Very small doorways, such as priests' doors and those that gave access to stair turrets or through internal walls into rood lofts, might be pointed, square-headed or of ogee shape. In the last instance, a depressed ogee was favoured. Jambs and shafts very much followed the pattern of the main doors but were plainer, and the doors rarely had hood mouldings or the various features associated with them. Priests' doors were the exception, in that they might be decorated and even canopied.

This was the period of the niche, so it is not surprising that doorways were regularly surmounted by such recesses. Adjacent places for niches included the jambs and the heads of the doorway arches, and in the wall on either side of the opening. In the former position they were very small but nonetheless frequently included figures. Niches might be given an ogee-shaped head, or a projecting canopy in any of a number of decorative configurations. Such canopies might be triangular or several-sided. Sometimes they were included within a straight-sided, gabled moulding, as if it were a pediment, so that they became a visual part of the doorway below. Wherever it was placed, there was always the opportunity for the niche to be embellished and inhabited. A characteristic niche of the early fourteenth century might have an ogee head terminating in a three-lobed floral finial and having foliated crockets along its upper edges. The sides might have a cinquefoiled head, following the general shape of the outer ogee, with ballflower decoration in the hollow. There is an example of this type at Combe (Oxfordshire). Mouldings in the shape of pediments were put up above doorways, providing the potential to apply tracery shapes within the resulting triangle. This created spandrels, which could be enriched with other geometrical or naturalistic motifs of the time. As the style progressed, so did the abundant use of crockets and foliage, especially that of a large, three-lobed, fleshy leaf type. Floral motifs and the customary ballflower were used to decorate hood mouldings and the hollows between arch mouldings.

Doors of the period were built of vertical planks of oak, banded by richly ornamented ironwork that took floral designs in the later years. What was achieved depended very much on the ability and creativity of the local smithy. Decorated panels were introduced into the woodwork of doors in the fourteenth century, and eventually richly carved with tracery, both reticulated and flowing.

During the fourteenth century, buttresses were better proportioned than ever before, although they were still commonly built in either two or three stages. These were separated by set-offs or string courses that sometimes worked in conjunction with each other, or with a string course that ran around the exterior walls of the building. In such instances the string course might be carried around the buttress, beneath a set-off. Occasionally a string course, running close beneath a window, takes a sudden vertical dive in order to continue at a more aesthetic, horizontal level. While many buttresses were plain, except for a chamfered arris, they were more frequently decorated. In buttresses that were not decorated throughout, it was usually the upper stage that bore embellishment, where there might be tracery-style panels or a niche.

*Lyddington, Rutland. Built late in the fourteenth century, in Perpendicular style, and of local ironstone; note the heavy corner buttresses rising through three stages, and the strong string courses tying it all together.*

The latter might be trefoiled, cusped, or constructed with an ogee head, frequently canopied and decorated with crockets and a finial. Any surface of the buttress was considered to be suitable for panelling.

Buttresses were also wider than they were previously. Their bases projected further away from the walls, and they were sometimes tapered as they ascended, in order to increase the illusion of height. They were either plainly chamfered or heavily moulded. There was some innovation, and a characteristic development involved placing pairs of identical corner buttresses diagonally at the point where two walls met at right angles, but not so that the angle was enclosed. In another design, a single buttress was put up, enclosing the point at which the walls met, at an angle of 45 degrees to the corner. Towers, in particular, occasionally featured both of these types. At ground level there might be a pair of diagonal buttresses, which eventually died into the wall. These were continued above by an angle buttress that partly rested on the set-offs of the former or was corbelled out from the wall. It was not unusual for the head of a buttress to be continued above through any battlements, or to be occasionally ornamented by a small niche at the point of intersection. Niches were the innovation of the period, and they might appear anywhere, even on relatively small or single-stage buttresses. In some instances, a Decorated buttress might have the appearance of being put up solely as the carrier for an ornamental niche. These typically had a full complement of gables, engaged angle shafts, pinnacles, trefoil- or quatrefoil-headed tracery and a whole forest of foliation by way of crockets and finials. The head of a fourteenth-century buttress typically ended with an upper weathering, inclined away from the wall, or a triangular or gable-shaped head.

During the Decorated period the parapet achieved its full complement of parts: coping, parapet wall, moulded cornice, or a string course and corbels. They were a pleasant way of breaking up the skyline and tying together the tops of buttresses and pinnacles. Since the latter were used quite sparingly and tended to be concentrated at certain points in the building, a parapet helped to bring an element of cohesion to the top of the wall, in a similar way to that achieved by string courses lower down.

*Edington, Wiltshire. The much battlemented exterior of William of Edington's cruciform church, built c.1352–61, is still Decorated in essence but blended with Perpendicular by inclination.*

The big priory church at Edington (Wiltshire) has the overall appearance of a small castle, largely because its walls are topped by a battlemented parapet. These features could be particularly beautiful where they were built along the sloping sides of roof gables, such as those of Higham Ferrers (Northamptonshire). In many churches parapets have niches at the points at which they run over the heads of features such as windows; in these instances the base of the niche was sometimes incorporated into the dripstone.

As embattled parapets became a feature of the period, such decorative motifs as the quatrefoil in relief were eminently suited to the merlons on which they appeared. There might be ballflower ornamentation in the cornice associated with a parapet, wandering four-leaf decoration or small heads. The parapet wall could be pierced with trefoils, quatrefoils, flowing tracery of innumerable forms, or an openwork representation of the four-leafed motif. A favourite alternative was to place the trefoil within a triangle and repeat this, sometimes alternately inverted.

Builders and masons began to see the outside of the church as a blank canvas, full of potential for decorating. The west front, in particular, provided a façade, into which niches could be inserted, with fine figurework to fill them. The doorway and the great traceried window above were sometimes enclosed within a deeply recessed arch. Large windows were put into the chancel walls, especially at the east end, where smaller windows might also be placed in the aisles. Internally, smaller churches were elevated by means of an arcade with a clerestory above; larger buildings might have a triforium between the two, lifting the church in three stages. Even then, the triforium gradually diminished in size and the concept was often abandoned altogether. Early English builders strove for height, but their successors decided they had gone far enough in that direction. It was only a temporary move but, for the moment, architects applied themselves to widening and opening out, and to flattening the roofs of aisles. This reduced the height of the walls beneath, thereby decreasing the amount of space available for stages of horizontal elevation. Decorated Gothic was much richer, considerably more mature and more closely harmonised with the genuine feeling of the times.

## Arches and arcades

Constructional arches were plain and pointed, although less acutely so than those of the preceding century. They were more spacious although not necessarily taller than before. Chancel arches were built of two or three orders and were plainly chamfered. They either continued to the ground or were supported by engaged pillars. Aisles tended generally to be more lofty, and there was a marked change in the pillars that supported the arcading between them and the nave. The abacus became the upper moulding of the capital, and an integral part of it. It was carved from the same block of stone, but usually retained a hollow quirk – even if less deeply cut than previously – as a reminder of its former autonomy. The Decorated period produced abaci that were octagonal, polygonal and circular, with a wide range of moulding configurations. Simple roll mouldings were popular on abaci, strings and dripstones,

*Boston, Lincolnshire. Building began here in 1309 but was not completed until 1390, when the nave was re-roofed. The tall Perpendicular arches are characteristic.*

and occasionally took a fillet. Also popular was the scroll moulding, in which the upper half of a roll overlaps the lower, like a scroll with a proud edge, the overlap having a flat underside. A form that included a well-defined square fillet has been called a *roll and fillet* moulding.

Beneath the abacus came the capital, although occasionally they were omitted in this period, or there might be no astragal – a single, semicircular, encircling moulding or bead – at the neck to give credence to the capital as a proper figure. The most common shape for the fourteenth-century capital was circular. It was generally narrower than its predecessor and comprised scroll or roll mouldings, ogee shapes and fillets. If the bells of capitals did not have geometrical moulding, they were usually covered in naturalistic foliage. Often this was done by following the contours of the bell and building upwards from stem to splendid leaf. In such instances, this enhanced the shape of the bell and gave it great dignity. But, as the fourteenth century progressed, the masons became so adept at naturalistic foliage that often they completely swamped the bell. It was all in sharp contrast to the stylistic and undefined flora that had gone on before. Little human heads were sometimes carved amidst a surfeit of ivy, oak leaves and acorns, berries, fir cones, maple and hawthorn leaves, and entwined running vines. Masons abandoned the idea of leaves that appeared to be growing on long stalks out of the shaft below. In many instances, stalks were completely disregarded. In their place, the foliage was grouped on stems that were not anchored to the pillar, as if growing out of the ground, but were included wholly as an intrinsic part of the design. Leaves increased in size and were carved in all different directions. The carver paid particular attention to the finish and, where his motifs stood away from the surface of the capital, their undersides and backs were smoothly worked. Later, a bulbous and unnatural curve occurred in even naturalistic foliage, simulating the opposing undulations of the popular ogee shape. Foliage on the capital usually just touched the astragal beneath but did not obscure or breach it. An astragal of the period was commonly a scroll moulding.

In cross-section, pillars became either diagonal, lozenge-shaped or a square placed diagonally. In larger churches, the compound pillars gave way to an arrangement of four or eight cylindrical shafts, set diamond-shaped on plan. The octagonal and cylindrical pillars were usually quite plain, and either might otherwise have a vertical fillet from cap to base. This decorative motif was particularly attractive when applied to the arrangement of cylindrical shafts that succeeded the compound pillar, as, from a distance, it enhanced the cluster effect. For added value, thin and thick shafts sometimes alternated when there was a total of eight in the feature. Towards the end of the period, there were a number of variations on the theme of four small shafts, set as it were at the corners of a square, and separated by deep hollows. This arrangement was occasionally associated with vertical, quarter round mouldings or more pronounced fillets. Any hollows tended to be small but deep. Because shafts were so much thinner and mouldings narrower than in the previous period, even

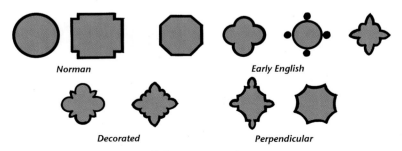

Column cross-sections.

relatively short pillars achieved the optical illusion of greater height.

This impression was further enhanced as bases were made deeper. This lifted the moulding that separated the pillar from the base higher than any previous level. At first, the bases were formed of two or three rolls, with a flat underside to the lowest, and decorative mouldings in the hollows. Later, they regularly comprised mainly reversed ogee shapes and wave mouldings, and closely followed the line of the pillar above, sometimes overhanging the shape of the plinth below. This usually occurred when the pillar and the plinth were not similar on plan, particularly when the former was made up of circles and the latter was an octagon or a composite shape roughly described on that figure. Fourteenth-century plinths might be constructed in several stages that were each set off against the one above and were either round, square or octagonal. Projecting angles in the arrangement might be a straight chamfer, a hollow, or otherwise distinguished by a narrow moulding. Despite their height, and the fact that the most common plinth was a double, they were usually smaller in ground area than before. This meant that they lost some of their prominence at the base.

Chamfers made in the fourteenth century tended to have less decoration at their terminations than previously. Many were plain and flat, and they frequently ended in a triangular shape that might be composed of little wave mouldings. The ogee curve was introduced into the chamfer, but by far the most popular end stops of the period were trefoils and quatrefoils. These were sometimes cusped and were occasionally enclosed within an ogee arch. Chamfers were, of course, hollows. In the fourteenth century, their convex cousin, the string course, commonly comprised a scroll moulding or some variation with an ogee as its lower curve. This was delicately done and resulted in a graceful outline. In most cases, a square fillet still formed the leading edge, and any hollows were always on the underside.

The innovation of the period was the ogee arch. In its simplest form, the ogee in cross-section is a single moulding inscribed as a protruding round or wave with a corresponding hollow below. This arrangement is called cyma reversa; the preferred version of classical architecture, in which the hollow is uppermost, is cyma recta. Occasionally in the fourteenth century part of the ogee might be a convex quarter circle or ovolo, which could have a quirk – a horizontal recess – along its upper edge or between the two elements of the moulding. A definition of the ogee shape is a continuous, flowing double curve that is concave above and convex below and springs from two opposing radii. Because the head of an ogee arch takes the form of two reversed curves, the feature cannot withstand heavy loads and is therefore unsuitable for use in a structural way. In about 1300 the ogee began to replace its straight-sided predecessor

*Stebbing, Essex. The traceried screen of three lancets – tiered, cusped, quatrefoiled and ogee-arched with ballflower decoration – was made early in the fourteenth century.*

as a canopy and then rapidly spread throughout the church wherever a decorative arch could be used. A depressed ogee was sometimes featured in window tracery, set beneath a pointed arch. An ogee arch might itself be cusped, framed by crockets, foliage decoration and ballflower, all flowing sinuously towards a crowning pinnacle at the head, itself decorated with crockets and finial. The ogee figure also appeared on tombs of the fourteenth century, in mouldings, cusping, niches, sedilia and piscinas, decorative arcading, on buttresses and in the head shape of Easter sepulchres. There is a fine example of the last at Hawton (Nottinghamshire). The design is all the more apparent because of the number of possible variations on the theme and the ways in which it lent itself to a range of decorative initiatives. The upper curves and lower curves might vary in length within their pairs, and they might be depressed or acute.

Most vaulting of the period was carried out in stone and only occasionally in wood, although relatively few vaults were constructed in either material after the middle of the fourteenth century. The more important ribs in an arrangement were likely to be thicker than the others, and any of the ribs potentially took decorative motifs of the period. Quadripartite vaults continued to be popular; transverse ribs and longitudinal ribs were sometimes not included in an arrangement, but there was an increase in the quantity of surface ribs. These might be between the diagonal rib and the cross springers, following the line of curve of the vault. Particularly in the south and west of England, a series of short ribs was put in, crossing between bosses and connecting them with the intersections of the principal rib and the ridge ribs. These members do not spring from imposts or attach to the ridge; they are termed *lierne ribs* and hence the area employing them is called a *lierne vault*. The construction results in very effective, and often quite complicated, star-like shapes. A combination of these additional short ribs gave the vault a net-like appearance.

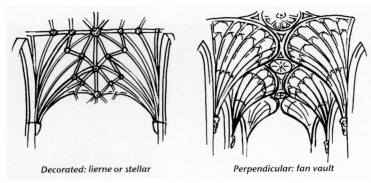

Decorated: lierne or stellar              Perpendicular: fan vault

*Vaults.*

## Roofs

Roofs of this time continued to be constructed of timber and were covered in stone roofing tiles, lead, or wood shingles made of split oak. By this time, builders better understood the optimum ways to support roofs. They were making considerable alterations in the arrangement of beams and subtle changes to the designs of some traditional supports. These changes enabled more efficient use of timber and at the same time offered scope for decoration and thereby an improved visual effect overall. A good example of this was the development of the simple tie beam. Now it was cambered, an alteration that helped to counter the additional loads imposed by more sophisticated roofing systems that might otherwise have caused it to sag. It might also be carved with plain mouldings or decorative motifs and, for added strength, be supported from beneath by arched braces that sometimes met in the centre. Otherwise, the principal rafters might now be continued in a curve beneath the tie beam. This created spandrels that were filled with pierced tracery, usually dagger motifs or some symmetrical arrangement based on elongated foils.

A similar arrangement formed the arch-braced roof, in which a pair of braces with continuous curves was set up between purlins on either side and the ridge piece. The thrust of the braces was relieved by placing wall posts beneath the principal rafters, which in turn prevented the roof from spreading. Another innovation was the insertion of a horizontal timber, known as a collar, between the principal rafters near their highest point. This enabled the conventional tie beam to be omitted in roofs that had a high pitch, and in some instances allowed an additional collar to be inserted even higher, for extra stability. This was the precursor to the elegant hammer-beam roof of the Perpendicular period.

## Mouldings and decoration

Fourteenth-century mouldings were numerous but were much less deeply undercut than previously. Early roll mouldings were small but increased in size with the years, and the hollows between became broader. The bowtell and triple filleted roll continued to be favoured, although the flanking fillets tended to be broader than the central one. By removing the projections and flattening the bowtell, the masons produced a beautiful form known as a *wave moulding*. This was an undulation that could be either gentle or severe, depending on the depth or angle of the hollow on either side in relation to the convex curve. Single wave mouldings, and pairs of wave mouldings with alternating hollows of various depths, were both common fourteenth-century features.

Take the Early English dog-tooth, tease out its teeth so that they look like petals and insert a ball; what you have is *ballflower*. This was the enduring motif of the Decorated period: the globular form of a flower with petals incurved so that they cup a central bead. Some of the figures were three-lobed, or the central globes might be pierced with three or four linked holes. Mostly, the ballflower was inserted in a hollow moulding. It was used universally and was particularly effective around small arches such as the mid-fourteenth-century niche at Combe (Oxfordshire) and the sedilia at North Luffenham (Rutland). Sometimes this ornamental device was put up in conjunction with a four-petalled flower or diaper flower, which might otherwise occupy a parallel hollow, thereby giving a particularly rich feel to the feature so decorated. In this case, the four leaves that curved outwards from a central bead formed a square. This ornamental figure was much favoured for cornices. The crocket came into its own during the Decorated period; the foliage was more leafy, more naturalistic, bulkier, and curved and waved in all directions. It was also to be found clinging more closely to the moulding beneath, when only its central section and the leading part of the leaf were raised.

Dog-tooth (Early English)

Ballflower (Decorated)

Running vine (Decorated and Perpendicular)

Square flower (Perpendicular)

*Carved mouldings.*

*Warfield, Berkshire. The riot of intricate decoration – seen here on the reredos – hides a 'green man' amidst foliage that continues around the sedilia and piscina; it was all done c.1340.*

In the fourteenth century internal features such as sedilia, piscinas, Easter sepulchres, niches and tombs were at their richest. This was due to the universal application of the ogee arch, crockets, ballflower decoration and decorative finials. All of these appeared on the features themselves and, where appropriate, on the carved stone canopies, which thereby became an intrinsic part. At the start of the period the piscina might still have two or three drains, but these soon went out of fashion in favour of the single outlet. It would be hard to find a better example of a church that has so many of the features just described, in such close proximity, than Winchelsea (Sussex). Less elaborate, but equally imposing, is the ogee-canopied arch above a tomb chest, pierced through the wall of the north chapel at Trumpington (Cambridgeshire).

## Development of windows

Windows became larger and, where the area of available wall space was not increased, occupied a greater percentage of wall. A greater number of windows was constructed. Prominence was given to the heads by making these wider and deeper, and through a greater range of designs executed with crisper tracery. Traceried windows of the time, which are flat-headed or only slightly arched, are usually quite early examples. Otherwise, the wider heads were acutely pointed, but most of the smaller ones were obtuse and, in some cases, square-headed. Whereas the pointed window more usually lent itself to trefoils, the mullions of its flat-headed cousin usually broke into a line of ogee-shaped ovals, enclosing pointed quatrefoils. In such cases, the trefoils were usually confined to the spandrels immediately beneath the flat, horizontal moulding at the top of the window. They also comprised the half figures that ended the row of oval lights on each side. In some fourteenth-century examples, the square-headed window might be surrounded by hollow mouldings, enclosing ballflower or some other decorative motif of the period.

At the beginning of the fourteenth century windows were mainly of two lights with simple *bar tracery* and a dividing mullion. *Y-tracery* was formed by dividing

*East Meon, Hampshire. The north window, of the fourteenth century, is an example of basic Y-tracery with two trefoil-headed lights and a quatrefoil above. Unusually, straight diagonals – instead of a curve – form the head of the window.*

a single mullion into two branches of equal length in the head. When this treatment was given to more than one mullion in the same window, the Ys overlapped, thereby forming *intersecting tracery*. The result was lancet windows below, and lozenge shapes in the head. At this point bar tracery was fully developed and took a number of different geometrical shapes and designs in the head. This was known as *geometrical tracery*: regular figures such as circles and quatrefoils to begin with, then lozenges, curvilinear and equilateral triangles. These were all described in the head of the windows, where they usually recurred, and were often combined with featherings, almost exclusively a feature of the larger figures. At this point, the tracery was ready to burst out of its geometrical confines into wild and intricate flowing forms. But for a while both existed side by side, often in the same window, and each achieved graceful curves and a considerable variety of form.

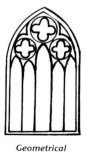
**Geometrical**

**Reticulated**

**Curvilinear**

*Decorated window tracery.*

*Warfield, Berkshire. (Left) A three-light window, showing how Y-tracery developed into intersecting tracery in the head, admitting a number of shapes – here including the ogee – that are further improved by attractive cusping. (Right) The five-light, fourteenth-century window is a combination of strict geometrical forms, admitting elements of free-flow and enhanced by crisp cusping.*

Windows in quite small churches of the period had up to four lights, and there were as many as nine in the larger buildings. Central lights were usually narrower and taller than those that flanked them, although this was by no means always the case. Occasionally, they continued the full depth of the opening, making for interesting figures in the spandrels. Tracery bars sometimes diverged upwards and outwards from the central light, resembling the head of the window arch inverted, and enclosed a circle – itself filled with tracery. The circle was a favourite figure of the time, placed centrally in the head of the window, and usually segmented or subdivided by smaller, similar geometrical figures. These also appeared elsewhere in the window, where they were no longer bounded by circles, as they had been in earlier tracery. A long-lobed, pointed trefoil was introduced initially where the confining arch was more acute, and rapidly spread throughout the head as a general feature of later geometrical work. Dagger decoration, shaped like the head of a spear, internally cusped and arched, also became a characteristic of Decorated window tracery. In smaller windows, the central figure was more likely to be a trefoil or quatrefoil.

One drawback of geometrical tracery was that it frequently produced odd shapes to be glazed between the main figures. The solution to this problem formed the basis of a whole range of infill devices based on the trefoil or quatrefoil. These shapes were being manipulated, extended and elongated into interesting figures that frequently took their own cusping. The round-lobed trefoil became a long-lobed type, which might be pointed or might be elongated into the spear shape, known as a *mouchette*. The quatrefoil became pointed and was given an overall ogee form, or had one of its lobes extended to a point or an ogee: this is called a *dagger motif*. There were other examples, such as cusped triangles, and ovals that appear to have been extruded on either side. And there were some that defy architectural description, like the spaces left in circular windows between adjacent trefoils and quatrefoils that had themselves been manipulated from the normal figures. It must have been laborious for glassmakers and artists, who had been experimenting with burning patterns on to glass and were getting to the stage where they might become more creative with

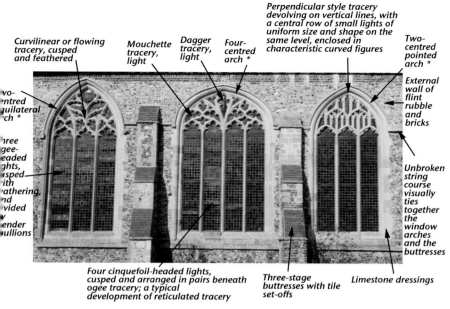

Curvilinear or flowing tracery, cusped and feathered

Mouchette tracery, light

Dagger tracery, light

Four-centred arch *

Perpendicular style tracery devolving on vertical lines, with a central row of small lights of uniform size and shape on the same level, enclosed in characteristic curved figures

Two-centred pointed arch *

External wall of flint rubble and bricks

Two-centred equilateral arch *

Three ogee-headed lights, cusped with feathering, and divided by slender mullions

Unbroken string course visually ties together the window arches and the buttresses

Four cinquefoil-headed lights, cusped and arranged in pairs beneath ogee tracery; a typical development of reticulated tracery

Three-stage buttresses with tile set-offs

Limestone dressings

*Decorated window tracery: a selection of beautifully executed free forms, showing the innovative treatment of the period. This is Little Dunmow, Essex.*

*\* A simple pointed arch is made up of two curves drawn from one centre. Two-centred and four-centred arches are based upon arcs whose radii rest along the springing line – the horizontal span between the points at which the vertical sides of the arch begin to curve upwards on each side. The two-centred arch is constructed around two arcs, the radius of each being equal to the span of the arch. The four-centred or Tudor arch is built around four arcs, where there are two centres on the springing line, and two more centres at some distance below it.*

colour and decoration. Their scenes could depict saints, biblical characters and foliage. In a way geometrical tracery assisted them in this, for, however complicated the window, it was composed entirely of individual pieces that never quite gave up their autonomy. Ogee arches and flowing curves broke away from all this.

*Reticulated tracery* was the first step in the transition from geometrical to curvilinear, the flowing form that began to free the window. The word derived from the setting of square stones to form a pattern based on intersecting diagonal lines and comes from the Latin description of a visual network. This was basically how reticulated tracery was arranged: by elongating quatrefoils into ogee shapes and repeating them in a honeycomb pattern that completely filled the head. Higham Ferrers (Northamptonshire) and Lady St Mary, Wareham (Dorset), have textbook examples of reticulated tracery. This form required at least three lights to produce the desired pattern, each being ogee-headed for the best overall effect. The figures were then repeated until they met the window arch. The effect of reticulated tracery becomes stronger as the lights below increase in number. It can be quite overpowering, particularly when all of the openings are cusped. The next logical step was to give a sharper point to the ogee heads of the main lights, and slightly change the vertical ogee shapes above into to form flamboyant tracery. Even so, this was rarely attempted in Britain but was taken to extremes in France, where, in essence, it corresponded with the rectilinear tracery of the English Perpendicular period.

*Flowing tracery* is exactly as it sounds; it originated where the recognisable geometric figures and ogee shapes were abandoned in window tracery and the lines

*Tilty, Essex. The arrangement of the five-light east window shows how the Decorated period allowed individuality to flourish; the main figure is a rose with internal linked roundels supporting a web of tracery.*

were allowed to branch off into undulating curves of exceptional beauty. In this, the mouchette was a principal motif, cusped and arched on the inside. This was particularly effective when used to infill a circular or *wheel window*, when movement was suggested by a sufficient quantity of curved mouchettes to fill the circle. There are also many examples of 'stationary' wheel windows whose openings are made up of straight-sided, elongated trefoils, extending from the circumference to some central motif, such as a quatrefoil. Wheel windows became more popular in the fourteenth century and are also known as Catherine or rose windows. In flowing tracery, the sinuous forms blended together and provided an almost infinite quantity of decorative possibilities. Many windows that had rich tracery also had mullions and jambs that were plainly chamfered. Otherwise they might be more richly moulded, studded by ballflower in the hollows of the jambs and in those of the tracery. It was not unusual for this to be included together with Early English nail-head motif. Pairs of lights in larger windows were occasionally enclosed in a sub-arch, whose jambs were entirely separate to those of the window. These formed a head above each pair of lights and might be treated independently with tracery. Many of the window mullions had shafts with characteristically moulded caps and bases. *Kentish tracery* is an interesting local variation in which the main figure is a four-pronged, star-like shape. In fact, it is formed of four elongated trefoils, set diagonally, and is cusped with small projections curving into the centre of the light.

When an aisle is thrown out, it further separates the nave from the windows in the side walls. The lower the arches of any intervening arcade, or the thicker the pillars, the more the natural light is reduced towards the centre of the building. One of the ways in which this was overcome was by putting in a clerestory, and these became more common during the fourteenth century. They enabled light to flood in from above, reflected and enhanced by the interior walls of the church. Natural light also better illuminated the wall-paintings, whose visual teachings were thereby more readily available for a greater part of the day. Evidence of changes in the pitch of roofs is frequently to be found in the west-facing walls above chancel arches, with a flatter roof pitch above. This is not to say that all builders of clerestories fully grasped their potential, even as late as the fourteenth century. Some of the lights to be found comprise only small trefoils or cinqefoiled openings; in these instances they are more decorative than useful. The most common arrangement was a row of relatively small single lights, which might be circles, squares, spherical triangles, trefoils, quatrefoils and sexfoils. Occasionally a single row would be a mixture of different shapes. During this period, the lights might include cusping and ogee shapes. In larger churches, clerestory windows usually had arched heads, were filled with conventional tracery, and were as tall and as wide as allowed by the dimensions of the clerestory and the rules of proportion. Some clerestories had two-light windows in each bay.

### Fourteenth-century fonts

Fonts of the period developed as octagonal bowls set on octagonal shafts, of which a typical early example is at Brailes (Warwickshire). There were some exceptions – notably the unmounted tub shape, the goblet style and the mounted basin – that took fourteenth-century decoration. Once the decorative potential had been realised, particularly with regard to octagonal bowls, there was a move to treat each side of the bowl, and those of the octagonal stem, in a similar way. This made for a very rich overall design. Arches were carved into each side, cusped and crocketed, given finials and accentuated by floral motifs in the spandrels. Shallow niches beneath were at first left empty, but were later given the likenesses of saints or biblical scenes. Window tracery was the type of decoration common to many font bowls.

At Ripple (Worcestershire) there is an early octagonal bowl of the Purbeck type, and there is another in Purbeck marble at St Mary, Luton (Bedfordshire). However, 'marble' proved to be a transitory fashion and in its wake came a return to freestone, which again increased the opportunities for embellishment. With the exception of granite, freestone was much easier to work. Even so, plain fonts continued to be made throughout the fourteenth century. The plain, square bowl at Herstmonceux (Sussex) is a late example. Others of this type include the octagonal bowl and base at Alstone (Gloucestershire), that at Harnhill in the same county, and that at Liskeard (Cornwall). In some instances, such as Bucklebury (Berkshire), the predominant decoration is the moulding.

The decoration on stone fonts had been limited only by the technical knowledge and abilities of the makers. Now that the popularity of square and circular font shapes was also on the wane, the alternative seemed to be a several-sided structure. The more flat surfaces there were to work on, the more complex, detailed and visually exciting

*Alstone, Gloucestershire. A plain, octagonal stone font bowl of the fourteenth century, on a convex stem, set on a chamfered base.*

*Shottesbrooke, Berkshire. An octagonal drum font, made in the fourteenth century; with ogee arches decorated with crockets and foliated finial, and slender buttresses with pinnacles.*

might be the finished work. The octagon became the most fashionable figure for the fourteenth-century font bowl, although some were even more ambitious. First the bowl, then the stem became octagonal. In some cases, an unmounted font might be wholly octagonal and compensated in other ways for not having sixteen surfaces to embellish. The potential of the octagonal bowl was being explored quite early; early examples are at Bakewell (Derbyshire) and Stowlangtoft (Suffolk). There are hardly any very early fourteenth-century fonts. The period begins with such fonts as the square bowl in local marble at Old Romney (Kent). There, the basic design, with circular corner shafts, moulded caps and bases, is essentially Early English, while the embellishment is Decorated. Early, too, are the bowls at Goldington (Bedfordshire), Brailes (Warwickshire) and Woodstock (Oxfordshire). Stansted Mountfitchet (Essex) has volutes at the angles. Harringworth (Northamptonshire) is square, retaining the customary shallow blank arcading left over from the period before. There are early examples with leaves at Wheathampstead (Hertfordshire), big ballflowers at Tansor (Northamptonshire) and nice tracery at Rickinghall Inferior (Suffolk). A font typical of the early Decorated period, but an oddity in that it incorporates the designs

*Woodstock, Oxfordshire. The Decorated octagonal drum has traceried arches on the sides of the font and a frieze of ballflower around the rim; the underside is plainly moulded.*

and influences of the previous two hundred years, is at Lostwithiel (Cornwall).

The Decorated period was the era of the niche. Niches were recessed by themselves and then appeared within arches, cusped and foliated with pinnacles, crockets and finials. Except in areas that could afford no more than a plain octagonal font, or one with the minimum of decoration, the niche appeared first on the bowl and then on the stem. The ogee arch was very soon introduced into the design of the niche. At the same time the several forms of window tracery, with trefoils, quatrefoils, mullions and transoms, made their appearance on fonts. There is some beautiful reticulated tracery on the bowl at Bedfield (Suffolk). At Honington in the same county the free-flowing curvilinear form predominates. Weobley (Herefordshire) is a good example of font tracery that illustrates a number of fourteenth-century patterns. Indeed, pattern-book examples appear frequently, as on the bowls of Milton Ernest (Bedfordshire), North Hinksey (Oxfordshire), Lanivet (Cornwall), South Normanton (Derbyshire), Kings Worthy (Hampshire), Little Hormead, Norton and Great Offley (Hertfordshire), Old-hurst (Cambridgeshire), in Leicestershire at East Norton, Goadby Marwood, Great Stretton, Stathern and Harby; in Lincolnshire at Authorpe, Linwood, Carlton Scroop, Great Gonerby, Heydour and Winthorpe, at Ecton and Stanford on Avon in Northamptonshire, at Normanton-on-Soar and Upper Broughton in Nottinghamshire, at Kinver (Staffordshire), and in Suffolk at Barningham, Barton Mills, Bedfield, Icklingham and Lawshall. The majority have a different pattern on each face. The decoration on a typical fourteenth-century font reflected all the new flamboyance in the surrounding church. Typical of the period was ballflower, which found its way around rims and was used as infill. In Bedfordshire there are fine examples at Goldington, Stagsden and St Paul, Bedford. Others occur at Swaton (Lincolnshire), Tansor (Northamptonshire) and Tadmarton (Oxfordshire). Throughout earlier periods, fonts predominantly featured arches and pillars; now the whole church was coming to life on the bowls. Gradually, the niches were filled with biblical figures, and whole stories were represented. Saints and apostles rested beneath their own personal canopies. Most of the carving was beautifully and delicately done, with extreme good taste.

Fourteenth-century font design is celebrated and epitomised at Patrington (Yorkshire). A desire to get in as much detail as possible is shown on the bowl at Hedon (Yorkshire), and the similar font at Holy Trinity, Hull. An interesting contrast to this plethora of carving occurs at Lapworth and Wootton Wawen (both in Warwickshire) and at Otham (Kent), where the corbels show considerable Norman influence. A font that is earlier than either of these is at Lowdham (Nottinghamshire). Weston under Wetherley (Warwickshire) has similar features where the heads are supporting the angles of the octagonal bowl, whereas the heads are large at Nether Alderley (Cheshire) and Bradwell-on-Sea (Essex). Heads protrude forcibly from the underside of the bowl at Snitterfield (Warwickshire).

Lowdham has one of the few Decorated bowls that are set on circular shafts. Its arches, separated by capped buttresses, are adorned with a feathery stiff leaf, with the finials over the upper moulding to the rim. The arches are the straight-sided, pediment type, here lushly crocketed with finials, and internally cusped. This characteristic early type might be considered to be a natural development of the thirteenth-century form at Lakenheath (Suffolk). Lowdham suggests a reasonable transition between that and, for example, the bowls at Hemingstone, Wickham Market and Wortham, all in Suffolk. There, the figures fill each face of the bowl, are multi-cusped and, other than at Wortham, double-arched with quatrefoils in the apex, tracery motifs in the spandrels and buttresses between.

A universal type of bowl, yet nonetheless more common in eastern counties, was the Patrington-influenced cup shape. These bore straight-sided pediments, with quatrefoils between and in the angles; they were cusped, foliated and crocketed with finials, and had angle buttresses resting on the heads of a decorative corbel course at the base. There are good examples of this at Hemingstone and Wortham in Suffolk. Both have plain, octagonal stems, although the connecting mouldings are more numerous on the latter. At Rattlesden (Suffolk), as at Great Offley (Hertfordshire), the straight-sided pediment became an ogee form, although it retained the basic decorative characteristics. A combination of the Hemingstone-style bowl and a traceried stem occurs at Wickham Market (Suffolk), where the panels have a double order of two trefoil-headed windows of the earlier period.

The canopied niche is a beautiful form that is nicely executed on the octagonal font and stem at Kessingland (Suffolk), where carved figures sit above and stand below, within ogee arches. These are buttressed on either side and are surrounded by foliated crockets and finials. At Fishlake (Yorkshire) there is a particularly delicate specimen incorporating a similar idea, the niches here being formed on their own piers with capitals and bases. The inhabited niche lent itself very favourably to the unmounted circular bowls of the fourteenth century. This tub form was not widely used, but the few extant include a wide range of decoration. St Michael, Oxford, for example, is richly buttressed and panelled, with figurework that includes bishops and saints. Ravenstone (Buckinghamshire) has a font that is both tub-shaped and an early example. The flat, trefoil-headed arches are a reminder of the preceding period, and the quatrefoils in the spandrels were a favourite motif from the fourteenth century. There is a juxtaposition of round-headed and pointed trefoils on the bowl at Aikton (Cumbria), and the pointed type within panels occurs at Mowsley (Leicestershire). On more ornate examples the sides of the bowl were divided by either buttresses or shafts, with pinnacles above. The bases of these dividing figures might be supported on heads or knots of foliage, which, in their turn, could be either corbelled out of the surface of the bowl or its underside, or set on the base moulding.

Above left: *Snitterfield, Warwickshire. There are a number of font bowls in the county that are carried on carved, corbelled heads. This shallow, octagonal font has eight of them, attached to a heavy stem, and was made in the fourteenth century.*

Above right: *Wootton Wawen, Warwickshire. The font was probably made early in the fourteenth century; it is octagonal with typically styled heads of the region, although it has shallower mouldings than others of its type, and hardly any stem.*

# Perpendicular
# 1350–1547

### Development of the plan

The plan of the church was influenced, to a degree, by the requirement of guilds, landowners and other individuals who either built their own chapels or took over some existing part of the church. In the latter instances, there was often no structural change within the building, but several chapels could be admitted under the same roof, where space allowed, by sectioning off areas. This might be achieved by means of parclose screens, which elsewhere in the church were used to protect tombs. Early parclose screens were constructed of wood, with blind panelling below openwork, traceried lights; they were carved, decorated and painted, yet were rarely as highly ornamented as screens with other applications in the church. Otherwise, space was made for chapels by extending the aisles of the nave eastwards, often ending flush with the east wall of the chancel, so that the basic ground plan of the church became a single rectangle. In some instances, the chancel was separated from its aisles by a low arcade of one or two bays, and even a clerestory might be added. A 'three-gabled' arrangement resulted from the aisles and the chancel, and in some instances from the aisles and the nave, being gabled to the same height.

Towers, aisles and porches were added during the fifteenth century. Rich landowners regularly added north porches because it was more convenient for them to enter and leave the church by the north door. Naves were lengthened and had their roofs raised in height, but flattened in pitch. As a general rule, this was true of

*Ingatestone, Essex. Impressive Perpendicular tower of red brick, with tall angle buttresses and imposing stair turret, stepped battlements above a frieze of corbels, and capped corner pinnacles.*

123

*Long Melford, Suffolk. A great East Anglian 'wool' church, completed in 1484, and of classic symmetry. Its lines are enhanced by the two-stage buttresses that define the bays throughout.*

all church roofs, which also tended at this time to disappear behind parapets. The same effect happened to aisles as they were widened and lengthened. This exercise was frequently carried out to the whole length of the nave and chancel, in order to admit large chapels. Sacristies were converted to smaller chapels, which in their turn became parts of larger ones. Little chantry chapels were built off large chapels, lining up to the east of rebuilt porches that might now be appearing with substantial upper chambers. Cruciform churches, especially those with small transepts, were made rectangular by building chancel aisles to the same width as the transept, and similarly widening the aisles of the nave. When redevelopers needed more space for an expanding congregation but wanted to maintain the character of an existing cruciform church, they might add or enlarge aisles and also raise and lengthen the transepts. Otherwise, the general programme of enlargement usually began with a north chapel, followed by one to the south. When towers were added from scratch, they invariably went up at the west end. This meant that the typical parish church would never be treated to the type of decorated façade that characterises large churches. The substitute was the amount and type of decoration that could be applied to the tower, or most particularly its western face.

Builders began to conceive their churches as a whole – an homage to spaciousness and light. The way in which shape, shadow and light interacted was no longer so much a matter of sculptural detail. High walls and large windows were designed to fill the church with a flat light that dealt similarly with all the interior surfaces and was most suited to illuminating the panels. In theory, this was a similar way of thinking to that which initially inspired three centuries of wall-paintings: that the surfaces were there to be plastered and illuminated with graphic depictions of whatever moral or religious teachings were currently in vogue. During this period, the shell of the church became the setting for a number of dominant features that reached their peak of creative excellence.

## Walls and parapets

The church grew taller in the Perpendicular period. Walls were raised, sometimes to admit a clerestory, at other times so that larger windows could be put in, or else

*Thirsk, Yorkshire. A large Perpendicular church built in the first half of the fifteenth century; it has distinguishing openwork 'lace' battlements, stepped and sloping buttresses to the tower, and a two-storey porch.*

they were simply built higher in the first instance. Where the masonry in the surface area was reduced to accommodate more or larger lights, this effectively weakened the fabric. However, the blocks of freestone used to build fifteenth-century churches were more uniform in size and finely tooled. This meant that they fitted together better and had a much more uniform appearance. Not everyone had access to good local stone quarries, however. Villages where freestone was not an option relied on flint or bricks, or sometimes a mixture of these and such stone as they could acquire. The trade in bricks had been growing for about two hundred years and was now a substantial one.

The horizontal, flat-topped parapet soon gave way to the embattled form. Builders realised the potential for treating embrasures and merlons more decoratively, and they either panelled or pierced the merlons, thereby adding to the overall appearance of the church. The embrasure – the space between the raised sections of battlements – is of material significance only on a fortified building. The embrasure was now simply a consequence of the embattled termination, and as such a contender for decoration. The width of a merlon was not necessarily the same as that of an embrasure. To begin with, the battlements were simply ornamented and, later, were either pierced with panel-shaped openings or similarly treated with surface carving. Trefoils, quatrefoils, multifoils and the four-leafed flower were popular. In some instances, a 'double tier' arrangement resulted, in which the merlons appeared to be twice the height of the embrasures. This was a very effective optical illusion, caused by repeating the way in which the merlons were themselves treated, with a continuous band of decoration that ran the whole length beneath. This might be further enhanced by building what was effectively a blind parapet with a row of entirely different, decorated panels immediately below. Indeed, battlements that are highly decorated are full of optical illusions. One example is the continuous parapet composed of blank and openwork members of equal dimensions: plain merlons alternating with pierced, but decorated, embrasures. Occasionally, in larger churches, one may come across an arrangement of double merlons adjacent to single openings. There are also embattled parapets in which double-depth merlons are treated as vertical rectangular panels, with horizontal panels, decorated differently, between them. In such cases, the 'embrasure' hardly exists; the top edge of the feature is entirely capped, and it is separated from the window course beneath by a moulded string.

A full parapet was constructed in three parts – coping, band and cornice – each of which might be richly decorated. Coping had hitherto been continued all around the leading edges of the battlements but gradually became confined to those that were horizontal. One commonly finds a blank band beneath richly carved or openwork battlements. The variety of gargoyles increased, although generally they were more slender than previously. The Tudors invented the down-pipe, but this did not diminish the popularity of the gargoyle, which had been, for centuries, a mirror of the surrealism, humour, anarchy and satire inherent in their sculptors. Even when they were not needed in a functional capacity, gargoyles continued to be put up.

## Buttresses

Fifteenth-century builders had a problem with buttressing. On the one hand, walls were thinner and roofs were flatter, which might have suggested lighter stresses and strains. On the other hand, the 'walls of light' were leaving less space for buttressing anyway. Two of the best examples of this, and themselves the finest fifteenth-century churches in the land, are at Long Melford and Lavenham, both in Suffolk. These are the magnificent Perpendicular wool churches of East Anglia, which show us how builders solved the problem: more buttresses, but narrower, rarely in excess of two stages along the nave and chancel, yet projecting even further away from the walls than ever before. If you look at the south face of either, you will see a series of façades, each treated as if it is a square-framed entity, built in some modular way and then put together as an integrated whole. In either case, the buttresses are visually part of the framework for the windows, although this is emphasised more by the proximity of the flat, plain parapets at Long Melford than it is by the glorious embattlements at Lavenham. At the latter, the builders took this idea one stage further by panelling the buttresses; so viewed straight on, they are the homogeneous uprights in set pieces. Elsewhere, one finds buttresses of the period embellished with niches, quatrefoils, panels, etc.

In construction, the upper stage of the buttress was either inclined towards the wall, some way below the parapet, or continued through it by means of a shaft surmounted by a pinnacle. Diagonal buttresses were put up at the right angles of aisle walls, with either larger pairs or bigger clasping buttresses supporting the end walls of chancels. Diagonal buttresses climbed the tower, their set-offs corresponding with each of its stages, before they either died into the wall just below the parapet or were capped by a gable at that point. Another technique was to build tower buttresses as pairs, right-angled to the faces at the corners but set back equidistant from the angles. This type commonly ended some way beneath the parapet, and often about halfway up the top stage of the tower. Particularly in the West Country, the uppermost set-off – and in some cases all of them – was continued upwards with the shaft and pinnacle arrangement. A further variation occurred when the angle at which corner buttresses met was filled with a diagonal projection for some way along its length, topped by a pinnacle. That other innovation, the flying buttress, continued to be put up in larger churches.

*Fotheringhay, Northamptonshire. Conspicuous flying buttresses support the walls of this Perpendicular church, renowned for its octagonal lantern crowned by battlements and pinnacles.*

*Northleach, Gloucestershire. The two-storey porch of the fourteenth-century 'wool' church; it is all pinnacles with crockets, buttresses and niches without, and panelled and vaulted inside.*

## Porches and doorways

The church porch continued to play an important part in religious and secular functions. Where big, elaborate porches were erected in the fifteenth century, as at Northleach and Cirencester in Gloucestershire, they were usually financed by trade and may have reflected a greater degree of secular activity. Many that were attached to larger churches were increased in both area and height. Where there was money to spare, a north and a south porch might be put up at about the same time. Nor was the south porch the automatic first choice for building or redevelopment. In many places the position and style of the porch was determined by its proximity to the village, its position in relation to the manor house, or its closeness to the most accessible approach for the most affluent landowner. Money spoke in this regard. It is likely to have been the case where the north porch is well decorated or the south porch is inferior. Sometimes there is proof positive of the porch's pedigree, in an heraldic shield above the opening.

The overall proportions of porches improved, and some of the larger ones were given some fine fan vaulting. Mostly, though, they had open-style timber roofs, occasionally with a tie beam, collar beam or king post, and arch braces. The porch

*Cirencester, Gloucestershire. The magnificent three-storey porch, built c.1490, has variously been the abbot's office and the town hall.*

*Steeple Ashton, Wiltshire. The two-storey south porch of a late Perpendicular church; inside the porch is a vaulted roof with a boss that depicts the Assumption.*

windows might be divided into lights with rectilinear tracery, and some had transoms and were of considerable size. They were typically built into the front walls of the porch; the sides were usually left unpierced, but often covered with blind panelling. Some of the openings in single-storey porches, which had no upper rooms, were flanked by large windows whose sills were just above the base mouldings of the porch, but whose traceried heads extended well beyond the height of the opening. Interior doorways were now made wider and flatter. They commonly had a square label above finely proportioned arch mouldings that might include multifoils, and a segmental pointed arch on the inside. Some were deeply recessed and had slender shafts with plainly moulded caps in the jambs, where they were frequently combined with other mouldings. Sometimes, niches were placed in the jambs. Many doorways had ogee-shaped dripstones beneath a pointed or square-headed hood moulding, or else the latter ran above a four-centred arch. The spandrels were richly decorated with feathering, rectilinear tracery, panelling, cusped circles, quatrefoils, coats of arms and foliage. Just occasionally, one comes across a Perpendicular doorway whose arch is so depressed as to be almost flat across the top, and curved only where the outer angles meet the imposts.

Panelling became a feature of the wooden doorways, where it was often elaborately traceried and cusped. The metal scrollwork that had hitherto been developed as a showcase of the local blacksmith's art gave way to wood-carving, and the smith continued to be responsible only for hinges, latches and handles. The wood-carver treated the door as a blind window, dividing the space with mullions and putting curvilinear or rectilinear tracery in the head. Sometimes,

*Blythburgh, Suffolk. Built in the fifteenth century, the porch includes a small medieval font relocated as a stoup, medieval angels on its pinnacles, which came from elsewhere, and a modern carving in a niche above the door.*

figurework or floral motifs were added in the spaces between the uprights.

A porch of two stages or more provided the opportunity for considerable embellishment. Stages were usually separated by string courses that were deep and richly ornamented. The walls and any buttresses were treated as an extension of the panel work that was now so prevalent in window tracery. These panels had quatrefoils that were cusped at the head of reticulated tracery. Even the simplest porches, erected against relatively small village churches, were rarely without niches. In larger structures, there might be three or four – stepped, canopied, or treated as an intrinsic part of a series of panels that decorated the front elevation. Spandrels, and the spaces between the elements of tracery, were regularly multifoiled and had figurework, vines, foliage and diaper patterns. Decoration continued above and beyond the parapet level. Here, there might be an arrangement of openwork battlements, stepped or level, and similar in style to those of the church tower. Alternatively, a triangular gable end was common, with a plainly moulded parapet. Pinnacles might be raised above the cornice or put up as an extension of buttresses.

## Clerestories

It was now that clerestories reached their pre-eminence, particularly in the fine wool churches of the Cotswolds and East Anglia. Previously, they had been put up as a means of getting extra light into the church through a number of windows high above the nave. The size of those windows, their quantity and the wide spaces between the openings frequently meant that the idea was better than the result. The usual arrangement was of two or three lights beneath segmental pointed or square heads. Although clerestories had been conceived as part of new church building for centuries, it was not until the Perpendicular period that their designers intended

Below left: *Melton Mowbray, Leicestershire. The largest parish church in the county is visually unified by its Perpendicular clerestory of three-light windows that run around nave and transept.*

Below right: *East Harling, Norfolk. Distinguished by the unusual flèche on its tower, this is an almost total fifteenth-century rebuild of an earlier church. The tracery in the heads of the clerestory windows is classic design of the period.*

129

the range to be viewed as a whole rather than as a number of individual windows. The clerestory was another feature of the church that responded well to financial sponsorship. In the best examples, windows were made larger than ever before and set closer together so that they seemed to form almost a continuous sequence – a wall of uninterrupted glass. When clerestories were built above the wall of an aisleless nave, the result was a magnificent two-tier arrangement of fenestration. It gave the church a bigger surface area of glass than of masonry. Several of the East Anglian wool churches have unusually large windows that are divided into a various number of traceried lights. Another feature of the period, as at Chipping Campden and Northleach (both Gloucestershire) was the insertion of a large window with typical Perpendicular tracery above the chancel arch. This gave the clerestory a return at the east end of the nave, thereby admitting all-round light.

## Roofs

A consequence of erecting clerestories was often the opportunity to remake roofs, particularly those over aisles. Trussed rafter and king-post arrangements were favoured at this time, as were braced tie beams. The principal rafters were connected a short distance from the ridge by a horizontal collar beam, which, in some roofs, had an upwards camber or might be supported by curved braces. Many of the timbers were richly carved, painted or gilded. Removal of a tie beam, particularly over a wide space, gave the appearance of height and spaciousness. It also admitted the *hammer-beam roof* – in effect a form of broken tie beam that is generally confined to the eastern counties. The hammers are short horizontal timbers that project into the church and are invariably supported by curved braces which spring from vertical pendant posts or wall posts. The latter effectively helped to reduce the thrust from above, with the hammers themselves partly countering the outward thrust on the walls.

A hammer beam rests on both the wall and the top of the pendant post, with an arched brace in each case giving support beneath its leading edge. In the absence

Above left: *Blythburgh, Suffolk. The painted medieval roof timbers, bosses, and flying angels with shields, some of which were destroyed when the spire collapsed in 1577.*

Above right: *Swaffham, Norfolk. A fifteenth-century double hammer-beam roof with long pendant posts and delicately carved rows of angels.*

Above left: *St Peter Mancroft, Norwich. The hammer-beam roof is partially concealed by stylised Perpendicular fan vaulting; there are angels on the decorated wall plates and the purlins.*

Above right: *Selworthy, Somerset. The wagon roof of the south aisle has angels with shields on the wall plates, and bosses at all the intersections.*

of a tie beam, the hammer-beam arrangement reduced the span without detracting from the height; indeed, it achieved quite the opposite visually in drawing the eye upwards by means of some quite sophisticated decorative treatment. The foot of the pendant post usually sits on a corbel that is at least simply moulded, although the overall design of the roof timbers and the applied richness usually determine its quality and style. Typically, a carved angel with outstretched wings might be placed on the leading edge of the hammer beams, or otherwise on the corbels beneath the wall posts. Heads, shields and foliage were also favoured. There are several worthy single hammer-beam roofs in Norfolk, of which Cawston and Necton excel.

When one tier of hammers was raised above another and connected to it by curved braces on vertical side posts, the result was a *double hammer-beam roof*. In many instances, as at March (Cambridgeshire) and Needham Market (Suffolk), much of the woodwork was also carved and decorated. This included the hammer beams themselves, with openwork or brattishing; the wall plates, which were effectively turned into cornices or friezes with several horizontal bands of decoration; the purlins, which often carried an upper frieze of brattishing; and the collar beams, which were also quite likely to be cambered high up in the roof. The spandrels of the bracket, formed by the arch brace beneath the hammer beam, if not open structures, were frequently embellished with elaborate tracery. Even the common rafters in this type of roof would, at the very least, be chamfered.

In the west of England, unbroken aisles ran the length of the church. Their roofs, together with those of the nave and chancel, were treated as a single expanse and given a characteristic *barrel* or *wagon roof*. This comprised curved principal rafters, seated on the wall plate and rising to the ridge piece. These might be almost semicircular or, as at Padstow and Launceston in Cornwall, slightly pointed. Rafters followed the lines of the principals, and purlins joined them at intervals, with the points of intersection being marked by carved bosses. The result of this was a series of timber-

*Athering-ton, Devon. A heavily engineered barrel roof, in a church noted for its rood screen, rood loft and bench-ends.*

framed square panels, which were either boarded or plastered. The simplest form of thin timbers with plain panels may be seen in Devon at Ashprington, and in Cornwall at St Neot, St Buryan, Mullion, Gulval and Breage. In some churches, however, the wagon roof was formed by a series of braces placed very closely together, as at St Endellion (Cornwall), which also has bosses at the intersections with the longitudinal timbers, and Altarnun, Ludgvan, Kilkhampton and Morwenstow, all in Cornwall, among others. In Devon, this arrangement was called the 'Devon cradle' and reached its peak at Lapford, where there are intricately carved panels and wall plate. The roof at Dunster (Somerset) is similar to the Cornish model of close-set beams and bosses. Zennor (Cornwall) is an example of both types: beams in the nave and panels in the chancel.

## Towers

Church towers were built for a number of reasons, not the least as a guide to travellers of one sort or another. That at Boston (Lincolnshire) – the famously unfinished 'stump', which is nonetheless nearly 270 feet (82 metres) high

– was a kind of daylight landmark for sailors. Merchant adventurers put up Dundry (Somerset) to help guide their waterborne investments up the Bristol Channel, and the tower at Minehead (Somerset) had a similar purpose. Church towers frequently dominate Cornish coastal villages and are in sharp contrast to the comparatively low church buildings attached to them, a sure sign that their purpose was to guide the local fishermen safely home.

The Perpendicular period was exemplified by its church towers. They were mostly still put up at the west end, and their basic shape remained square

*Boston, Lincolnshire. The lantern tower, with flying buttresses and crown of battlements with pinnacles and large Perpendicular windows beneath, is more than a nod towards continental flamboyance.*

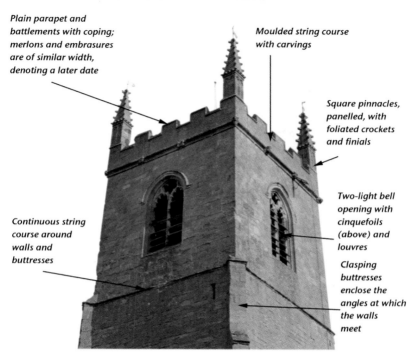

Plain parapet and battlements with coping; merlons and embrasures are of similar width, denoting a later date

Moulded string course with carvings

Square pinnacles, panelled, with foliated crockets and finials

Two-light bell opening with cinquefoils (above) and louvres

Continuous string course around walls and buttresses

Clasping buttresses enclose the angles at which the walls meet

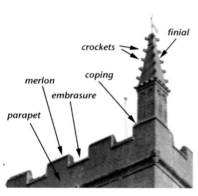

finial

crockets

coping

merlon

embrasure

parapet

*Features of a typical Perpendicular tower: Islip, Oxfordshire.*

on plan with embattled parapet and corner pinnacles. It was a period of unrivalled tower building by a number of local schools of builders and masons, who, between them, built a great variety of structures. New money was the catalyst for artistic innovation, and what they produced made spires almost unnecessary. The typical Perpendicular spire was plain, unambitious, and rose like a spike from well behind the parapet. Large west windows were put into the tower, which was opened up internally, admitting light into the back of the nave. Stair turrets became a standard feature of the tower. Sometimes they were an internal arrangement reached through a small doorway in the south interior wall. Mostly they climbed the outside of the tower, within an octagon that rose at least to parapet level, and frequently beyond, and might be finished with a spire. In other examples, the stair turret might end in an openwork octagon with traceried openings or be given a parapet of its own. Depending upon the style of the church, this could have battlements that were plain, panelled or

*Louth, Lincolnshire. The fifteenth-century tower and spire show understated tabernacle work in conjunction with the favoured ogee motif, the preference for crockets, and the visual value of flying buttresses.*

pierced. The lights in stair turrets tended to be small circles, triangles or squares, with tracery that was often cusped. With the magnificent local exceptions that will be described later, most towers built during this period were relatively plain.

Some, such as the one at Cricklade (Wiltshire), were heavily panelled. Flint and stone panelling was a feature of East Anglian church towers. Through local variations, we can best see how church towers were now conceived, designed and decorated as a harmonious whole. This is often shown in the ways in which the windows were arranged in each stage to complement each other, and how the masonry around them was treated in ways that were visually pleasing, drew the eye and enhanced the tracery.

*Cricklade, Wiltshire. The sixteenth-century tower was paid for by John Dudley, Duke of Northumberland, but he was beheaded before it was finished. It is much panelled and features large windows with intersecting tracery, polygonal buttresses, and big pinnacles separated by a stepped openwork parapet.*

*St Mary Magdalene, Taunton, Somerset. The late fifteenth-century tower dominates the church; it has an openwork crown with filigree-style battlements and traceried cage-pinnacles, and decorated mullioned and transomed windows repeated through each stage.*

## Somerset towers

Nowhere in England are there so many Perpendicular church towers with better proportions than in Somerset. Supreme among these is St Mary Magdalene, Taunton, a four-stage tower that embodies the spirit of Somerset design and virtually every physical characteristic of it. Elsewhere, the designs of many towers were influenced by those of Wells Cathedral and Glastonbury Abbey, and local quarries of good limestone were the means of achieving them. Masons were allowed to personalise and did so, particularly in the variety and scope of the windows and belfry openings. Several architectural historians have variously classified the results of all this, although the scale of conception, the variety of the designs and the amount of detail have always presented difficulties.

There are two main types of tower: those where vertical lines predominate, running through the belfry stage and continuing down the tower; and those where they follow the more traditional approach of separate stages with some means of visually dividing them. In the Somerset type, this was sometimes done by means of panelled tracery, typically the quatrefoil, in contrast to the more usual and less decorative string courses. Work of this kind can be seen at Curry Rivel, Huish Episcopi, Taunton (St Mary Magdalene), Kingsbury Episcopi and North Petherton. A wide course of blind quatrefoils immediately beneath the parapet might sometimes be repeated as a string course at the junctions of the stages below. The vertical line approach, after the west tower at Wells Cathedral, can be seen at Ilminster, Wells (St Cuthbert), Batcombe, Evercreech and Wrington. In the complete achievement of this style, everything above the roof line of the nave was regarded as an unbroken entity. However, there were some hybrids. Chewton Mendip is an example of verticals on the same plane, but nonetheless broken where there would otherwise be horizontal strings. Fine examples of towers that followed the developed style of the stages, but with string courses rather than bands of panelled tracery, occur notably at Isle

*Mells, Somerset. An early sixteenth-century tower with grouped blank windows and an interesting arrangement of buttresses and pinnacles working in combination for visual effect.*

Abbotts and Bishop's Lydeard.

As well as conforming to characteristic styles, Somerset's church towers of the period are also distinguished in certain decorative particulars. Foremost is the pierced battlements and openwork pinnacle arrangement, forming a top-heavy, tier-upon-tier, coronet effect, as at Taunton (St Mary Magdalene) and Dundry. This can also be seen in embryo at Huish Episcopi. Even in Somerset, embattled parapets were still most often blank but, where they formed a traceried parapet, the corner pinnacles were frequently treated as if they were rectangular cages. Such are to be found at Taunton (St Mary Magdalene), Chewton Mendip, Huish Episcopi, Dundry and Glastonbury. Slender, subordinate pinnacles might run through the central merlon of a pierced parapet; indeed, this is common to many of the county's major towers, irrespective of their basic style or other influences. In some instances, the main corner pinnacles were attached to slender subordinates at the angles by means of little flying buttresses, the subordinates being bracketed out on corbels. The typical Somerset pinnacle – and a whole forest of them might break the skyline – had crockets and finials, while the larger ones were virtual spirelets.

Two-light windows were usually put into successive stages of the towers, with greater attention being paid to the belfry stage. Notable exceptions are St Mary Magdalene, Taunton, where every stage has pairs of three-light windows, and Huish Episcopi and Kingsbury Episcopi, where the single windows beneath the belfry stage have the greater number of lights. Belfries characteristically had two or three two-light openings, often divided by transoms and filled by masonry pierced with sound holes. The openings might be flanked by pinnacles, carried on shafts above the buttresses, or arranged as pilasters, there and between the openings. When belfry openings did not extend the full width of the stage, they were sometimes included in panelling or blind tracery that extended on either side. Irrespective of how the belfry stage was treated, a single two-light (occasionally three-light) window usually went into the stage below. Mells and Chewton Mendip are fine examples of staged towers that have three- and two-window arrangements respectively, which mirror those of the upper stage.

### Cornish towers

The greatest influence on the church towers of Cornwall was the prevailing material: the intractable granite. Generally, this partly accounted for low, ponderous and fairly plain towers that rarely reached beyond three stages and were battlemented, with or without pinnacles. Some were given excessively tall pinnacles, carried well above the parapet, as at Germoe, where they are also corbelled out in a manner common to Breage, Ludgvan and St Ives. Elsewhere, there is a peculiar form in which a sloping inner surface

*Launceston, Cornwall. A typical town church of the far west, built early in the sixteenth century, but retaining the fourteenth-century tower and higher stair turret of an earlier place of worship. The porch is a riot of carving.*

creates an optical illusion that the whole structure is leaning. Occasionally, as at Lelant and Madron, corner buttresses were built behind the embattled parapet. The tower at Towednack, although fourteenth-century, is about as low as Cornish towers get, and that of Sancreed is typical of the conservative size and design. St Buryan is noteworthy among the handful of rare four-stage towers in the county. The standard Cornish tower had a single two- or three-light opening in the upper stage, and little else of note. Those of this period were typically unbuttressed, or, if buttresses were present, they might be of the set-back type. St Austell illustrates this perfectly and is also distinguished by having inhabited niches on each face. Other examples of this style of buttressing occur at Callington (where they do not rise to its full height in order to admit the pinnacles), St Cleer, St Ives, Breage, Ludgvan and Kilkhampton. Where external stair turrets were attached to the towers, these were usually square or rectangular on plan and tended to rise beyond the parapet stage. The glory of Cornish towers is at Probus, where the whole piece is overtly of the Somerset type, with pinnacled buttresses at every stage, quatrefoil and reticulated tracery, both pierced and blind, and sub-pinnacles attendant on the corner shafts above the parapet. In fact, the Somerset type can also be found occasionally, possibly with local variations, in Cornwall, Devon, Wiltshire, Gloucestershire and Oxfordshire.

## Devon towers

Colaton Raleigh, where the fifteenth-century tower is made of soft red sandstone, is typical of Devon. It is also an example of the village type: at the west end, embattled, unbuttressed, with little two-light belfry openings and a demi-octagonal stair turret rising high above the parapet at one corner. East Budleigh is similar. This arrangement, with or without buttresses, was also the favoured local design in towns: for example, St Stephen, Exeter, and Sidmouth. Many of Devon's towers were built in the fifteenth century and share with Cornwall the set-back arrangement for buttresses. A few have diagonal angle buttresses, as at Salcombe Regis, and even fewer have pairs of buttresses set right on the corners at right angles to each other. The impressive tower in granite at Ashburton conforms in general to the local type and may in its turn have helped to inspire that at Totnes. At Widecombe in the Moor, the church is of Cornish influence throughout, and the tower is of the imposing, heavy-pinnacled type. There are also a number of Devon churches that are distinguished by the height of their towers and the large, double bell openings, each of two lights and ornamented in Somerset style. The four-stage tower at Chittlehampton has these, as does Combe Martin, where there are pinnacles on the set-offs of the buttresses. The 130 foot (40 metre) tower at Hartland, also four-stage, is the

*Chittlehampton, Devon. Built c.1480, this four-stage tower is one of the county's finest; it has Somerset-style, double two-light bell openings at the belfry stage.*

tallest in the county. Ipplepen is a fine example that was built in 1440, and Totnes, of about a decade later, has elaborately traceried belfry windows.

External stair turrets became very common in Devon during the fifteenth century; most usually they were placed at one corner of the tower, but not uncommonly they were positioned along one side. Quite often they are slender but out of scale, rising high above an embattled parapet and ending in battlements of their own. This type occurs at Colaton Raleigh, Landkey, Harberton and Woodbury. In another design, the stair turret was placed in the centre of one of the faces, in which case admitting a small belfry window on either side. A third type placed the stair turret not equidistant from the sides of a face, nor gave it so much space, so that in either case the belfry opening was made to one side and was therefore restricted in size.

## Gloucestershire towers

The Perpendicular period began at Gloucester Cathedral and in 1539, close to its end, the bell tower was built at Evesham (Worcestershire). This is worthy of comparison. The tower at the former soars in a profusion of two-light windows, ogee shapes and blank panelling, culminating in a coronet-style pierced parapet and big, square-on-plan openwork pinnacles. At Evesham all of the elements are still there, if done more crisply, more slenderly and with more grace. The influence of Gloucester on Cotswold church towers can be seen throughout the period, not in that individual features were necessarily copied, but in the ways in which a general impression of the cathedral tower was conveyed through local styles. There was also an interchange of ideas between Gloucestershire and Somerset, and both areas benefited from the wool trade. It also clipped north Wiltshire, as evidenced by the fine tower at Colerne, which has a Somerset-inspired belfry stage, but panelling below in the Gloucestershire style.

## Windows

Fifteenth-century windows were all about achieving light, and in so doing they created monotony. They provided business opportunities on an unprecedented scale

*Evesham, Worcestershire. The Lichfield campanile, a clock and bell tower completed in 1538, showing the favoured style of panelling and ogee motif.*

*Thaxted, Essex. A splendid church, built successively from 1340 to 1510; a wall of typical Perpendicular windows illuminates the Lady Chapel on the south side of the chancel.*

for the glassmaker and the glazier, yet the result was often no more than glass panelling. It is impossible to better the late fifteenth-century porch at Cirencester (Gloucestershire); yet there the treatment is really diaper-work panelling in stone and glass. Horizontal transoms were introduced which divided the main lights and allowed the upper and lower sections to be dealt with independently. Where these sections were not of equal depth, once divided, the upper portion was the taller division. Perpendicular windows were square-headed, semicircular, segmental or pointed, and they were commonly four-centred. They were never actually pointed, nor were they ogee-shaped, although this favourite fourteenth-century curve was still used elsewhere and within some tracery motifs. The arch became depressed, which meant that either the tracery in the head was depleted, or it was carried below the points of spring of the arch. Stone mullions ran vertically from the cill to the head. These formed the main divisions of the window, as well as the limits of the individual lights. The heads of the lights were formed of thinner tracery bars, resulting in rectilinear tracery – essentially a series of panels of lights, quatrefoiled and cusped in the heads and admitting lozenge shapes in the spandrels.

Rectilinear tracery opened up a whole new world for the glassmaker and the glass painter, and engendered widespread co-operation with the masons. The glassmaker had difficulties fitting the flowing forms of Decorated tracery, and the fourteenth-century painter was required to paint small figures in awkward spaces. It meant that masons could design their windows to accommodate the glass painters, who in their turn were often able to treat the windows as a single theme. Once mullions were carried right through into the head, the painters were able to develop their designs

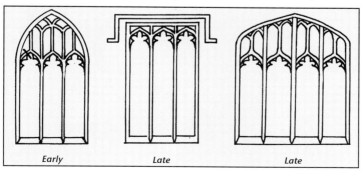

*Early*  *Late*  *Late*

*Perpendicular windows.*

*East Harling, Norfolk. The five-light east window has twenty biblical cameos, on glass that was painted in the fifteenth century, plus other decorative motifs; these include (top left) the red squirrel symbol of a family that took over the manor in the sixteenth century.*

as a whole and decorate them accordingly. It also provided a much bigger area and enabled ideas to be carried out on a much wider scale and, overall, many large pictures were produced. These included whole landscapes with buildings, and sophisticated tableaux centred around biblical figures. The composition of rectilinear windows also meant that the divisions formed by the glazing bars in the head could be developed as panels of niches. Small windows, as well as individual sections of larger ones, were filled with angels, saints and their emblems, and heraldic devices. The colour in the rest of the church complemented, but could not match, that of the glass; nor were the figures more beautifully portrayed than in the windows. There was a great difference between the sun shining on the painted walls of the church and the sun shining through the painted glass in them. Where it was not painted, the thin translucent glass of the fifteenth century let a silvery light into the church. Not many complete examples of painted windows have survived, and often only fragments remain that have been collected from more than one source and subsequently put together.

### Pillars, bases and plinths

During the fifteenth century the ground plan of the church developed outwards about as far as it could. The church was now a series of rectangular rooms that had been built to fit the dimensions of what was already there. Thus, in general, the chancel

*Thaxted, Essex. A flattened arch, almost a semicircle, separates nave from transept; a more pointed arch of the period lies beyond.*

*St Peter Mancroft, Norwich. An arcade of slender Composite pillars accentuates the height of the fifteenth-century nave.*

had been built or remodelled to the width of the nave, and north and south aisles to its length. Chapels were put up on either side to correspond with the width of the chancel, and the depth of the aisles. Theoretically, the all-encompassing rectangle that now enclosed these rooms might have been opened out, and new chapels built beyond its walls; but, except in the instances of small chantry chapels and porches, this did not happen. Instead, the Perpendicular period was all about building upwards, increasing the height of external walls, taking out the west wall of the nave and inserting a high arch into the tower, and rebuilding the nave arcades in the new style. Experiments in proportion on a grand scale succeeded those that had hitherto been carried out in the play of light and shade.

This also enabled an enhanced visual illusion of height to be achieved by flattening out the crown of the arch and thereby bringing the capitals of the pillars closer to it. As the fifteenth century progressed, arches became more obtuse. The four-centred, or Tudor, arch appeared. This is a particularly English innovation in which the sides of a depressed pointed arch are straight, being suddenly curved on the outer angles where they meet the imposts. The Tudor arch was very popular by about 1485 and was used for doorways and windows as well as in arcades. Arch mouldings were wide and shallow and sometimes continued unbroken right around the arch and down the jambs to the floor. In these instances, there might be a sub-arch, decorated with a band of quatrefoiled panelling. Sometimes a small cap was placed on the inner moulding, purely as a decorative feature.

Octagonal pillars continued to be built throughout the Perpendicular period, particularly in smaller village churches, and it is difficult to distinguish these from their predecessors. Even the plain, circular pillar continued to survive. More ambitious examples comprised clusters of four columns that were lozenge-shaped on plan. The prevailing type, however, was tall and considerably more slender. In larger churches, the popular arrangements were of clustered columns, or groups of four, eight or more engaged columns set against a larger central core. Thick shafts alternated with thinner ones, and there was a wide variety of shallow, concave mouldings between them. The arch mouldings above a composite pier were frequently a continuation of the shafts carried individually above independent caps. Until the fifteenth century the shaft and the point of spring of the arch were separated by very distinct architectural elements. Masons in the Perpendicular period went for an arrangement that, in effect, merged abacus, bell capital and any astragal or necking, effectively creating a single feature.

Perpendicular capitals were generally narrower and taller than those of the Decorated period and were often quite plain in smaller churches. In larger buildings, particularly earlier in the period, the elongated bell might be covered in large, shallowly carved leaves. These were generally stiffer than previously and were

141

*Dedham, Essex. The tower was built in 1519; the roof of the Galilee porch entrance beneath it is lavishly decorated with ogee motifs, rosettes, heraldic devices, portcullises and the Tudor rose.*

formed into rectangular shapes that fitted well into the sides of an octagonal bell. As the style progressed, where the bell retained a more or less circular shape, or the capital followed the form of a cluster of shafts, a more naturalistic type of leaf was developed. This spread in a horizontal wave around the feature. Sculptors attached angels to the sides of their capitals and gave them shields or other heraldic devices to hold. Such heraldry frequently related to patrons of the church, although much that was associated with angels tended to be symbolic bearings of religious significance. Instruments and emblems of the Passion also commonly appeared on capitals.

Where the shape of a composite pier effectively facilitated a number of caps adjacent to each other, both upper and lower mouldings usually continued unbroken all around. Above it all, the abacus ceased to be an important component of the capital and generally took an octagonal shape, even when the pier below it was circular. The moulding might be a roll, an ogee shape or one that began as a chamfer and then developed into a rounded edge or square fillet with an ogee quarter round beneath. When the abacus was octagonal, its sides often took a slight hollow. One unusual form exists in which an octagonal, embattled capital was put up in conjunction with a frieze of four-leaved flowers, thus giving the appearance of a crown.

At the foot of the pier, even simple octagonal bases were considerably increased in height, and some were double. Quite often, each section of such a two-tier structure carried a different design, the lower one being projected out by a reversed ogee moulding. This might be a single string, or a double arrangement with a bead between the two. Where the pier above was composed of several shafts, each might have an independent base, although the group was usually treated as one in the matter of mouldings. These were more pronounced on the base, where the double ogee was a particular survival, often embellished with a quirk. The lowest moulding of the base often overhung the top of the plinth. Plinths usually closely followed the line of the lowest element of the base.

### Panelling and general decoration

Builders lost interest in any practical advantage to the triforium. Although its course was sometimes followed by panelling, its depth was reduced, and any clerestory was mostly divided from the arches below by a narrow string course. However, string courses were often omitted altogether from village churches put up in the fifteenth and sixteenth centuries; otherwise the mouldings were angular, with wide but shallow hollows. Bands of quatrefoiled panels became popular, frequently running around towers, or included in conjunction with an embattled parapet. Internally, panels ran around walls and were formed of mullions and tracery. Vaulted ceilings of the period were sometimes almost entirely covered in panelling. These lent themselves well to admitting the shields and heraldic devices of the age, the likenesses of monarchs, and general, more secular enrichment. Smaller panels might enclose squares, circles, quatrefoils, etc, and were frequently designed so that they enclosed a centrepiece, such as an heraldic shield, in a profusion of tracery. Larger, rectilinear-style panels were also headed by multifoils. In all instances, the foils might be cusped, and these sometimes ended in minute flowers or foliage.

Floral decoration was either stylised, or bulbous and undulatory. It was used less frequently than in the preceding period and was now redrawn unnaturally, either in order to fit the described shape more closely, or for the purpose of symmetry. This was particularly true for decorated, square or rectangular panels. In the spandrels formed by the main figures, there might be the emblems of saints, shields,

armorial bearings and badges, beasts and birds. The square, four-leafed flower was initially popular but later developed into the Tudor rose and portcullis. Canopied niches, usually inhabited, were put into the fabric of the building, both inside and out, and tiers of statues were a favoured treatment for a reredos, which often occupied much of the east end, inside larger churches.

## Vaulting

The peculiarly English form of decoration known as *fan vaulting* was pre-eminent. This may be described as a trumpet-shaped, inverted cone of masonry formed by a series of ribs that diverge equally in all directions from a common source. There was usually a capital, corbel or vaulting shaft attached to the

*Sherborne, Dorset. The magnificent fan tracery combined with lierne vaulting that was the supreme decoration of the Perpendicular period in England.*

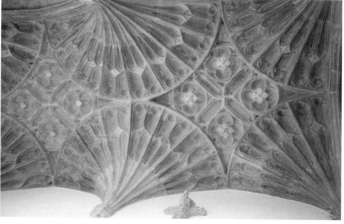

*North Leigh, Oxfordshire. Delicate fan vaulting in the Wilcote chantry chapel, which was begun in 1439.*

143

side walls, at the points of spring. Fan vaulting is not groined, and the pendentives were usually put up in pairs along the roof, and arranged so that the extreme ribs of each conoidal figure met at the centre. At that point, there might be a boss or a drop pendant, or both. The vertical ribs were equally spaced, and some fans also included horizontal ribs, the spandrels between being treated as a series of rectilinear, traceried panels. Most frequently, these panels were trefoiled above and so described below to fit the shape of the converging fan at that point. This usually meant that the lowest row was a series of daggers. Fan vaults are commonly to be found across aisles of the period, and above chantry chapels and tombs. There are fine examples at Ottery St Mary (Devon) and in the south chapel at Cullompton (Devon).

## Screens

Fan vaulting was also used at the head of muntins, the vertical members of carved screens, as at Plymtree, Ipplepen and Lapford in Devon, and at Bishop's Lydeard and Westonzoyland in Somerset. Indeed, these screens exemplified the rise of the carpenter and the wood-carver to a similar craft status to that of the masons. Until now, timber had been almost universally functional in its use for framing and bracing. Wood came down into the body of the church, although stone screens also continued to be erected during the period. The screen now achieved its full development. It might have an embattled or brattished cornice or, more usually, one that was deep, coved, stepped and intricately moulded. This comprised a frieze of several narrow horizontal bands of decorative motifs, divided by plain moulded strings or fillets, and characteristically topped by a cresting of dentil moulding. The bands were treated as a continuous sequence, which meant that running vines with delicately carved bunches of grapes were extremely popular; they tied the whole thing together from end to end. Oak leaves, acorns and berries, linked by little stalks, also lent themselves to this kind of treatment. The effect was always a series of minute figures repeated at intervals, as if it were horizontal diaper work. As a general rule, the higher the screen, the fewer were the bands of moulding, and the narrower was the cornice.

Occasionally this was no more than an upper rail, surmounted by brattishing.

Beneath the cornice was a top rail; this frequently included several plain mouldings, stepped downwards to meet the upper frame of the bays and the stiles – the outside vertical members of the square frame. Cresting and the top rail were often linked by slender, curving ribs, which sprang from the muntins below and ran right through the cornice. The position of the opening in the screen was usually determined by the total width available, coupled with the best aesthetic use of bays. In this regard, bays with two lights divided by slender muntins were favoured, so carpenters tried to build this arrangement to the best possible proportions. If a suitable effect could be

*Charlton-on-Otmoor, Oxfordshire. The early sixteenth-century painted rood screen and rood loft, with a cross of evergreens; the coving has flowing tracery and the muntins and stiles are banded.*

achieved with an odd number of bays of equal width, the opening was usually placed centrally. An even number of bays usually resulted in fewer lights to the left of the opening. In some instances, where space allowed, openings were put in which were double the width of the flanking bays. Pierced carved tracery was applied to the heads of the lights and also those of the openings, thus providing horizontal canopies of decorative openwork that bound screens together visually beneath their top rails. This tracery was either cinquefoiled with minor motifs in the spandrels, or rectilinear after the prevailing fashion. Typical decoration of this time, applied variously to screens, included tabernacle work, panels, columns and pinnacles, niches and statues. Beneath the bays carrying lights, there were usually plain or blind traceried panels, sitting on a bottom rail and ultimately a deep plinth. In earlier examples, ornamentation was larger than latterly and was applied to the panel; later in the period it was much smaller, more intricate, and carved into it. Occasionally, the opening was turned into a doorway, as if the church was not quite ready to relinquish centuries of closure before the chancel and explain the sense of mystery about exactly what took place there. Where screens crossed aisles, small doors might be put in, usually no wider than a bay. After the carpenters came the painters, decorating the screens in bright colours and frequently painting figures on the flat panels. There is an extraordinarily fine example – although one that is unrepresentative of the period in that it comprises a wall of single lights – at Charlton-on-Otmoor (Oxfordshire).

Wooden screens that form the only division between nave and chancel and extend the full width of the church across nave and aisles are particularly characteristic of the far west of England. The widest of this type in England is at Dunster (Somerset); the longest is at Uffculme in Devon. Local style in the West Country generally produced low screens that had thick stiles and muntins but were lavishly ornamented. The rood screen at Totnes (Devon) is of stone with a number of different designs and was put up in 1459. Cornwall has particularly fine rood screens of the period, notably at Altarnun, Gunwalloe, Ladock, St Buryan, St Ewe, St Levan, St Winnow and Tintagel. Awliscombe (Devon) is an example of a relatively simple screen of the period, while those at Dunchideock, Bradninch and Swimbridge in the same county

*Ranworth, Norfolk. The fifteenth-century screen shows a series of apostles and saints, male and female, painted in hierarchical order within decorative panels with blind tracery.*

*Ellingham, Hampshire. The Perpendicular wooden screen that separates nave from chancel has single multifoiled lights with trefoils in the spandrels and reeded muntins (the uprights), dentil moulding on the cornice, and boarded lower panels.*

represent fifteenth-century screens at their best. In Somerset, Carhampton's screen is an especially attractive web of tracery, done in perfect proportion with exquisite lightness of touch, and tier upon tier of the most intricately carved decoration. Other examples are at Halse and Minehead.

## Fonts

A considerable amount of copying, especially between poorer parishes in the same vicinity, resulted in a rash of rather stereotyped and generally uninspiring fonts throughout the Perpendicular period. There are a number of local types in design, artistic content and execution. At Potter Heigham (Norfolk) and Chignall Smealy (Essex), brick had to be used. It is still possible to come across a font such as at Sandon (Staffordshire), which, even at this advanced date, might cursorily have been placed much earlier because the style is so rustic. Then there are those fonts in the far west, notably at Padstow and St Merryn in Cornwall, that hark back

*Ufford, Suffolk. The fifteenth-century tower of crowns font cover – tier upon tier of openwork tracery – is topped by a pelican picking her breast to feed blood to her young, and stands nearly 20 feet (6 metres) high.*

to the Romanesque style of Bodmin, and those in Devon, as at Lifton and Marystow, that are of Launceston type.

Most fonts were coloured and would still be but for the indifferent ways in which the layers of whitewash that were applied at and since the Reformation were removed. Masons tended to copy not only the better ideas but also those that were mediocre. With the exception of the Seven Sacraments fonts of East Anglia, there were few good, original ideas. Wiltshire, for example, has hardly a commendable Perpendicular font. Many places took the opportunity to remake their existing Norman fonts, especially if there was little decoration on them. Elsewhere, some fairly unprepossessing bowls and stems were raised on decorated steps, so that some quite respectable pieces were formed.

The most common shapes for the fifteenth-century bowl were octagonal and square, and there were usually plain, recessed panels or niches on each side. The panels were either square or rectangular, the latter sometimes subdivided into two squares each. Others might have leaves at the angles, or little round shafts with caps and bases. In these examples, there was unlikely to be any more decoration than a sequence of plain, narrow mouldings at the rim. This was the common style of rim for most Perpendicular fonts, although a shallow band of minor motifs is sometimes found, set between two conservative mouldings. *Tudor flower*, the flat, upright, triple-leaf form that lent itself so well to cresting later in the period, also found favour around the rims of fonts constructed in the fifteenth and sixteenth centuries.

The more ambitious divisions between the sides of the bowl were made by ornamental buttresses that sometimes ended in crocketed pinnacles. Where the buttresses were stepped, they replaced the single, vertical straight line and, at the same time, provided several flat surfaces of their own that might each be decorated. Some of these little buttresses were given niches, and these were occasionally pinnacled or canopied, with tiny figures in the hollows below. When the division between each surface of the font was emphasised by a miniature representation of some structural feature to be found elsewhere in the church, it was sometimes used as the point of spring for arches or vaulting, which then formed the head of a panel.

Tracery forms were commonly used in the panels. Cinquefoils, ogee arches or delicate tabernacling, with canopies and minor decorative motifs wherever spandrels occurred, were set against rectangular panel work. Panels containing quatrefoils sometimes alternated with those containing trefoils. A favourite treatment of the former was to link the quatrefoil with a circle, encompassing a small shield. Otherwise, plain shields, or those bearing heraldry associated with local landowning families, were used to decorate the panels. The shields might be held by angels. The emblems of Christ, the instruments of the Passion and the symbols of the Evangelists were also popular subjects for the surfaces of Perpendicular fonts.

In many instances the panels on the bowls were filled with sophisticated figurework, in quantities that had not been done since the twelfth century. This was motivated by different values and aesthetics from that of the earlier period. It was of considerably better sculptural quality and nicely proportioned, although the degree of excellence and the quantity present on a single font was proportional to the amount of money that could be raised for the project. Even though there was a lot of figurework, it was solemn, and its purpose was to instruct in ways that were neither spontaneous nor entertaining. Just as fonts of this time can often be dated fairly accurately by the coats of arms on them, it is often possible to identify the characters depicted in the figurework.

Sometimes the panels of the bowl were treated as tableaux, with scenes sculpted beneath canopies with finials, often with rectilinear tracery in the spandrels. Each face might have a different scene to its neighbour, depicting either a biblical message or a point in the life of a saint or martyr. Less sophisticated panels might have just one or two figures.

The surfaces between the sides of the bowl and the top of the stem were, at their best, an arrangement of plain mouldings and hollows. More often, the underside of the bowl comprised a shallow downward inclination, formed into a hollow with a single line of patera. This tended to be of one sort: commonly either four-leafed flower, Tudor flower, a vine, or winged angels' heads in relief. Occasionally, associated motifs, such as slightly different pieces of floral decoration, were carved together; but rarely were the motifs entirely different. Less common were grotesques and vaulting. Occasionally, two horizontal bands of decoration were placed between the bowl and the stem. When the underside of the bowl was corbelled out at the corners, there was rarely any other decorative motif in the spaces between. The corbels were commonly angels' heads and wings, although grotesques were sometimes used, and in some instances little arches sprang from the corbels.

There are some instances in which the sides of the bowl are shallower than the undersides, and the latter are completely filled with either large flowers or angels'

heads with outspread wings that overlap each other. This treatment is in contrast to the prevalent move towards smaller, more detailed sculptures. It cannot be called barbaric, because of the subject matter, but the treatment nonetheless is more than a nod back to that of earlier periods. Other than this, the underside of the bowl was rarely enriched to any great extent, although, technically, any panels here held the same potential as those on the sides of the bowl. Some were corbelled out from the stem on the backs of angels.

Stems or pedestals of the period were either octagonal throughout, or octagonal at the bowl and square where they met the base. They might be quite plain, or decorated by an upper or lower moulding, below the bowl and above the base. The angles were sometimes decorated with thin shafts with little capitals and bases, or with buttresses that might be stepped. Occasionally, animals seated on their own personal plinths appear to be supporting the bowl. The sides of the stems, if decorated at all, might have shallow, trefoil-headed arches in one or two tiers on each face. Where the bowl and the stem were treated as a piece

*Stalham, Norfolk. Figurework in pairs in framed panels around the bowl; the ribs of a lierne vault cover the intersection between the bowl and the stem of this fifteenth-century font.*

*Idbury, Oxfordshire. The octagonal Perpendicular font with quatrefoils around the bowl, and blind traceried arches, pinnacles and corner buttresses about the stem.*

and decorated accordingly, the result was a most pleasing unity of design. Interesting, too, are those fonts in which the underside of the bowl and the stem beneath are decorated as a piece, usually with an arched canopy at the head of each face. It is not unusual to come across fonts of this period whose stems appear to be quite inadequate for supporting the bowl. One may make comparisons with earlier fonts, especially where the stem is thicker than average in comparison to the bowl, and the chamfer on the underside is shallow. Aesthetically, this is less pleasing than the strictly segregated arrangement since, from a distance, the bowl appears to be proportionally squat. But it is reminiscent of early bowls, or at least of how an earlier bowl appears if it has been ornamented at a later date. Bases were either square or octagonal and were usually quite plain. Tall plinths were usually decorated on each side by double or triple rows of panels with pierced or blind traceried quatrefoils, sometimes set diagonally, encircled or cusped.

The whole structure might be raised on one or more steps, which were either plain or divided into panels that sometimes contained heraldry or geometric designs. These included circles, quatrefoils within circles, foliated quatrefoils, wheel motifs, and rectangles and squares, almost any of which might also have geometric figures

inscribed within them. In some instances, steps quite out of proportion to the rest of the piece were erected.

Some of the finest Perpendicular fonts are the Seven Sacraments group of more than thirty in East Anglia. These are all octagonal bowls on which are depicted baptism, confirmation, Eucharist, extreme unction, penance, ordination and matrimony, in variable sequence, leaving the eighth side to be filled by some suitable teaching from the scriptures. These fonts were raised above a number of steps, which in some cases took the form of a Maltese cross and were characteristically decorated.

*Badingham, Suffolk. The octagonal Seven Sacraments font, of 1485, is notable for the scenes packed with characters and the amount of detail contained within each; all is acted out beneath ogee arches with extended, canopied heads.*

# Renaissance and Classical
# 1547–1830

**The Classical orders and their ornamentation**

The Classical period was also known as the pillar and portico era. A *portico* is a roofed area, open on at least one side, the roof being supported by an arrangement of columns. The word is Italian, derived from the Latin *porticus*, and has come to mean a walkway that is associated with any number of free-standing columns supporting some sort of entablature or pediment. Typically, the columns stand in front of the Classical building and are usually raised above the ground, either on a wall or above steps. They may run around the outside of the structure, more usually in the case of one that is circular, or around the inside, thus forming a cloister-like arrangement. Four columns put up in this way form a tetrastyle; six comprise a hexastyle; eight an octostyle; ten a decastyle. The upper frontage was the *pediment*: a low-pitched, triangular, ornamental gable that might be finished with classical urns at its apex and sides. Many pediments were enclosed within a cornice that ran horizontally above their base mouldings but followed the chosen shape of the pediment above.

Pediments were also used to describe the similar, if smaller, figures above doors and windows, even though, in the case of the latter, they are unlikely to be associated with any sort of portico. Most cornices were unbroken and were not particularly ornate. However, the typical triangular type offered tympana that might be left blank or enriched with escutcheons, garlands, figurework, or Classical sculpture in relief. Some included a circular window. It was the closed, triangular pediment that appeared mostly on the outside of the building, whereas those above doorways were rather more ornamental. A *broken pediment* is one in which the base moulding is incomplete but is finished as projections returning inwards above the columns on either side. The *segmental pediment* is shaped like one quarter of a circle, round side uppermost. If this side is incomplete, the figure is called an open segmental pediment. Rarely are the mouldings of segmental pediments simply interrupted at the top, as may occur along the lower moulding of their triangular counterparts. Instead, the plasterwork of the tympanum is frequently chased into a design that links the two broken mouldings. An open pediment with a moulding that ends in whorls is said to be *scrolled*; and those that have graceful, flowing curves to their sides, which end almost in finials that resemble birds' heads, are said to be *swan-necked*. The space between the mouldings in an open pediment is likely to have some small Classical motif that helps to bind the figure together.

The arrangement of portico and pediment was put up as the main entrance to most of the Classical churches designed by Wren, his followers and successors. But the pediment is to be found elsewhere: as the gable on relatively small porches, as at Shrivenham (Oxfordshire) and on wall monuments and memorials everywhere of the Classical period. In many instances, coats of arms were placed in the tympana. Where particular statements were to be made, broken triangular pediments allowed the bearings to burst from the confines of the triangle. Pediments on large memorials were frequently adorned with urns or obelisks.

The architecture of imperial Rome was more elaborate than that of ancient Greece, on which it was based. The constructional arch was unknown to the Greek builders, and it is certain that in ancient Rome brick arches that rested on columns were at first introduced behind the entablature. This was the horizontal superstructure above a Classical column, composed of (from the top down) cornice, frieze and architrave – and the style of the supporting pillar. Both have particular characteristics, and the

St Paul, Covent Garden, London. The church was built in 1631–8; it has a deep portico, an exaggerated overhanging pediment, two square angle pillars, and two Tuscan columns between them.

entablature was later modified to accommodate an open arch. The elements involved were not confined to load-bearing pillars and might appear, in whole or part, around the upper sections of interior walls.

Otherwise, the architecture of the time was based on Doric, Ionic and Corinthian, the names the Romans gave to the three classical orders of ancient Greece. They added two of their own: Tuscan and Composite. An *order*, insofar as it applies to Classical architecture, may be defined as a column, including its base, shaft and capital, plus the associated entablature, in whichever style. There might be an abacus between the capital and architrave, and an astragal between the capital and the shaft. The whole field of Roman architecture was set out in the ten-volume *De architectura*, a treatise by the first-century architect and writer Marcus Vitruvius Pollio, known as Vitruvius. He gave his name to Vitruvian scrollwork, a continuous band of what appears to be stylised waves in the sea, much used in Classical architecture. It was Andrea Palladio's study of Vitruvius' writings that inspired his own work, giving rise to the Palladian style of modern Italian architecture, which followed that of the Italian Renaissance. And it was this that was taken up by his followers, including Inigo Jones (1573–1652), who worked very much after the examples of Vitruvius. He imposed a characteristic variation to create his own interpretation of the Italian Renaissance. Jones's church of St Paul, Covent Garden, London, built in 1631, was the first wholly Classical parish church in England. Yet, without its furniture, it is a simple room of the period: its windows, flat moulded ceiling and gallery on Doric columns are more reminiscent of a town-house ballroom. Outside, there are pure Tuscan columns of exaggerated entases and a pediment that overreaches itself.

The oldest and plainest of the Greek orders was *Doric*. In this, the shaft was tapered and might be fluted by horizontal hollows or channels, each with a sharp edge or *arris*. The frieze above could include vertical blocks known as *triglyphs*, containing decorative angled grooves. In a Greek Doric frieze, these blocks were regularly positioned to one side, whereas in their Roman counterpart they tended to be centred above the column. The spaces between the triglyphs are called *metopes*, and these were usually left quite plain in their original forms. In Roman examples, however, this was rarely the case. Flat, oval decoration and animal skulls with floral trails were common to later metopes. Rectangular projections (square in the Roman interpretation) known as *dentils*, from the Latin for 'little tooth', are features of most Classical orders. These are often present beneath a plain moulding in the capital or cornice.

The lowest part of the projecting mouldings in a Classical cornice is a *corona*. Attached to the *soffit* or underside of the corona there might be a series of rectangular blocks. These may also appear beneath the *tenia* – the fillet or band running along the top of the frieze, which in all orders other than Doric is called the *cymatium*. These blocks, called *mutules*, run lengthways, with the appearance of horizontal dentils, and are moulded out from the feature above. They are either plain or may be decorated on their undersides by tiny dentils, or cone-shaped drops known as *guttae*. There are other differences between Greek and Roman Doric: typically that the ratio between the base diameter of the column and its height is greater in the latter, and the Greek column may have no base. The latter is also most likely to have a square, plain abacus. It may also have flatter mouldings, for the Greek *ovolo*, which in particular formed upper sections of the cornice, was cut on less of an angle, with an upper quirk. By comparison, the Roman alternative was usually a full quarter-round scroll. The ogee form of moulding was widely used, frequently also cut with an upper quirk which helped to give extra emphasis to the flow of the wave. The convex section of the ogee was always uppermost in Classical architecture – *cyma reversa*, in contrast to *cyma recta*, in which the head of the feature is the hollow of the ogee.

The *Tuscan* order was a Roman innovation, although it was considered to be derived from the Greek Doric. In effect it was a mixture of this and the Roman Composite, and it became extremely popular in English Renaissance architecture. This was an extremely striking style, which, in modern parlance, would aptly fit the saying 'less is more'. There were no decorative motifs on Roman Tuscan: here were plain mouldings at either end of a big, plain shaft. The columns generally had a wider diameter than those of the other orders, and the mouldings were better placed for harmonious visual effect. This also helped to give the whole structure the appearance of strength and elegance. At the foot of the column, there was likely to be a square plinth surmounted by a roll moulding, or *torus*. Both Doric and Tuscan bases commonly comprised a fillet or shallow astragal above a torus. Between the capital and the entablature there might be a single fillet or astragal; otherwise both were composed of plain mouldings as described above.

The *Ionic* order is instantly recognisable by the characteristic volutes at each

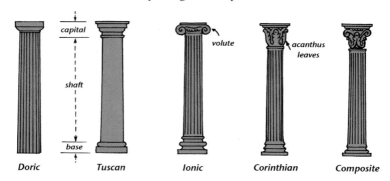

*Classical columns.*

*St Pancras, Euston Road/Woburn Place, St Pancras, London. The neo-Grecian church by W. and H. W. Inwood, completed in 1822 with its distinguished portico of six Ionic columns, also has a run of caryatids designed by Rossi.*

corner of the capital. These spiral scrolls were also used in Corinthian and Composite examples, in association with the characteristic ornamentation of those orders. Volutes might be flat against two opposite sides, or – particularly if they are later examples or of predominantly Roman influence – angled out from beneath the abacus. In this way, all four faces of the capital appear to be treated exactly the same. In some English examples, the volute can be quite overpowering. A favoured decorative motif of the Ionic order was the *echinus*, the continuous band of egg and dart, or one of its close derivatives. This might appear along the upper edge of the volute, or between the scrolls. In general, the whole piece was widely decorated with interlinking or running vines on the capital, miscellaneous foliage, flowers and trails, or the favoured acanthus leaf, which was to become such a feature of Corinthian and Composite. Figurework was often carved into the frieze, and the Ionic corona was sometimes bracketed out on flat, leafy scrolls, called *modillions*, which were also widely used on the Corinthian and Composite orders. While the main elements of the entablature were flat and plain, the typical Ionic cornices, friezes and architraves were separated by dentil mouldings, fillets or strings of beads, floral motifs or V shapes. The columns were fluted with shallow hollows and slender fillets between. The plinth was square and shallow with an *Attic* base above. The latter typically comprised a hollow moulding, or *scotia*, between two round mouldings, or tori, the lower torus being the wider of the two. In other examples, there might be two narrow astragals with a scotia hollow above and a large torus below.

In the Greek *Corinthian* order alone, the capital was higher than its width and was distinguished by the mass of spiky laurel, olive or acanthus leaves that were piled one on top of the other, spreading upwards and outwards in a number of tiers. This produced an overall bell shape that terminated in small volutes, named *caulicoli*, beneath a narrow abacus. These, in effect, bracketed out the latter. Whereas the foliate decoration on the faces of the bell might be interwoven, or might assume that design around a central motif, the edges beneath the volutes regularly comprised tiers of separate acanthus leaves. The abacus might comprise a quarter-round scroll moulding, a concave moulding and a fillet, each of which could be decorated. Similar work is often to be found along the cornice, sometimes in association with the ubiquitous dentils, and occasionally with modillions at the corners. It is not unusual to find two or three horizontal bands of entirely different decoration abutting each other in this order, whereas in Classical architecture this is otherwise rarely the case. Corinthian columns are usually fluted and have, at their base, an arrangement of two flattened tori on either side of double hollows that are sometimes associated with fillets.

The *Composite* order was the Roman mixture of Ionic and Corinthian. Except for

153

*St Mary, Marylebone Road, Marylebone, London. The portico of Corinthian columns and Corinthian pilasters, above which there is a typical baluster parapet.*

the capitals, it might be considered as a little more subdued than the latter. The capitals retained the tall characteristics and tier-like effect of the Corinthian: outwardly curved acanthus leaves surmounted by volutes beneath a plain, narrow abacus. The elements of the entablature were all retained, although they were plainly moulded and included fewer, narrower, more conservative bands of decoration between them. Both dentils and mutules are likely to have been put up in association with each other and, in this order, the frieze might be decorated to its full depth. Composite columns were also fluted with hollows and had, at their bases, simple concave and convex mouldings in varying depths. The occasional fillet might be inserted, invariably above a convex moulding.

Classical ornamentation was bold and deeply cut, giving a crisp outline. Favourite motifs included foliage, birds, cherubs, faces, shells and masks. Floral decoration was both stylised and naturalistic, but delicately done and lusciously depicted, whether in high relief or flat against the surface of the masonry. Human or cherubic likenesses looked healthy and well-fed. Almost as instantly recognisable as the English oak leaf is the upright Classical acanthus leaf that adorns Corinthian capitals, cornices and friezes. The multi-lobed anthemion, or honeysuckle, the bay leaf and the lily were also commonly included in decorative arrangements, as were similar arrangements with palmettes. Foliage and fruit were combined in short, fleshy trails known as festoons, or were worked up as wreaths or garlands that enclosed panels. Loosely folded material was also carved in masonry: a piece on its own might be a riband, or it could be looped, as on pegs, to form a swag. There were several Classical variations on the scroll or wave motif, as was the case with the egg and dart or egg and tongue themes. Closely resembling these were styles of bead and reel – a kind of diamond and fillet device. The Greek key, fret or lattice was frequently used, as were reeding and fluting; and an interlaced banding of Flemish origin, called strapwork, became popular. Then there was the guilloche: two loosely plaited strands running horizontally, and often enclosing a small flower.

*St Katharine Cree, London. A Laud-inspired preaching room of 1631, with Corinthian columns carrying high, round-headed arches; nave and chancel areas are as one, with clerestory and ribbed ceiling with heraldic bosses.*

### The Great Fire of London and Christopher Wren

Few churches were built in the one hundred years or so before the 1660s, and only a handful during the first half of the seventeenth century. These were plainly and solidly done in a strange mixture of Gothic and Renaissance styles. The latter was mostly learnt second-hand by masons who had seen drawings of Classical Roman architecture, or who had witnessed the work of Italian sculptors employed in the great houses of England. Some would have seen the fine tombs in Westminster Abbey and elsewhere; by now, these included the work of at least two generations of Classical craftsmen. Then, on 2nd September 1666, began the fire which was to burn London and destroy eighty-seven of its churches. This presented the opportunity to establish Classicism in England at a stroke. It might otherwise have taken decades to integrate sufficiently with, and ultimately supersede, Perpendicular Gothic, had not the decision been taken to rebuild fifty-one of the lost London churches on their former sites within what was left of the medieval lanes of the city. Christopher Wren, son of the rector of East Knoyle in Wiltshire, was just thirty-four years of age when the fire raged. He was anxious to try out his own interpretation of the Baroque style, and he put forward plans that were never carried out for rebuilding the whole of London. Wren began work on the churches in 1670, and most of them were brought to the point where the interiors, fixtures and fittings were completed within a decade.

Wren never studied the Italian Renaissance at source but was influenced by some of its exponents. These included Gianlorenzo Bernini, creator of the bronze baldacchino in St Peter's, Rome, whom he met when the sculptor was in Paris at the behest of Louis XIV. Wren was steeped in Gothic tradition and, although he occasionally built in the late Perpendicular style, he cared little for it. Even so, he did put rood screens into a couple of his churches: All Hallows (now at St Margaret Lothbury) and St Peter upon Cornhill. And there was something very traditional about his spire for St

Far left: *St Margaret Pattens. The early eighteenth-century tower with angle pinnacles and balustrade, and the medieval-style polygonal spire with its spirelights, are an unusual combination for a Wren church.*

Left: *St Benet Paul's Wharf. Built 1677–83 of red and blue bricks with stone quoins and stone dressings; the church has a hipped roof, dome and openwork drum with spire.*

Below centre: *St Mary-le-Bow. The beautiful steeple, with its wide, rusticated doorway at street level, was finished by 1680; it has pairs of pilasters at the bell stage, and a balustraded parapet with openwork volute pinnacles beneath the characteristic arrangement of drum, dome and spire.*

Below left: *St Bride, Fleet Street. Wren's famous 'wedding cake' stone spire, from the church he built in 1671–8, has been internally reconstructed since much of it was destroyed in 1940.*

Below right: *St Dunstan-in-the-East. The angle pinnacles, above diagonal buttresses, are spirelets in themselves; the spire, with stepped buttresses of its own, hangs above flying buttresses; and the whole Gothic-style crown has crockets and finials.*

Right: *St Vedast, Foster Lane. Diagonal groups of pilasters at the angles of concave sides are carried in two tiers beneath the spire of this late seventeenth-century steeple.*

Far right: *St Michael Paternoster Royal. The tower, of 1713, is plain until the parapet stage, which is pierced rather than balustraded, and has, recessed above, a pretty little colonnaded octagon beneath smaller, pierced drums.*

Right: *St Peter upon Cornhill. The tower is of brick, with round-headed openings throughout, a campanile-style upper stage, a copper dome, and a little spire on an open drum.*

Far right: *St James Garlickhithe. Another plain Wren tower, with similar detailing above the parapet stage to that of St Michael Paternoster Royal.*

Margaret Pattens, London. The Gothic influence is also shown in the proportion of his steeples and the way in which, where space allowed, he designed a traditional arrangement of nave with flanking aisles. But Wren's London churches are, in several respects, a compromise. There were balances to be struck as a result of the various ways in which the works were financed. The fabric of the buildings was to be paid for by a tax on coal, but they were fitted out at the expense of the individual parishes, or from private donations. It was to be well into the eighteenth century before steeples were added to some of the Wren churches that had been in use for years.

Also, the change in liturgy to the central preaching requirements of Protestant worship impacted on the ways in which he perceived the purpose of the building. Liturgy and preaching had to be successfully combined in ways that had not previously concerned church architects. Wren had to allow for the projected sizes of the congregations and yet work within the varying sums of money that were available for each building. Because London had grown around its medieval churches, and before the fire many buildings pressed hard upon them, it was difficult to design for many of the sites. They also occupied sites between medieval streets that were cramped and presented less than ideal standards. Other rebuilding was also taking place simultaneously in close proximity. In an overcrowded area, there were two important considerations for Wren: the appearance of the churches at street level, and the visual impact they made when people looked upwards at the broken skyline. Because most of the churches were put up in areas that were already overcrowded with buildings, it was important that the steeples should also stand out from a distance and be recognised individually as landmarks.

With this in mind, Wren built steeples in lead and stone, to which justice can hardly be done by describing them in architectural terms. He built from the ground with little decoration below the roof line of surrounding buildings, thereafter distinguishing each one. The London skyline was changed by towers and spires that frequently combined Gothic and Renaissance features. They rose in stages, with curving sides, cupolas and domes, supported by square or round colonnades, or diagonal columns, and embellished with balustrades, obelisks, urns, and parapets with corner finials. Each stage was treated individually, and many took the form of an opening, flanked by free-standing or engaged Classical pillars, with or without a pediment. This arrangement is known as an *aedicule*, and in many instances the spires of Wren's churches are a diminishing succession of aedicules or cupolas that end in either an obelisk or a spirelet with finial. The overall effect is of a spire of parts, certainly more intricate than ever before, but criticised in the nineteenth century. In visual terms, the more ambitious steeples were tier upon tier of symmetrical Classicism – the ultimate expression of a vibrant mind creating the ultimate symbol of ecclesiastical rebirth.

This is not to say that a hallmark Wren steeple was universally applied. He put up spireless towers, with or without corner pinnacles – occasionally pure Gothic, with either balustraded parapets or those that were blank or pierced. There was the occasional traditional spire, as at St Margaret Pattens. Or a design might be Wren transitional: a dome and cupola above a Classical tower, as at St Benet Paul's Wharf. So apparently recognisable of Wren, yet most uncharacteristic, are the five drums in diminishing stages – the wedding cake effect – that comprise his highest tower: that of St Bride, Fleet Street. Most medieval in concept is that of St Dunstan-in-the-East, where a spirelet is supported by arched buttresses which spring from above the tower, behind big corner pinnacles. St James Garlickhithe, and St Vedast, Foster Lane, have very Baroque steeples, the lantern sides in both instances appearing to be concave, by means of projecting columns set on the diagonal at St James, and similarly arranged clustered shafts at St Vedast. The top of St Stephen Walbrook is very similar to St James, except that the corner columns are set square.

Wren rebuilt his London churches in Portland stone and brick. The designs were mostly based on a traditional, single rectangular plan with one or two aisles. Internally, they were arranged as a square or oval space, or in the shape of a Greek cross. Many had galleries, vaults, arched recesses, or central domes, as at St Stephen Walbrook, which is the very best of Wren's Baroque-style London churches (1672–9). In effect, this was Wren's development of the auditory plan: halls built to ensure that everyone could see and hear everything that was taking place. Pillars that had previously supported pointed arches were replaced by free-standing pillars, which in Wren's churches supported flat ceilings of rich plasterwork above a decorated entablature. Carved and painted altarpieces were put up, in order to enhance further the importance of the altar. High-backed pews were arranged to give fine views of the richly panelled pulpit with carved and decorated tester, frieze and sounding board. Large windows, full of clear glass, flooded the interior with light.

The architect had to divide his time between the individual craftsmen. Much of the work considered to be characteristic of a Wren church was put there by some of the finest craftsmen of the day. These included the Dutch wood-carver and sculptor Grinling Gibbons (1648–1721) – maker of the fine font cover at All Hallows Barking, and creator of some exquisite altarpieces – and the painter and politician Sir James Thornhill (1675–1734). The emergence of named architects and builders, both professional and amateur, was a product of the seventeenth century. So was the way in which groups of individual craftsmen, who were themselves the inspiration for schools of excellence in their fields and commanded their own imitators, worked together under Wren or Hawksmoor. Despite the unsurpassed quality of the work, not all of Wren's City churches survived up to 1939. Others were destroyed during the Second World War, including St Vedast, which was rebuilt, leaving just twenty-three in place. These are St Andrew-by-the-Wardrobe; St Anne and St Agnes, Gresham Street; St Augustine, Watling Street; St Benet Paul's Wharf; Christ Church, Newgate Street; St Clement, Eastcheap; St Dunstan-in-the-East; St Edmund the King, Lombard Street; St James Garlickhithe; St Lawrence Jewry; St Magnus the Martyr; St Margaret Lothbury; St Margaret Pattens; St Martin Ludgate; St Mary Abchurch; St Mary Aldermary; St Mary-at-Hill; St Mary-le-Bow; St Michael Cornhill; St Michael Paternoster Royal; St Nicholas Cole Abbey; St Peter upon Cornhill; and St Stephen Walbrook.

*St Stephen Walbrook, London. Completed in 1679, this is Wren's best parish church; the south-west corner, beneath the great dome, shows the characteristic arrangement of Corinthian columns and entablature.*

## Auditory plan

'Auditory' is all about hearing, and an auditorium is defined as the space in which an audience sits in a building intended for public meetings or performances. And that was exactly the idea in the seventeenth century, when greater prominence was given to the area forward from the pulpit. The idea was that this would be best facilitated when everyone taking part in the service was accommodated in a single, undivided interior. Not only should they be in the same room, but ideally the congregation was to be as close to the preacher as possible. It might seem a particularly secular way of describing the part of the church that we have hitherto thought of only as the nave. Yet the word 'nave' is itself derived from the Latin *navis*, meaning a ship, and the meaning in which it was applied to the public area of the church was as much symbolic as practical.

Just as a ship is a reasonably secure area surrounded by treacherous waters and sailing on a journey, so was the physical body of the church building a place of safety from the more earthly dangers outside on the journey through life. The two themes are inextricably linked in coastal churches, where some aspect of the sea may be depicted on the fixtures and fittings within the nave.

In village churches all across England, it became a matter of shifting around furniture within the existing plan, although a number of arcades were rebuilt during the seventeenth century, with Classical columns supporting high arches. Tuscan columns were favoured because they were the plainest, and psychologically they were the nearest Classical approximation to the bulky columns and piers they were replacing. When the guilds and chantries were suppressed, altars disappeared from aisles and transepts. The long-standing ones often had piscinas built into the walls close by, and these were allowed to remain. To this day, it is often possible to identify where a lost altar was formerly placed by the presence of such an ornamental drain – notably at the eastern end of an aisle. Here, the east wall itself might still have the remains of a defaced reredos that formerly stood behind the side altar. In the countryside, too, the main altar came into the nave. Those churches in which altars had been removed from aisles and transepts found they had extra space, and the congregation could be accommodated all around the newly positioned table in the nave. When altars were eventually reinstated at the east end, that part of the church was sometimes rebuilt with an apsidal ending, and a reredos was set up behind the altar. There was a need to try to ensure that, by making such a feature of the replaced altar, there was less chance of it being moved again. There was also, perhaps, an element of trying to make peace with God for the disturbance.

Of course, the nave was not lost by the seventeenth-century architects working under the auditory plan, but simply reshaped and, in some cases, rearranged. Most significantly, churches were made wider, whereas increasingly large congregations

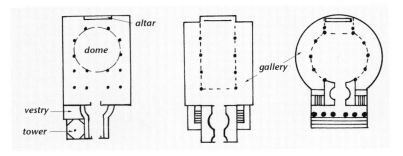

*Classical plans: (from left) St Stephen Walbrook, London; St Bride, Fleet Street, London; St Chad, Shrewsbury, Shropshire.*

might previously have been accommodated by lengthening the nave where possible, thereby placing those at the back even further from the mumblings at the east end. If it was not possible to shoehorn the congregation in on one level within the physical confines of the plan, architects discovered what we might today call 'the mezzanine floor approach'. Although they were never as frequently built in England as elsewhere, small galleries for accommodating people have been put up in the country's churches since the eleventh century. Now, six hundred years later, Classical architects were building deeper galleries – often around three sides of the room – supported on free-standing pillars. These not only accommodated a proportionally large overspill of worshippers, they also facilitated a much more economical use of space and brought more people than ever before closer to the pulpit.

## Renaissance architects and provincial churches

In 1711 Parliament passed an Act authorising the building of fifty new churches. In the event, only twelve were built. They were mostly designed in Baroque style by, or with the help of, Nicholas Hawksmoor (1661–1736), who was Wren's pupil and a friend of Sir John Vanbrugh. Notable among Hawksmoor's contributions in London were St Mary Woolnoth in the City; Christ Church, Spitalfields; St Alfege, Greenwich; St George-in-the-East, Stepney; Christ Church, Stepney; and St George, Bloomsbury. His churches were very original, and solidly overpowering. In this they contrasted with those of James Gibbs (1682–1754), who studied in Italy and who created with a lighter hand. Good examples of Gibbs's work are St Mary-le-Strand and St Martin-in-the-Fields in London, and All Saints, Derby. Other architects who designed churches in the Baroque style in London and the provinces over the next few years included Thomas Archer (1668–1743), who was a pupil of Vanbrugh. Among his fine churches were St Philip, Birmingham, St John, Smith Square, Westminster, and St Paul, Deptford (London). John James (1672–1746), who designed St George, Hanover Square, Westminster, was a pupil of Gibbs, and was also influenced by Hawksmoor. However, the later decades of the seventeenth century were almost entirely given over to building great houses. The rebuilding of London's churches had been more or less completed, and there was no political impetus to carry on at such a rate. Churches were soon to pass through a comfortable drawing-room stage, and to emerge as little more than halls. George Dance the Elder (1700–68) built in the Classical style; notably extant are St Botolph Aldgate, and St Botolph Bishopsgate, both in London. Of Gibbs's school, too, was Henry Flitcroft

*St George, Hanover Square, Westminster, London. This church, designed by John James, went up in the third decade of the eighteenth century, with its great pedimented portico, and its solid belfry adorned by swags and pairs of Corinthian columns.*

*St Botolph Aldgate, London. A building of 1744 by George Dance the Elder; it is of dark brick with stone quoins, a tower that might almost be stylised medieval, and an interior that is wholly Classical.*

(1697–1769), who is probably best known for St Giles-in-the-Fields, Holborn, and St John, Hampstead, also both in London. None of these architects possessed Wren's genius. Their buildings had imposed grand façades into the streets.

Some nice work was done in the provinces after these influences, albeit sometimes conservatively, as at Frampton (Dorset), where the Perpendicular-style tower of 1695 has tiers of great Tuscan columns at its corners. Usually, though, the churches outside the capital were more or less equal to the demands made on them, though they had been ravaged, stripped of their treasures and deprived of much visual splendour. This was because they were no longer at the centre of community life, and there was little to be said for many who preached in them. As a result, there are few village churches of the Wren period, and hardly any that resemble those being put up at the time in London.

*Willen, Buckinghamshire. A Classical country church, built of brick with stone dressings in 1680, and with a tower parapet topped with pineapple finials.*

*Above left and right: Blandford Forum, Dorset. Built in 1733–9 by John and William Bastard, this town church has typical baluster parapets, Georgian windows, and a distinguishing cupola that was put up in lieu of a spire that never materialised. Inside, the moulded entablature is supported by large columns with Ionic capitals, made of Portland stone; the chancel is tunnel-vaulted; and the nave roof is a Gothic-inspired tripartite vault.*

Although there are strong claims that Wren at least advised on the design of the church at Farley (Wiltshire), through his personal association with its builders, it is not a Wren church. That at Ingestre (Staffordshire) is the real thing, however. Just as Wren completed St Stephen Walbrook, up went Willen (Buckinghamshire), under the influence of the Renaissance. In 1717 the delightful church at Wolverton (Hampshire) was built in Baroque style with a red brick tower. Elsewhere, some country churches were built to the medieval plan, but with some internal arrangements of the Renaissance: perhaps an arcade of Classical pillars and round arches, divided from the clerestory by a decorative cornice. From now on, the work was in the hands of named architects and craftsmen, professionals who paved the way for a great tide of gifted amateur designers to work in the provinces. One of the finest provincial churches of the early eighteenth century was begun in 1732 at Blandford Forum (Dorset) by John and William Bastard, also under the influence of Wren.

## The eighteenth-century exteriors

Nicholas Hawksmoor and James Gibbs were the great church architects after Wren. Of Hawksmoor's six London churches designed under the 1711 Act of Parliament, the front elevations of Christ Church, Spitalfields, and St George, Bloomsbury, are quite different, and both are supreme. The former is Palladian with large Tuscan columns and a stylised, scaled-down version of the ground storey in the second stage. The latter is a single pediment carried by the most wonderful Corinthian columns. Hawksmoor's interiors are distinguished by their spatial awareness and high arches,

163

*St George, Bloomsbury, London. Nicholas Hawksmoor's stepped tower of c.1730 is topped by a statue of George I and has modern lions and unicorns at its base, recreated and restored by the sculptor Tim Crawley.*

as at St Alfege, Greenwich, which were sometimes round and sometimes depressed. His tower for St Michael Cornhill is a mix of Wren's work on St Mary Aldermary and St Alban, Wood Street. The little steeple of St George, Bloomsbury, is a cheeky addition with its statue of George I topping a blunt pyramid, above square sides formed of colonnades, corner columns and pediments. Externally, St Mary Woolnoth is an example of how Hawksmoor managed to get a massive, brooding structure into a relatively small space and, although authorities have called it bold overall, the rustication is decidedly municipal. Internally, large semicircular windows provide a clerestory of light above the central area. The entablature that sits above the Composite columns at Christ Church, Spitalfields, seems almost to float in the air.

All of this, however, was a far cry from what was going on in the countryside. Three-quarters of the way through the eighteenth century, a few country churches were being built in a Georgian Gothic style. This was a mixture of Perpendicular-style tracery in eighteenth-century walls that were plain and had no string courses. The proportions of the soaring Gothic towers fell out of fashion, although some still included features such as broaches and small flying buttresses. Whereas tall pinnacles

at least, if not spires, had hitherto pointed the way, single-stage or two-stage towers now had only the thrust of small lanterns or blunt and abbreviated cupolas. Renaissance towers were square on plan, sturdy, plain and largely unbuttressed. Where buttresses existed, they might be of bricks and were otherwise quite plain. Yet the flat *pilaster* not only survived but was given a Classical cap and base and became a feature. Now used as a vertical punctuation on both inside and outside walls, flat pilasters marked the extent of bays, and they frequently flanked windows. Internally, they were sometimes put up in line with a row of free-standing columns, where previously there might have been responds to the nave arcade.

*St Mary Woolnoth, London. A Baroque Commissioners' church by Nicholas Hawksmoor, built 1716–27; its rusticated lower west front is a feature, beneath a belfry stage with Corinthian columns and twin balustraded turrets.*

164

*Great Packington, Warwickshire. A brick rebuild of 1791, in Italian style, with a heavy cupola turret at each angle and lunette-style lights.*

To some degree, the strings were replaced by moulded cornices that invariably stopped where they encountered the lower section of a steeple. *Cornices* replaced corbel tables, which had hitherto run around the top of the building and the tower. They were frequently topped by a plain parapet or one that was partly pierced and included turned *balusters*. The latter were small, circular columns that were wider in the middle or at their base, and had been commonly used in the former style in Romanesque architecture up to about the twelfth century. Their main function at that time was to separate the lights in tower windows, as the forerunner of mullions. After an absence of four centuries, the baluster was favoured once more. It reappeared externally in parapets and window dressings, and inside the church around galleries, and as altar or communion rails. When a run of balusters was put up, it formed a *balustrade*. The parapets or balusters hid lead gutters and frequently masked the lines of shallow-pitched roofs. Typically, there was an urn or obelisk at each angle, which sometimes rested on plinths that were the same depth as the parapet. This arrangement effectively replaced the medieval battlements, and the eaves beneath were supported by a moulded cornice.

Large, regularly shaped ashlar blocks of stone were used to construct walls. Otherwise, churches were increasingly built of bricks, with either stone quoins or the corners formed of alternating bricks and pieces of stone. The corners were sometimes formed as a pillar of rectangular blocks, placed one on top of the other, and ascending the full height of any tower. It all gave the appearance of great strength. This was enhanced when the cornerstones were rusticated, to give a false impression of the type of extra stability formerly associated with buttresses. The corners of buildings might be capped by urns or Classical

*St Paul, Birmingham. Built in 1777–9, with a western spire added in 1823, this is a typical Georgian hall with rusticated quoins; a modern stained glass window recalls that it is at the centre of the city's Jewellery Quarter.*

figures, which might also be raised on plinths above the cornice or on the flanking edges of the gables at either end of the church. Stone was used for banding if the tower was divided into stages, as dressings around windows and for minor decorative accessories; thus it contrasted strongly with the brickwork. There is an example of this type of building at Farley (Wiltshire). The Classical styling, with its associated pediments and columns, enabled the west end of the church to be designed as an integrated façade: an arrangement of colonnaded portico and pedimented doorway perhaps, beneath a large pediment. Even when the steeple was in the way, in the sense that its lower section was built out from the surface at the west end, the new-style symmetry enabled the façade approach to integrated design. Where the west end featured a pediment, the steeple rose above and behind it, typically topped by a drum or cupola. In some instances, an otherwise towerless church might be distinguished from surrounding architecture by a small drum and dome carried above it at the west end, on open arches.

The east and west ends of most churches had been gabled for centuries; now this was incidental, being replaced by pediments on the elevations. The sloping roof lines were largely hidden behind the square-topped fabric. The gables of porches also became pediments, and the south doors they protected were put up in a more central position. Not that porches of this time were common in the provinces; the one put up in 1765 at Glynde (Sussex) is typical of the utilitarian type. The porch at Shrivenham (Oxfordshire), c.1764, is an oddity: pedimented to the west with doorways in its north and south walls. In larger town churches the traditional-style porch was succeeded by the Classical portico. This was typically an arrangement of between four and six columns across the main face of the building, with perhaps two or three returned at right angles on either side. Some porches were semicircular on plan with six or more columns supporting either a flat or a domed roof. In such cases the entablature would be curved, admitting no pediment above. This would also be the case when the entablature was surmounted by a balustrade. The typical Classical-style doorway had curved arches, sometimes springing from moulded abaci and composed of large, occasionally oddly shaped voussoirs. Keystones might be flat, projecting or exaggerated. The door openings were flanked by flat, set-back pilasters with Classical caps and bases, or scrolled brackets known as consoles. There were usually closed pediments above, either triangular or arched, and the tympanum might be recessed.

Even by the early eighteenth century the elevation of many churches resembled contemporary domestic architecture, such as in the treatment of windows. Carved panels or decorative swags of fruit or foliage were sometimes put up over windows. Windows in towers were generally square-headed or round-headed, and of one or two lights. There was a subtle change in regard to clerestory windows, hitherto needed to give additional light in the church generally. Upper rows of round-headed windows were put in

*St Mary Magdalene, Bridgnorth, Shropshire. Designed by Thomas Telford, and built in 1792–6 in Classical style, it features a landmark cupola tower, and a portico with square pillars at the angles.*

*Croome d'Abitot, Worcestershire. The church was built in 1763, with interior and tracery designed by Robert Adam, who put in this Y-tracery window with cusping beneath an ogee arch.*

specifically to illuminate the galleries. The heads of fairly large windows that were not divided by flat mullions or transoms were either semicircular, depressed or flat. Hardly any cusping was done after the middle of the seventeenth century. There were flat dressings, and often an exaggerated keystone at the crown. Wren's churches sometimes included stained glass and, although a small amount of glass painting was carried out during the eighteenth century, windows were more commonly filled with small, rectangular leaded panes of clear lights. Other kinds of windows used in Classical buildings include the oval opening, the semicircular lunette and the *Venetian window*. The last comprises three lights set side by side as a piece. The larger, wider central opening has an arched head, while the thinner flanking lights are square-headed. *Oval windows* were popular at first-floor level, in clerestories and at the bell stage of towers. *Lunettes* were also featured at clerestory level, or might be put in above the altar. Here, high altar pieces, with panels of paintings and texts, or an equally overpowering carved reredos meant that it was unnecessary to create a big east window after the Perpendicular fashion. Even relatively small, round-headed windows put in behind the altar were often partly obscured.

At this time, the squire might be financing the rebuilding of parts of the medieval church, adding galleries and

*Gaulby, Lincolnshire. The nave, and the tower with its exaggerated pinnacles, were designed by John Wing the Elder and put up as part of a rebuild in 1741; the chancel remains from a previous rebuilding in 1520.*

*St Martin-in-the-Fields, Westminster, London. A masterpiece by James Gibbs. Semicircular arches spring from the entablature-bearing classical columns, beneath the barrel-vaulted ceiling and the exquisite Rococo plasterwork.*

furnishing his own sumptuous pew; effectively family pews took over from chantry chapels. His architect might be influenced by the work of Wren and his followers, especially after the Reformation, and took on board the kind of drawing-room style that the squire had in his newly built country house. Of course, there were fine named architects working outside London, and much was put up following the Palladian revival of around 1720. Examples are St Nicholas, Worcester, by Thomas White; St John, Gloucester, by the Woodwards; the mid-century St George, Portland (Dorset), by architect/builder Thomas Gilbert; Moreton (also Dorset), by James Frampton; Mistley (Essex), by Robert Adam; Wanstead (London) by Thomas Hardwick; and John Wood of Bath's church at Hardenhuish (Wiltshire). The church at Ingrave (Essex) is a good eighteenth-century church but the architect is unknown. The influence of Wren, Gibbs or Archer is evident in so many like these, and also in those towers that were rebuilt around the countryside during this time.

In 1728 James Gibbs published his influential *Book of Architecture*, which positively affected the way in which people viewed Palladianism. In 1713 he had been appointed to the Commission under the 1711 Act and set about St Mary-le-Strand, which was a strange but impressive fusion of Wren, Hawksmoor and Italian Renaissance; yet it was remarkably harmonious without, and incredibly decorated within. There were others, of course, but Gibbs's masterpiece is St Martin-in-the-Fields, which stands in Trafalgar Square. It is Hawksmoor's St George, Bloomsbury, and Wren's St James Garlickhithe, but relatively conservatively done and beautifully balanced. Inside it is all barrel-vaulted, with exquisite plasterwork ceilings.

### Eighteenth-century interiors

Certainly in the provinces, Gothic arches were still being put up around the rearranged interior; the nave arcades were in the traditional style, but with arches in the Classical style. Typical arches of the Classical age were semicircular and elliptical, and high enough to allow the glory of the columns and capitals to be fully appreciated.

*Tetbury, Gloucestershire. The Perpendicular-style nave, with its slim columns of wood around iron cores, and its vaulted roof, was built by Francis Hiorn of Warwick in 1781.*

They allowed the maximum amount of light into the hall and enabled it to be used as efficiently as possible. Ordered arches disappeared after the Perpendicular period, to be replaced by those with perfectly flat soffits or undersides. A feature of larger churches, such as St Andrew Holborn (London) by Wren, his St Bride in Fleet Street, and Gibbs's St Martin-in-the-Fields, was the barrel-vaulted ceiling, erected either throughout the church or at the east end. Sometimes put up in association with this was a run of transverse barrels, echoing the shape of windows in the outside walls, and inscribed laterally above a series of entablatures with Classical columns beneath. Just as the medieval barrel-vaulted ceilings of the West Country were frequently divided into square panels, so too were those of the Classical age, now framed or covered in decorative plasterwork to various degrees.

By the seventeenth century, fashionable ceilings were of moulded plasterwork, such as might be seen in the great houses of the day. Ribands, wreaths, swags, fruit and foliage, patera and healthy cherubs adorned soffits, panels and spandrels everywhere. Deep, rectangular ceiling panels were admitted, a style of feature that is said to be coffered. Panels might be painted, usually in white, gold or pastel shades. General designs and individual motifs were all of a secular nature. They originated with the big houses and transferred to the church. A riot of gold and white plasterwork and flamboyant and gilded stucco became the Rococo

*Great Witley, Worcestershire. An eighteenth-century Baroque church which has a painted ceiling by Verrio, a monument of 1735 by John Michael Rysbrack, and this painting of the Resurrection by Antonio Bellucci.*

successor to Baroque, roughly throughout the second third of the eighteenth century. It was still popular in the 1750s when Palladianism was on the way out, as architects became disenchanted with something that had been based on an interpretation of a Classical style, rather than the real thing at first hand.

## Fonts

Old fonts were among the great losses of the English Civil War and the Reformation, when they were often replaced by basins made of pewter or tin. However, at the Restoration, many original pieces that had been put to secular use or hidden from the destroyers were reinstated. This is why we may sometimes encounter medieval bowls on post-Reformation stems, or post-Reformation bowls on Gothic stems. In other instances, older bowls will show evidence of having been damaged when the clasps, by which they were once locked to protect the holy water from theft, were wrenched out and the lids destroyed. There was little of the Gothic tradition in the design of the seventeenth-century font, which, although typically octagonal or hexagonal, might be made of polished marble. Irrespective of their overall diameter, the bowls tended to be shallow with a relatively small hollow for the baptismal water. Others were chalice-shaped, with thick, concave stems, or took the form of a shallow bowl on a sturdy Baroque baluster. It became fashionable, especially in the years that immediately followed the Restoration, to carve the date of manufacture on one face of the bowl, and perhaps add the names of the churchwardens of the time. Most bowls were not decorated, except for an upper band or frieze of some Classical motif, and the occasional single pieces of flora. Others, such as at Willen (Buckinghamshire) and Castle Bromwich (Warwickshire), were given chubby cherubs' heads. On deeper bowls, there might be an arcade of plain, round-headed arches. There are a few wooden fonts remaining from this period, as at Stanford-in-the-Vale (Oxfordshire).

*Right: Tredington, Gloucestershire. Plain, moulded and chamfered stone font of c.1700 with wooden, ribbed, pyramidal font cover.*

*Below: St Margaret Lothbury, London. The white marble font, which stands on a baluster stem, has winged angels between carved biblical scenes such as a representation of Adam and Eve in the Garden of Eden.*

# Victorian
# 1830–1900

## Introduction

We tend to place the Victorian approach to churches into one of two categories: either it represents a massive and fairly universal programme of restoration throughout the country, or new building in the Decorated style. It is very easy to malign both, but there is no mistaking a Victorian church, irrespective of the period of architecture it pretends to be. Nineteenth-century restorers could be unsympathetic and heavy-handed. They were often intolerant of the ways in which craftsmen of the past patched up their own inheritance, and they swept away what they considered to have been done piecemeal. Today, much of this would be rustic beauty that we would want to preserve. But by the nineteenth century many medieval churches presented such a poor state of repair that there was little choice but to undertake wholesale rebuilding. This approach saved many churches that otherwise would not be standing today, and some restoration was extremely good; a competent architect with empathy for the spirit of medieval church building could achieve much.

Gothic was never entirely abandoned, even after the Restoration, and it is possible to see neo-medieval work from virtually any time. Indeed, country areas that were isolated from centres of taste and learning might be up to half a century behind. In the early days they did not so readily attract architects who were influenced by one or other of the Classical revivals, and they might miss out altogether on those architectural vogues that were particularly short-lived. Obtaining success with new churches in a medieval style was always rather more tricky. On the one hand, most people were ignorant of the purely functional origins of church building and, although they did not really understand how pre-Reformation symbolism had developed, they nonetheless regarded it with a romanticised view. On the other hand, builders were trying to reproduce the work of a former age with the experience of hindsight, and improved tools, materials and technologies. What they could not emulate was the 'soul' of the original work – the religious feeling that inspired medieval masons to do their work in the first instance, and their successors to develop it in a similar spirit.

At the beginning of the nineteenth century there were old people whose parents had seen the rebuilding of London's churches by Wren, his disciples and successors; they had themselves known the full force of Baroque in their youth and had lived through the Palladian revival. And now church building was going through a frivolous approximation of Gothic. In 1747 the writer Horace Walpole (1717–97) moved into a cottage in Twickenham (Middlesex), which, over the next quarter of a century from 1750, he systematically enlarged and Gothicised. He named this mixture of villa, castle and folly Strawberry Hill, and his work on the building inspired literary romanticism and influenced architectural taste. In some quarters the spirit of medieval chivalry was being revived, together with a vogue for follies that were much less practical than Strawberry Hill. These might be Gothic, Classical or ancient Roman, and for a while the balance might have gone any way. There were other influences, of course; the birth and establishment of nonconformity was a difficulty that impacted heavily on the established church, both from within its own ranks and outside.

One of the biggest changes taking place was the emergence of architecture everywhere as a profession. The main practitioners took on assistants and then pupils, many of whom became well-known in their own right, usually working after the fashion of their mentors. Most successful practices kept long hours, and the apprentices might spend at least a decade learning their craft. Nor was this desk-bound tuition; they might travel extensively at home and, with the continuing, if fluctuating, vogues for various neo-classical approaches, could spend some time studying at first hand abroad. It gave a marketing edge to their practices and at the same time helped to keep alive foreign architectural influences. Even so, many provincial churches were designed by amateur architects, diverse in their approach, and often following the designs of the masters. The distinctions that had made for local styles in church building were becoming blurred. The new architects were developing their own designs and required builders to create them in brick and stone exactly as instructed. In this way, architects came to be recognised as a professional body.

In 1803, Parliament passed the Gifts for Churches Act (amended 1811): 'to promote the building, repairing or otherwise providing of Churches and Chapels, and of Houses for the Residence of Ministers, and the providing of Church Yards and Glebes'. These Acts also provided for 'decent and suitable accommodation for all persons of what rank or degree soever... and whose circumstances may render them unable to pay for such accommodation'. Thinking people at the time had much to occupy their minds. The authorities were still focused on the effects the French Revolution might have in Britain; there was the rise of nonconformity and the pressure for civil and religious rights for such sects, and there was the emergence of alternative religious thought.

Industrial expansion meant population shifts to the new centres; nationally, the population began to increase at an unprecedented rate, and many of the larger towns and cities expanded considerably to accommodate workforces at the new industrial works. Suddenly there was a need for additional churches, and for new ones in areas where there had previously been no requirement. Country churches saw their congregations decline as villagers began to recognise that financial stability would be found elsewhere, and the future lay rather more in industry than agriculture. Town churches had a pressing need to accommodate their immigrants. The rigid structure within the Church of England meant that it could not extend its old parochial system to the new centres of population. The clergy generally did not have a good reputation, the whole system seemed in imminent danger of collapse, and little was being done by the established Church to cope with new social conditions. Where the Church of England was absent, nonconformity stepped in.

### Greek and early Gothic Revival

The evangelical approach of the early nineteenth century prompted a more subdued style of Strawberry Hill Gothic. At the same time, there was a brief return to the neo-Romanesque forerunner of a stronger revival in the 1840s. The Greek Revival in church architecture corresponded in timescale with the Regency style for public and domestic architecture during the second decade of the nineteenth century. The scene had been set much earlier, when James Stuart and Nicholas Revett studied in Greece in the early 1750s, and then published *The Antiquities of Athens* in 1762. There was no immediate rush to apply the concept to English church architecture, and it was not until the 'Elgin Marbles' arrived in 1801 that interest in Greece was stimulated. While John Nash (1752–1835) worked under the influences of the Italian-inspired Robert Adam (1728–92) and his Palladian-minded colleague Sir William Chambers (1723–96), architects such as Henry William Inwood (1794–1843) were crossing between secular and ecclesiastical architecture. Influenced by ancient Greek buildings at first hand, Inwood designed St Pancras (London). Thomas Hardwick (1752–1829), although he restored St Paul, Covent Garden (London), in Palladian style, nonetheless put up St Mary, Marylebone (London), in Greek Revival style.

A Parliamentary Commission for Building New Churches was set up in 1818, partly in response to the unprecedented speed with which the Industrial Revolution was taking hold. One million pounds was set aside under the Church Building Act to construct new churches in London, the industrial Midlands and the north of England. These were known as the 'Million Churches'. This amount of money was

*St Mary, Marylebone, London. Thomas Hardwick's Greek Revival church has a steeple with a drum of free-standing columns supporting caryatids and a cupola – Corinthian columns on the portico, Ionic columns inside.*

woefully insufficient for all the work that needed to be done. It meant that economy was paramount, and the focus was on halls that could hold large congregations. The designs for what were known as 'Commissioners' churches' had to be approved by the authorities and were executed either as Greek Revival or a type of neo-Gothic that was inferior to that of the preceding century. These stereotypical 'Commissioners' churches' provided opportunities for many young architects who had previously been articled on public buildings and private houses. This was good on-the-job training in ecclesiastical conservatism and, because of the nature of the work, not too taxing. The potential attracted both amateur architects and others with little experience of church design. Many were quick to realise how the new need for

*Penzance, Cornwall. Designed by Charles Hutchens of St Buryan, built in 1832–5, the church has aisles as tall as the nave, and a galleried interior.*

173

churches might enable them to prove their worth in another area, establish their own practices and make their fortunes. Even so, a good many Gothic churches were designed and built in the provinces between the 1820s and 1840s, mainly by regional architects. For example, St Mary the Virgin, Penzance (Cornwall), was designed in the mid 1830s by Charles Hutchens of nearby St Buryan. St Gregory at Dawlish (Devon, 1824) was by local architect Andrew Patey, as was the neo-multi-period Victorian effort at Teignmouth in the same county.

There were, however, architects who had their own preferences. In 1844 Benjamin Ferrey (1810–80) built a wholly neo-Norman church at East Grafton (Wiltshire). William Railton (1801–77) worked in the provinces and favoured the Early English style; George Webster (1797–1864) spent a third of a century building and restoring churches in the north-west of England, and H. J. Underwood (1804–52) typified the Victorian approach to church building at the time. Peter Atkinson (1776–1843) spent a decade or so almost exclusively designing numerous churches for the Commissioners. He specialised in lancet windows, but his interiors were dull. John Loughborough Pearson (1817–97), the architect of Truro Cathedral (1879–87), had been in business for only two or three years when he designed St James, Weybridge (Surrey), in the mid 1840s. Forty years later, he was the architect of nearby St Peter, Hersham (Surrey). He was to become well-known, both as an originator of churches, of which his best work was achieved in the suburbs of London, and a restorer of cathedrals. Bristol, Canterbury, Chichester, Exeter, Lincoln and Rochester all felt the hand of Pearson. Truro came just after his spacious London masterpiece, St Augustine, Kilburn. Pearson built at times in Early English style and often in the French style of the thirteenth century, and he produced some of the very best nineteenth-century churches. These were frequently large and high, and many were distinguished by beautiful stone vaults with brickwork between the ribs.

Soon the clamour for 'correct' Gothic buildings favoured those who were prepared

*Hersham, Surrey. Designed in Early English style by John Loughborough Pearson, the designer of Truro Cathedral, and built of Bath and Bargate stone, 1886–7; the nave features alternating octagonal and circular pillars.*

*All Souls, Langham Place, Marylebone, London. John Nash's church of 1824 is an arrangement of circles: a circular portico of Corinthian columns, circular balustrade, and a circular drum of free-standing columns beneath the spire.*

to study and design in sympathy with the prevailing thought. Overall, the Commissioners' buildings came to be less favoured by the users. Later, various groups of thinkers formulated very definite views on the ways in which they felt architects should approach church design, and tried to impose their own criteria. The Church Building Society, formed in 1818 and incorporated ten years later, proved to be of great financial assistance in building and repairing Anglican churches.

In the thirty-eight years that followed the Parliamentary Commission there were as many Church Building Acts. Throughout the 1830s, most new churches had a Gothic flavour mixed with Georgian styling. Some early Victorian churches were of Georgian dimensions and symmetry, yet included Romanesque decorative motifs. This was followed by a brief flirting with architecture of the thirteenth century, but of a type that might have been influenced by several overseas sources.

The Act occasioned several London churches in classical Greek styles: notably Nash's All Souls, Langham Place, Marylebone, with its distinguished circular portico on Corinthian columns. Sir Robert Smirke (1781–1876), a pupil of Soane, travelled extensively in Greece and Italy. He settled on the style of the former for St Mary,

*Holy Trinity, Marylebone Road, Marylebone, London. The portico on Sir John Soane's south front has four Ionic columns, a square tower with paired columns at the angles, and, above, a tall cupola with free-standing columns.*

*Horbury, Yorkshire. The architect John Carr, who lived at Horbury Park, designed this classical south porch with its large pediment and Ionic pillars.*

Wyndham Place, Marylebone, where the portico, although semicircular, reflects Nash's design, and St Anne, Wandsworth. Others included St Luke, West Norwood, by Francis Bedford (1784–1858) and the imposingly Doric St Matthew, Brixton, by Charles Porden (1790–1863). Sir John Soane (1753–1837), the bricklayer's son who became England's great classical architect, designed just three 'Commissioners' churches'. Holy Trinity, Marylebone Road, Marylebone, has a portico with four Ionic columns, and a steeple not unlike several of Wren's. He also designed St Peter, Walworth, and St John, Bethnal Green.

Meanwhile, Gothic designs were creeping back into churches, particularly externally and in a non-structural capacity. This approach was used to give what some architects considered to be a sense of authenticity. A stonemason in his father's firm, John Carr (1723–1807) turned architect and builder and started developing a reputation for Palladian-style mansions, mostly in his native Yorkshire. By 1765, he turned his attention to churches, building that at Horbury (Yorkshire), and becoming one of the earliest of the Gothic revivalists. It was, however, a movement that did not achieve the anticipated success in its time. Very little church building took place during the latter part of the eighteenth century or the early years of the nineteenth. More pressing were matters relating to the French Revolution and the Napoleonic Wars. Architects such as William Porden (1755–1822) were designing Gothic buildings in the provinces. The industrial architect John Dobson (1787–1865) had a long career during which he either designed or rebuilt many churches in the north of England. Unlike the stricter architects to come, he began the nineteenth century by putting up Classical churches according to the fashion until about 1830, changed to early Gothic when this became fashionable and, later still, pleased the Ecclesiologists with good work in the Decorated style. During the second decade of the century, Henry Hake Seward (1778–1848) built a succession of small, simple Gothic buildings.

### The spirit of Gothic

It might be said that a Gothic revival began in 1813 when Sir James Hall published his *Essay on the Origin, History and Principles of Gothic Architecture*. Four years later, a self-taught Liverpool architect, who was one of the first to attract the Church Commissioners' patronage, Thomas Rickman (1776–1841), published *An Attempt to Discriminate the Styles of English Architecture from the Conquest to the Reformation*. This was a seminal work: a classification based on the gradual lowering of window arches. Rickman had been building Georgian-style, neo-Gothic churches since the start of the nineteenth century and continued to do so until about 1840. He was at his most prolific in the sixteen years from the formation of the Commission, working mainly in the Midlands, and remaining faithful to the Georgian plan.

Until Rickman, 'First', 'Second' or 'Middle' and 'Third Pointed' had been the definitions for the Early English, Decorated and Perpendicular periods, and his re-classification met with some opposition. Indeed, although Rickman had an unrivalled knowledge of medieval architecture, and presumably the kind of empathy with it that must have inspired his interest, he rarely built his economical churches in one or other of its styles. When he did, Perpendicular was favoured. Other architects, particularly Edmund Sharpe, divided Rickman's 'Decorated' into 'Geometrical' and 'Curvilinear' by the appearance of the ogee arch, and substituted 'Rectilinear' for the next period. All of these terms remain in common usage to describe styles within each of the two later Gothic periods, but Rickman's terminology was accepted. It was left to his contemporaries to give real impetus to the Gothic revival. The great medievalist Edward Blore (1787–1879), for example, was a big influence on the first half century of Victorian church architecture. He put up Romanesque, Early English, Decorated and Perpendicular churches.

## The movements of change

During the 1830s, two organisations were formed that proved to be a force for liturgical change in the established Church and influenced the architecture of the buildings. The Oxford Movement, otherwise called the Tractarian Movement, known by its supporters as the Catholic Revival, was founded in 1833 in response to the government's abolition of ten Irish bishoprics. The inspiration for the Oxford Movement was the 'National Apostasy' sermon which John Keble (1792–1866) delivered in the same year. Their subsequent printed *Tracts for the Times* were aimed at the clergy, although they were not approved by many of them, or by politicians. These works espoused High Church values and urged that theology, ecclesiastical history, liturgy and evangelism should be comprehensively studied as an integrated whole. The *Tracts* were begun by the Oxford vicar John Henry Newman (1801–90), who published several and determined with college fellow Richard Hurrell Froude (1803–36) to uphold the integrity of the Prayer Book.

Opposition was not surprising, because the Tractarians' aim was to elevate the Church above the State and re-establish the Church of England, with full Catholic doctrine and ritual, as a reformed member of the Catholic Church. Their standpoint was that a Gothic revival in church architecture was fundamental to a return to pre-Reformation forms of worship. They preached that the Church should ally itself to this as well as to religious doctrine and ecclesiastical history. The High Church approach was controversial, and sermons delivered in the provinces argued a case for the then prevalent Low Church alternative. There was also an evangelical element in the Anglican Church who believed that it was far more important for large numbers of people to hear what was being said in the pulpit, rather than to see High Church rituals being enacted in the newly favoured deep chancels. The churches that were commissioned from the Low Church architects were much less ambitious and, although Gothic in nature and form, nonetheless facilitated evangelical requirements. As topical matters of theology and ritual were now being openly aired through the pulpit, a wider cross-section of people was being exercised in the matter than at any other time. At the same time, the decline of standards within the church, and the need for a properly ordained priesthood, were also being discussed. Many of those being ordained were scholar priests of independent means. Their private wealth financed much church building and restoration. Newman eventually abandoned his stance on Anglicanism, embraced Roman Catholicism and was eventually created a cardinal. Meanwhile, the theologian Edward Bouverie Pusey (1800–82) joined the Movement in 1834, soon became one of its leaders and began to issue his own *Tracts*.

In 1839 an undergraduate named John Mason Neale (1818–66) became the founding leader of the Cambridge Camden Society. This was a group of ecclesiologists who were concerned with the science and study of church liturgy, archaeology, history, architecture, art, furniture and decoration. Their principle was that the form, practice and spirit of medieval religion were the blueprint for Christian architecture and worship. For them, medieval Gothic architecture was the only true Christian and inspirational type, and churches needed to be used as they had been before the Reformation. Hence they took their name from the scholar historian William Camden (1551–1623), whose approach to understanding the past underpinned the work of seventeenth-century historians. In 1586 Camden secured his reputation as a scholar by publishing *Britannia*, then *Remains Concerning Britain* almost two decades later. One of the Camden Society members was Richard Carpenter (1812–55), who built St Mary Magdalene, St Pancras (London), in Decorated style, exactly halfway through the nineteenth century.

Within two years, the Camden Society had begun publishing a monthly magazine, *The Ecclesiologist*, which was to last until 1868. In 1846 the Camden Society changed its name to the Ecclesiological Society, largely as a result of opposition to their High Church beliefs. The very nature of reviews in *The Ecclesiologist*, and its descriptions of the buildings and liturgy, positioned it as the major influence on how new churches were designed to facilitate the Society's preferred style of High Church ritual. This affected church design from the 1840s, and also the ways in which existing churches were furnished and arranged internally. Neale himself, a clergyman and composer of hymns, was also writing on aspects of church history and furnishings. In addition, the group issued a number of pamphlets that were fundamentally concerned with religious controversy. The Camden Society argued that everything has a beginning, middle and end: these equate with experiment, maturity and decline, with the middle section supreme as the most vigorous and pure. Applied to Gothic architecture, in terms of Rickman's classification, it meant that Early English was the experimental stage and Perpendicular was decadent. Decorated was identified as the most desirable, epitomising English Gothic at its best. Strict guidelines were

drawn that maintained that only original materials should be used to build churches. They also stated that the work should be done only by architects who were Christians with apparently impeccable morals. What had never been properly decided was the point at which medieval Decorated architecture was at its peak. If funds were available, a late Decorated/early Perpendicular transitional style was favoured. Elsewhere, some Norman or Lombardic-style churches were built in the 1840s, and these continued to be put up in country villages throughout the decade.

From 1833 the theoretical leader of Gothic Revival in England was Augustus Welby Northmore Pugin

*St Mary, Derby. A. W. N. Pugin converted to Catholicism in the mid 1830s, and this was the first Roman Catholic church he designed; it is in Perpendicular style and was built in 1838.*

(1812–52). He was the son of Augustus Charles Pugin (1769–1832), Wyatt's pupil, artist, architectural designer and teacher. Pugin senior published *Specimens of Gothic Architecture* in two volumes – a work that provided the inspiration for his son's own books. This, and other of his publications, were among the first to feature accurately drawn figures of medieval architecture. He also had his own pupils, notably Benjamin Ferrey (1810–80), who built St Stephen, Westminster, in the favoured neo-Decorated style of the late 1840s. Pugin junior was a brilliant eccentric, a convert to Roman Catholicism at the age of twenty-one, who was obsessed with the effects of morals on architecture.

In 1836 he began to provide Sir Charles Barry with architectural drawings for the Houses of Parliament and published *Contrasts: or a Parallel between the Architecture of the 15th and 19th Centuries*. This was also the year in which the Ecclesiastical Commissioners were established and were given wide controls over matters of finance and property. They also had the ability to pursue sweeping administrative reforms. Pugin's *Contrasts* included heavily biased illustrations ranging between what he believed to be the true Gothic as exemplified by Decorated architecture and the prevailing neo-Gothic. Pugin argued that fourteenth-century architecture in England resulted from the Christian faith in its purest form and was therefore the only true Christian style. In his values are the seeds of our own misguided conception of the Victorian attitude to religion. But Pugin was also seeking to demolish what he felt to be fundamental errors of taste in the work of some of the great architects who preceded him, and also in that of certain contemporaries. His suggestion that Perpendicular was debased to the point of being pagan might appear to be unjustified to our minds, and his theories may now appear confused. But they were born of his belief that the better society is in terms of Christian values, then the better the architecture that results. Such theories clearly have especial significance in church building. They certainly defined 'correct' Gothic for the Victorians and gave impetus to a programme of building that was no less ambitious than that in medieval England, even if it lacked its quality and spirit.

There were no half measures acceptable to the advocates of strict taste in the 1840s and, without a spirit of compromise, there was no doubt that by Pugin's conversion to Catholicism the Anglican Church lost what might have been an inspired source of new buildings. Pugin designed some Roman Catholic churches, including the cathedral of St George at Southwark. In 1841 he published another influential work, *The Principles of Christian Architecture.*

From that moment, people became wedded to Pugin's favoured medievalism and his conviction that, in matters both structural and spiritual, the Gothic approach was superior to the Classical. In this he had the support of the Ecclesiastical Commission, the Oxford Movement and the Camden Society.

*Cheadle, Staffordshire. In 1846, a decade after he was received as a Catholic, Gothic revivalist A. W. N. Pugin completed this church, adding golden lions – the symbol of the Talbot family, who commissioned the work – to its west door.*

*All Saints, Margaret Street, Marylebone, London. Built in the 1850s to the design of William Butterfield, leader in the Gothic Revival and the use of polychromy, in accordance with the ideas of the Ecclesiological Society.*

## Architects of revival

The Oxford Movement's greatest tangible embodiment was the kaleidoscopic and frighteningly ornate All Saints, Margaret Street, Marylebone (London), begun in 1850 and designed in the Decorated style by William Butterfield (1814–1900). Of exactly the same date is his much less impressive contribution at Yealmpton (Devon). An active member of the Camden Society, he designed both buildings and the furniture that went in them. More than any other architect, Butterfield built in the Gothic Revival style in an uncompromisingly individual way. His first important building was St Augustine, Canterbury, but it was All Saints that established his reputation. He chose natural materials in construction and natural colours. He used polychromy on an unprecedented level. This was the colouring of walls and other architectural features using different-coloured bricks, stone and marbles, etc, arranged to create an ornate surface pattern. St Augustine, Kensington (London), is another fine example of Butterfield's work. Polychromy became one of the main features of high Victorian Gothic. At All Saints, the colours come at you as if trying

*All Saints, Margaret Street, Marylebone, London. The structural polychromatic backdrop to the entrance courtyard; patterns picked out with coloured bricks contrast with the cream stone of the crisply pointed windows and the tracery.*

*Helmsley, Yorkshire. The murals in the north aisle were designed by the Reverend Charles Gray (vicar 1870–1913), were painted by Gast of London, and relate to local ecclesiastical and parochial history.*

to escape the reverential gloom of Victorian foreboding. Butterfield favoured lofty steeples, and his work could be angular and austere. Internally, he used a more permanent style of structural decoration, so even the passage of time hardly lessens the harsh effect on the eye.

Polychromy and garishness went hand in hand and, although some acquire a taste for it, others find it very difficult to reconcile such spirit with either the perceived attitude of Victorian England towards religion or the styles of medieval church architecture to which it is apparently attached. Pink and grey brick in juxtaposition, black and yellow, and honey and red were favoured amongst a seemingly endless palette of colours: bright roofing tiles, highly polished marbles of contrasting hues, and the seemingly ubiquitous encaustic tiles. The designers were so taken with the possibilities presented by the machines of the Industrial Revolution that they were blinded to the ghastly result. Polychromy is at its most unsympathetic in the bright, polished marbles that some of the artists set up against centuries-old stonework. The only way to tone it all down was to cover it over in much the same way as the original polychromy – the medieval wall-paintings – had largely been obliterated. In some instances this was done.

A revivalist who worked for the Commissioners in the provinces was Sir Charles Barry (1795–1860). He took time off between studying and setting up his own practice in 1820, during which he travelled to Italy and Greece, the Middle East and

181

North Africa. He returned to do a crash course in Commissioners' Gothic – a style in which he worked between 1822 and 1846 – and his first important church was St Peter, Brighton (Sussex). Barry was unsympathetic towards the Ecclesiologists' preference for deep chancels separated from the nave by high rood screens. Some of his churches were Italianate and, when the guidelines were tightened in the 1840s, he turned his attention to public buildings.

Sir George Gilbert Scott (1811–78), by sheer weight of numbers, did more than any other church architect to popularise the Gothic revival. A Pugin convert, he studied medieval architecture during the 1830s and then built profusely in those styles; at the same time he made his name as the originator of Tudor-style workhouses, together with W. B. Moffat. It is thought that, following his first church restorations at Chesterfield and Stafford in 1840, he had a hand in over seven hundred churches, although he offered little originality, and much of his work was dull. His first London success was the Early English-styled St Giles, Camberwell, and perhaps his grandest neo-medieval exterior is the much pinnacled and crocketed spire of St Mary Abbots, just off Kensington High Street. Nowhere in England is far from a church by Scott. By 1847 he was restoring Ely Cathedral, which led to around forty similar commissions. At Swindon (Wiltshire) Scott designed St Mark (1845) in Decorated style, and Christ Church (1851) in Early English; also of the latter period was his church of Holy Trinity, Cirencester (Gloucestershire; 1847). The canal network had helped to convey building materials greater distances, but the establishment of railways, which happened just as Scott got going, revolutionised the transport of freight. At the same time, wherever the railway industry established its works, or to a degree provided stations that helped to open up greater areas to settlement, new churches might be needed. As at Swindon, Scott could take advantage of this,

*Wilton, Wiltshire. Italian-style Romanesque with distinguished campanile, designed by T. H. Wyatt and D. Brandon and built in 1841–5.*

providing places in which the new railwaymen and their families, or increased populations, could worship. For him, there were no boundaries and he built, added to and restored throughout the length and breadth of the country. The architect did not cut an unopposed swathe, however. In 1877 William Morris, a trained architect turned decorative artist and poet, with a particular liking for Gothic architecture, founded the Society for the Protection of Ancient Buildings as a protest against what he considered to be Scott's drastic restorations.

Another active Ecclesiologist was Scott's former assistant George Edmund Street (1824–81), who paid considerable attention to interior colour and polychromy, and produced his best churches in high Victorian Gothic during the 1860s. These included the exceptionally ornate St James the Less, Westminster, built right at the beginning of this period, and, in contrast, the considerably more conservative, but nonetheless original, St Mary Magdalene, built near its end in Paddington (London).

Fond of the Italianate, too, was Thomas Henry Wyatt (1807–80), who designed the Lombardic parish church at Wilton (Wiltshire) in the early 1840s, in direct contrast to the edicts of the moment. At the same time, he was also building to Georgian proportions and undertaking wholesale restorations of little note. As time went on, a number of architects were influenced by the kinds of styles from abroad and use of materials that the Ecclesiologists had at first been unable to accept. During the 1850s Italian work became a brief inspiration in English church architecture, and in 1855 Street published *Brick and Marble Architecture of the Middle Ages in Italy*. The prominent Gothic Revivalist William Burges (1827–81), whose best-known contributions to small church architecture, done a decade before his death, are at Skelton (near Ripon) and Studley Royal (Yorkshire), went in for approximations of thirteenth-century France, a style that was more solid and simple than its Early English counterpart. Meanwhile, Scott's pupil George Frederick Bodley (1827–1907) was a major influence in reviving the late Decorated period. The churches at Eccleston (Cheshire), Hoar Cross (Staffordshire), Pendlebury (Lancashire) and Chapel Allerton, Leeds (Yorkshire), are examples of some of his best provincial work. Bodley began with simple Gothic and developed a more sensitive use of colour and materials than many of his contemporaries. His very best work followed Street's and was done between 1890 and the end of the nineteenth century. By the 1880s, architects were once again copying English work of the thirteenth, fourteenth and fifteenth centuries.

# Church furnishings and features

**Wall-paintings and dooms**

In 1871, what are believed to be the oldest church wall-paintings extant were rediscovered in the vaulted chancel, the nave and above the chancel arch at Kempley (Gloucestershire). They have been dated to the first few years of the twelfth century and were partly painted directly on to the wet plaster – which sections are therefore frescoes – and partly added after the plaster was dry. Even the ceiling of the chancel is covered, and the paintings include Christ in Majesty, the Evangelists, angels and various heavenly hosts, the world at its moment of creation, and a vast amount of symbolism. Early as it is, this painting clearly shows most of the elements that were to be included by the painters of church walls throughout the medieval period, and gives us a good idea of how completely all church interior walls were covered with what amounts to illustrated biblical teaching aids. It is now thought that all interior surfaces, including window splays, columns and capitals, were once painted.

Copford (Essex) is an example of wall-painting from the middle of the twelfth century to Victorian times. The pictures here include Christ in Glory, scenes from the New Testament, numerous biblical figures, and all manner of decorative motifs and symbolism. The tiny church at Inglesham (Wiltshire) also has paintings that were done between the thirteenth and nineteenth centuries, including a fourteenth-century doom on the east wall of the north aisle, and a range of written texts.

Of all the teaching murals that decorated the inside of the church in medieval times, those showing the Last Judgement – the so-called 'doom' paintings that

depicted the weighing of souls according to how they had led their lives – are possibly the most engaging. They were meant to instil a sense of right and wrong, and of fear. Dooms were usually created around the chancel arch, chosen because it stood above the portal between the secular nave, which belonged to the people and was therefore the worldly domain, and the chancel, which was occupied by the clergy. The paintings were made either directly on to the wall or on boards. Although most were whitewashed over or removed at the Reformation, a good number have been recovered – often together with other wall-paintings – during or after restoration in the nineteenth

*Kempley, Gloucestershire. Executed c.1130–40, the wall-paintings in the chancel are unique and amazingly beautiful. Christ in Benediction is the centrepiece of the ceiling, and the walls are packed with figurework and symbolism.*

*Above left: Pickering, Yorkshire. This fifteenth-century wall-painting of the martyrdom of St Edmund is one of a series that also includes a depiction of the Passion and moments in the lives of St George, St Christopher, St Thomas of Canterbury and St Catherine of Alexandria.*

*Above right: Breage, Cornwall. The large wall-painting of St Christopher carrying the Christ child, on the north wall.*

century. Some seventy are said to exist, including a number that are very large indeed, and very graphic in their subject matter.

The example at St Thomas, Salisbury, is typical. It shows the good souls that have been saved rising towards heaven, where Christ sits in Majesty, while the bad souls are driven towards hell – the place of the damned. The doom at Oddington (Gloucestershire) is on the north wall of the nave. At Clayton (Sussex) there is a benevolent God, painted early in the twelfth century, above the chancel arch, flanked by groups of white-robed apostles, with souls making their way in processions on the north and south walls. The 'ladder of the salvation of human souls', done at about the same time at Chaldon (Surrey), is a frightening illustration. It depicts the weighing of souls by the most fearsome creatures and shows the punishments that await those who do not get to climb the ladder to where the angels wait with a welcome to heaven. Cambridgeshire has some very explicit dooms. These include Great Shelford, where Christ sits with the instruments of the Passion, angels blow the last trump, Mary intercedes for sinners, and the lost souls are dragged in chains to hell. At Broughton (Cambridgeshire) there is a fifteenth-century version along similar lines, but with a number of other characters.

Fragments of wall-paintings, often single figures, are to be seen quite often, St Christopher being a popular subject. He is often shown, as at Breage (Cornwall), where he has adorned the north aisle since c.1470, carrying the infant Christ. Here, too, are paintings of St Hilary, the mythical Cornish bishop St Corentine, St Ambrose or St Gregory, and the Christ of the Trades. You are likely to encounter scenes from the Bible, cameos of the lives of the saints, depictions of the commandments, legends,

beasts mythical and imaginary, and morality and allegorical scenes – all done from the earliest times in red and ochre, and sometimes white, yellow and black. The fascinating fragments that remain on the walls at Barton (Cambridgeshire) are an amalgamation of the weighing of souls – which involve St Michael and the Virgin Mary – and scenes from Jesus' life, collections of saints, and knights and devils. Above the north arcade at Ickleton (Cambridgeshire) is a fine run of tableaux depicting martyrdoms and scenes from the Passion, painted in the twelfth century.

Wall-paintings were sometimes painted over or replaced with fresh images. At the Reformation and afterwards, the newly whitewashed walls were painted with biblical texts. In Victorian times, arcades were sometimes given colourful borders of running vines or diaper motifs, and occasionally friezes were painted the length of walls.

### Stained glass

The church at Fairford (Gloucestershire) has a full complement of twenty-eight medieval stained glass windows. They were made in England, probably using Flemish

painters, at the end of the fifteenth century, and are remarkably rich – in content, detail and colour. So important is this collection that the windows were removed at the outbreak of hostilities in 1939, stored in vaults beneath the house in Fairford Park, and put back in the church between 1945 and 1947. Together, they show us exactly what stained glass was meant to impart at a time when church services were conducted in a language that was incomprehensible to the lay worshipper, and when almost the entire congregation was illiterate. Here the life of Christ and the lives of the saints were illustrated; here were their deeds presented in graphic form, and in colours that changed and shifted to startling effect with the ambient light. At its best, as at Fairford, stained glass was all about manipulating the images with the play of

Above left: *Deerhurst, Gloucestershire. St Alphege was a monk here in the tenth century; his stained glass window is dated c.1450.*

Above right: *St Martin-le-Grand, York. One of the numerous panels in a large, five-light window whose fifteenth-century glass depicts scenes from the life of St Martin; in this one the devil carries his prayer book.*

light on colour, and bringing them to life.

It is likely that people discovered how to make glass, probably by accident, nearly three thousand years BC. Colouring was achieved using metallic salts and metal oxides. Cobalt oxide imparted shades of blue; copper oxide gave shades of red; greens and yellow were produced by iron oxide; manganese oxide produced purples. By the first century, windows were being glazed, and the Romans popularised coloured glass in their villas. By the end of the Roman occupation of Britain, window glass was being used decoratively, and there are examples of glass being used in English churches in the seventh century. Most early glass was pot metal – coloured all through while in a molten state – and this was imported from the continent until well into the seventeenth century. Pot metal was thick and contributed a dense colour that did not admit much light; this was eventually solved by thinly coating pieces of clear glass with coloured glass, a technique known as flashing. Flashed glass was typically red.

By the tenth century, the designs had become decorative and sophisticated, and were moving away from the single figures that had hitherto been depicted. The early work, too, was frequently confined to medallions, or took the form of dull grisaille diapering. This involved picking out the image in monochrome shades of mostly grey or brown, occasionally given a little colour by way of tints, and arranging the glass in geometrical order or patterns of lozenge shapes or strapwork. At Chartham (Kent) and Stanton Harcourt (Oxfordshire) there are notable examples, and more thirteenth-century glass adorns the lancet windows of Chetwode (Buckinghamshire). Small symbols and foliage were popular, and heraldic devices began to find their way on to windows in the thirteenth century. A favoured theme was the genealogical Tree of Jesse, which remained popular until the fifteenth century. Good examples of such windows can be found at Westwell (Kent), Margaretting (Essex) and Leverington (Cambridgeshire).

*St Wilfrid, Church Norton, Sussex. Modern glass, designed by M. C. Farrar-Bell in 1982, which shows wildlife to be found on the nature reserve created out of mudflats in Pagham harbour.*

By the fourteenth century, figurework had become a popular subject for windows, and, just as stone effigies were presented beneath decorated canopies in the body of the church, so were the stained glass figures enclosed in niches, canopies and the like. There is fourteenth-century glass in the Lady Chapel and clerestory at Edington (Wiltshire). The approach had hitherto been inherently atmospheric; by the fifteenth century, windows began to be dealt with as a whole rather than as a number of individual lights. Figurework became more realistic; and the scenes became more extensive, creating narrative windows. The scenes were frequently bordered with architectural frames of diaper patterns. Heraldry and symbolism became even more popular. There is fifteenth-century glass in some of the smaller lights at Chipping Campden (Gloucestershire); a fine collection may be seen at Long Melford (Suffolk), and there is some at Steeple Ashton and Lydiard Tregoze, both in Wiltshire.

Stained glass can look so vibrant because of any number of techniques used to create and make the pictures. For example, minute points of light were created by using a brush to stipple vitreous paint lightly on to sections of clear glass. In the fourteenth century, silver stain was added to the catalogue of reds, blues, violets and whites, which produced luminous gold and yellows when fired. It is silver stain that gave its name to stained glass. An example of the action of silver stain on blue, producing green, is evident in the fine fifteenth-century windows at St Peter Mancroft, Norwich. In contrast to being entirely fired through with colour, glass at this time was sometimes coated in it. The fifteenth century was also a time when lozenge-shaped clear quarries – square or diamond-shaped panes of glass – were decorated with heraldic devices, and any number of small creatures drawn on them. Saints remained popular subjects; there are thirty-two of them shown in the fifteenth-century stained glass at Winteringham (Lincolnshire). After the Renaissance, windows were treated to areas of coloured glass enamel paint. From then onwards, naturalistic poses, a better drawing of perspective, and the gradual move towards Classical architectural figures and motifs made the scenes much more realistic. Throughout the seventeenth century, roundels and quarries remained popular; there is fine heraldic glass of this time in Bath Abbey. Lydiard Tregoze in Wiltshire also has seventeenth-century glass.

Named individual glass-painters became well-known, and, from the eighteenth century onwards, they were often to sign themselves by way of monograms – the equivalent of mason's marks – in some corner of the window. This became particularly popular during the nineteenth century, when the art of stained glass window making re-emerged as medieval churches were restored. Well-known artists and craftspeople became involved in designing new church windows, and much devolved on the exponents of the Arts and Crafts Movement. C. E. Kempe, for example, signed himself with a wheatsheaf; a wheatsheaf with a tower marked the work of W. E. Tower.

There are many churches, such as Ludlow (Shropshire), that still have fine medieval stained glass windows, and many more that have only fragments of old painted glass in place, or windows that have been restored. Some remain from the twelfth and thirteenth centuries, such as that in Canterbury Cathedral that shows the miracles of St Thomas, everyday life, and the ancestors of Christ. There is a little glass from the thirteenth century in St John's Chapel in Cirencester church (Gloucestershire) and much good glass of the fifteenth century elsewhere in the building.

## Memorials

### Monumental brasses

The church at Stoke D'Abernon (Surrey) has several monumental and inscriptional brasses, including one of 1277 in the chancel: it is 6 feet (1.8 metres) in length, bears the likeness of Sir John D'Abernon, and is said to be the oldest church brass in England. Nearby is a family scene in brass, of 1592, depicting Thomas Lyfield and his wife and daughter in the clothes of the period. There are no brasses extant in England's churches from before the thirteenth century, and it is thought unlikely that there ever were. Brass sepulchral memorials were produced instead of stone- or wood-carved effigies.

They are made either of brass, or of a mixture of brass and bronze, or of latten, a brass-like copper alloy. There was no brass manufactory in England before the middle of the seventeenth century, so the material had to be imported, was relatively expensive, and was not readily available. For monumental brasses, the metal was milled into thin sheets; it was cut to the appropriate size; incised by chisel with the written and illustrative memorial; and riveted into an indentation in an underlying stone slab, sometimes on a bedding of melted pitch. The job was finished by working a black resin into the cut lines, and, in the case of intricate designs, by picking out the background ornamentation with colourful enamels. The early inscriptions were done in a Lombardic hand in the Norman French language; from later in the fourteenth century, Latin was used, then English done in a heavy script; Roman lettering became common after the Reformation.

Today, church brasses may typically be found *in situ* on altar tombs, in the floor of the building – often in the chancel – and about the walls, where they have most likely been relocated. They may be 6 feet (1.8 metres) long or 6 inches (15 cm). Some are demi-brasses, with just the head and upper part of the body shown, like the early fourteenth-century example of Sir Richard Boselyngthorpe at Buslingthorpe (Lincolnshire). Until the sixteenth century, the likenesses of the deceased were more likely to be representational, with perhaps some personally discerning feature, such as a moustache or beard; from the sixteenth century, a degree of portraiture was introduced into the faces. Many brasses are hidden by mats, other fixtures and fittings, or are in virtually inaccessible

*Northleach, Gloucestershire. Late fifteenth-century memorial brass showing the wool merchant John Taylor, his wife, Joane, and groups of children; beneath, there is a sheep standing on a woolpack.*

positions. A regular rectangular indent or matrix in a stone slab is a possible indicator of where there was once a brass that has since been moved, or stolen for the value of its metal. There are thought to be around four thousand brasses of all sizes and types remaining in England's churches.

Because they could be cut with the most intricate of detailing, church brasses provide a wonderful insight into a wide range of armour, civilian costume, symbolism and heraldry over hundreds of years. The early ones are of churchmen, or they depict knights in full armour; civilian clothes were represented from the fourteenth century. The carefully drawn likenesses of Sir Roger de Trumpington, 1289, at Trumpington (Cambridgeshire) and that made in the mid fourteenth century of Sir John de Creke and his wife Aleyne at Westley Waterless (Cambridgeshire) are good examples; both are so well done that each element of the armour worn by the men can be identified and named. There are brasses, too, of skeletons (Hildersham, Cambridgeshire, 1530); some represent babies (Lavenham, Suffolk, 1631), and there are oddities, such as the brass depicting a medieval Forest of Dean miner at Newland (Gloucestershire). At Crewkerne (Somerset) are two sixteenth-century brasses; one shows a monkey and the other is an hour-hand brass showing the exact moment of death.

There are many fine brasses around East Anglia, perhaps because of the medieval merchants who grew rich there on trade with the continent. Examples of good brasses, covering military and civilian types, and spanning three centuries, can be found at: Acton, Suffolk (Sir Robert de Bures, 1331); King's Lynn (St Margaret), Norfolk (Robert Braunds, 1364); Chipping Campden, Gloucestershire (Thomas Grevel, 1401; and Sir Baptist and Lady Elizabeth Hicks, 1629); Herstmonceux, Sussex (Sir William Fiennes (1402); Cobham, Kent (Sir John de Cobham, 1407); Felbrigg, Norfolk (Sir Thomas Felbrigg, 1416); Stoke Poges, Buckinghamshire (Sir William de Molyns and his wife Margaret, 1425; and Edmund Hampdyn and family, 1577); Childrey, Oxfordshire (several, from the early fifteenth century to the mid sixteenth); Northleach, Gloucestershire (John Fortey, 1459); Stoke-by-Nayland, Suffolk (Lady Catherine Howard, 1465); Cirencester, Gloucestershire (William Prelatte and his two wives, 1462, and Sir Richard Dixton, 1478); Little Easton, Essex (Viscount and Countess Bourchier, 1483); Lavenham, Suffolk (Thomas Spryng, 1486); Hunstanton, Norfolk (Sir Roger l'Estrange, 1506); Preshute, Wiltshire (John and Maryon Bailey, 1518); Blewbury, Oxfordshire (Alice and John Daunce, 1523); Plumstead, Norfolk (Sir Edward Warner, 1565); Hindolveston, Norfolk (Edmund and Margaret Hunt, 1568); Long Melford, Suffolk (Roger Martyn, 1615).

*Post-reformation memorials*

The whole approach to monuments and tombs changed dramatically after chantry chapels were removed and the Reformation took effect. Previously, effigies were laid on their backs and, while there was usually some symbolic representation of their status or main occupation on earth, that was

*Dennington, Suffolk. The Bardolph chantry chapel is surrounded by a wooden parclose screen with loft. The effigies are of William Bardolph (died 1441), with his feet on an eagle, and his wife, with her feet on a wyvern. William was treasurer to Henry V, and a hero of Agincourt.*

*St Botolph, Aldgate, London. Monument to Robert Dowe (1522–1612), a merchant tailor, whose likeness is presented in a niche beneath the armorial bearings of the worshipful company to which he belonged.*

not the main thrust of the pose. The whole piece was geared to the life hereafter. These recumbent medieval figures were reverently craving a passage into God's kingdom. Expressions were natural; the eyes were closed and the hands were either clasped in prayer, rested across the body or were placed at the sides. Fairly early in the sixteenth century, figures began to kneel. This was a pose to be adopted later by effigies of attendant weepers, as well as other members of the deceased's family, particularly children. There are excellent late sixteenth-century kneeling effigies of the main figures among a fine array of monuments in the church at Lydiard Tregoze (Wiltshire). Favourite family pets sometimes formed part of the tableau, the inclusion of animals formerly being mainly of a symbolic nature. Examples of these included the dog footrest, signifying a woman who had remained faithful to her husband, and the lion on which rested the feet of the effigy of a courageous man.

As religious thought declined in the laity, its place on monuments was often taken by a list of the reasons why the deceased should be eligible for a place in the Kingdom of Heaven. This was a verbose *curriculum vitae* in marble and stone, partly a reminder of the character that had been lost to those remaining, partly the inspiration for others to emulate during their time on earth, but also a catalogue of desirable human characteristics. Graphically, the styles of lettering were arguably at their flamboyant best, and the set of references that accompanied this lengthy catalogue of the deceased's worldly virtues was usually an exquisite accomplishment of the calligrapher's art. Nor were many wall memorials or the fashionable cartouches – stone likenesses of scrolls of parchment with their curled edges – treated much differently. Whatever excellencies could be squeezed into them were incised by impeccable hands. Such wall memorials were done in white, black or colour-veined marbles or alabaster, and frequently a combination. Both native 'marbles' and others imported from abroad were used. Individual features such as a cornice, shelf and columns were frequently made of black marble, in order to achieve the visual effect of a black border to the piece, when viewed as a whole. Black- and white-veined marbles and pure white marbles were favoured in the eighteenth century.

*Stow Bardolph, Norfolk. The wax likeness of Sarah Hare (died 1744) is kept in a mahogany cabinet in the family mausoleum; the effigy is dressed in her own clothes.*

*Lamport, Northamptonshire. Memorial to a benefactor; the monument by Scheemakers to Sir Justinian Isham, who died in 1737, having previously added a chapel beside the chancel, and under whose bequest all but the tower was rebuilt in the 1740s.*

Some wall memorials were small tablets that recorded the barest details, and they might be of almost any shape, although that of the sarcophagus became a favourite. Other memorials included only the arms of the deceased, set in a roundel or carved in relief above the inscription. More commonly, however, they adopted the Classical style throughout. The bearings were either placed within a triangular or segmental pediment, or rose through it. The cornice beneath might be supported by Classical pillars of any order, flanking the inscription, and the whole piece rested on a shelf with brackets below.

Coupled with this was a general increase in the size of interior memorials, in particular the amount of wall space the larger ones took up, and the overtly secular poses of the figures in them. No longer was heaven the supplicatory hope of pious men laid on their backs; these subjects were forcibly portrayed as they almost commanded their entry, on the basis of the lists that accompanied them. They stood, often surrounded by the tools or symbols of their trades, and were either depicted engaged in their calling or seemingly watching the church. Somehow, medieval monuments were always in keeping with the fabric of the church. But the great white marble monuments that went into medieval churches in the eighteenth century were always quite inappropriate. Many overpowering representations, built against a wall in the chancel or put up at the end of an aisle, still dominate otherwise small and unprepossessing country churches, in a very unsettling way. An example of this is the fine white marble monument of 1786 to carpenter Thomas Spackman at Clyffe Pypard (Wiltshire). From the late seventeenth century it became popular to dress the subjects of memorial sculptures in ancient Roman clothing, and later in Classical draperies. During the eighteenth century these likenesses became even more irreverent. The subjects might be heavily bewigged and given semi-recumbent postures. Beautifully dressed as many of them were, they nonetheless lolled about or adopted theatrical poses.

Nor were these Classical pieces confined to imagery of the deceased. Tombs and monuments might have moulded canopies in the form of open pediments, along the sides of which there might be reclining, symbolic figurework. These often represented some desirable aspects of the deceased's character, in which visual biographical representation they were not wholly removed from the medieval wall-painting ethic, the difference being that one had to have experienced a Classical education in order to appreciate the subtlety, so the information was being given to the peers of the departed rather than the general populace. At its apex, the pediment most likely had an urn finial, and either urns or vases were typically set up at the end of each sloping side. Beneath the pediment might be a cornice or full entablature, supported by Classical pillars of all orders. Chubby, winged angels, cherubs or medallions adorned canopies.

Free-standing urns might appear almost anywhere within the tableau, standing on bases that could be used for some forms of inscriptions. Classically draped angels and damsels were used structurally, decoratively and symbolically, sometimes as caryatids in the place of pillars, and often in the guise of corbels and brackets. Ribands, bows, garlands, curtains, swags, scrolls, floral motifs and strapwork were put up as cresting or supporting decoration. Any representation of the tomb was likely to be sarcophagus-shaped, with the deceased lounging upon it, seemingly engaged in conversation, reading or writing. Great attention was paid to clothing, draperies and the representation of soft furnishings. Figures would be dressed in some form of Classical costume and anyone depicted on the piece would appear to be very much alive. The sculptors particularly wanted the effigies to appear as comfortable in death as they would have been in their own drawing rooms. And latterly, the furnishings of such interiors were finding their ways into the family pews of the era.

## Hatchments

The other type of memorial commonly put up at the time was the hatchment. These were diamond-shaped mourning boards, the panels painted black and white, either singly or in various combinations to denote the type of person the deceased was, and his or her marital status or position. Central to the hatchment was the appropriate coat of arms, the elements of which were picked out in their usual colours. Hatchments were a visual record of the passing of a person of note, not unlike a modern-day illustrated obituary notice. They hung outside the deceased's house for several months, before being removed to the church, where they were usually put up in one of the spandrels of the nave arcade or on the interior of the west wall. Their design conformed to strict rules and used divided shield shapes throughout, except where a deceased spinster or widow was represented. In these cases, the single bearing that denoted the former and the split bearing representing the latter were done on a lozenge shape. In the case of a married person, the diamond was divided vertically down the centre; the man's arms were always to the left and the woman's to the

*Breamore, Hampshire. A collection of Hulse family hatchments, dating from the eighteenth century, adorns the walls of the crossing; this is said to be the most in any parish church.*

right. The bearings of the dead person were drawn on a black background, with a white background for those of the surviving partner. The all-black background and single coat of arms were used for a bachelor or a spinster; the widow or widower had a divided coat of arms against an all-black background. In the case of a deceased bishop, the lozenge was also split vertically, with the heraldry representing the see to the left on a white background, and the personal arms of the deceased prelate on a black background to the right. Only in the case of the late wife of a bishop were the arms of the surviving churchman set, together with hers, on the black background. Those of the see remained on the white background to the left.

## Coats of arms

Heraldry plays a prominent part in the decoration of individual elements in the church; it was important to the families involved and gives some insight into the social history surrounding the parish. However, it is of greater interest to the local historian and the liturgist than the church visitor or student of architecture. It might be said that the most fundamental bearings are the various sacred Christian symbols and emblematic or attributable heraldry ascribed to God, Christ, biblical characters and saints. All of this symbolism is worn like a badge and is present wherever Christian themes are depicted in carvings, stained glass and wall-paintings. Long before warriors and landed families were known by their armorial bearings, an arrangement of symbols was used to define and illustrate major characters in the history of Christianity.

There are two kinds of coats of arms most commonly seen in churches: royal arms and family bearings. Royal arms – and also those of the Commonwealth – were usually painted on boards or canvas and typically hang above the chancel arch, above a door, or at the west end of the nave. They are distinguished by the prominent crown, the emblems of the British Isles, and the motto. From the moment of Henry VIII's break with Rome, it became necessary to underline the monarch's acquired status and this was done by substituting the king's arms for the rood. All royal arms extant result from this act, and almost all monarchs are represented up to Victoria, although

*St Peter, Salisbury, Wiltshire. The royal arms of Elizabeth I.*

hers is rarely found. Queen Anne is popular, though her reign was short, and the arms of the first three Georges frequently appear. Palimpsest arms, in which the original has been once, twice or three times over-painted, can often be seen.

Personal coats of arms were incised into ledger stones, but most often appear in stained glass, on the sides of tombs, on wall tablets, on hatchments, on memorial brasses, and in the pediment or cornice above free-standing memorials. Stained glass typically has the bearings of important churchmen. The whole subject of coats of arms, crests, badges, insignia and cadency symbols to be found on church fixtures and fittings bears detailed study that is far outside the scope of this book. Often, the presence of coats of arms is a clue to who benefited the church, and an indication of when the parish was financially sound, and it is allied to some of the best work of the period to be found there.

## Seating

Seating was introduced into churches in the fourteenth century, although it was by no means universally applied. The design was developed from that of the wooden stalls in the chancel, although, unlike many of them, it was neither compartmentalised, ornamented nor canopied. Seating in the body of the church became more common during the fifteenth century and, once it had been designed, the shape of the common pew or bench never changed in anything but minor detail. These were fixed seats, overall some 3 feet (1 metre) in height, with a horizontal plank placed about halfway up, between two uprights known as bench-ends or standards. In early or rustic examples, the standards might comprise square-framed close boards with no ornamentation. The seats were typically narrower than the width of the bench-ends but, when wider, tended to have curved or chamfered ends. In examples of this type, the leading edge of the standard was cut away to allow the curved edge of the seat to be inserted. In the case of richly carved bench-ends, there was rarely a single top rail; in most other instances an integral bench and back rest was usually capped by a moulded top rail. Fitted at right angles to the back of each might be an armrest, to

*Dennington, Suffolk. The nave has box pews, and some finely carved bench-ends that depict animals and mythical beasts on the heads and the sides.*

support the elbows when kneeling. There was often an integral kneeler board below. Depending on the status of the church and available finances, the backs of pews were typically close-boarded, although some might have decorative carving such as trefoil-headed openwork, or blind applied tracery. The front pew might be carved in this way, even if those behind were treated less ostentatiously. Blind tracery was often featured on the back of the very last pew, which would be seen by everyone coming into the church, as at Morwenstow (Cornwall). The ends next to the aisles were decorated and those next to walls or wainscoting were left plain.

Often the pew ends were square-headed, although carved finials such as poppyheads or their derivatives, for example the winged angels at Talland and St Ives (Cornwall), were always popular. In contrast to the previously plain standards, an array of carved, panelled and traceried bench-ends was erected during the fifteenth and sixteenth centuries, nowhere with quite such exuberance and variety as in Cornwall. Those at Altarnun, of which seventy-nine remain, were put in place during the first third of the sixteenth century and are extremely richly carved. Late, too, are more than sixty bench-ends on predominantly religious themes at Launcells; over fifty at Gorran; the instruments of the Passion at Poughill; and others even later, but packed with saintly symbolism, at Kilkhampton. St Winnow has one that tells the story of the saint in a boat being blown to Cornwall by a strong wind. The jester appears at Mullion, where there is a wonderful set of bench-ends. At St Levan, tracery and floral motifs are mixed with fish, emblems of the saints, a shepherd and other local people. Other Cornish churches that have fine bench-ends *in situ* include Davidstow, which, like Altarnun, includes a man playing bagpipes, St Mawgan-in-Pydar and Morwenstow. Elsewhere in the county, they are often to be seen now built into some other fitting within the church. Cornish bench-ends are the equivalent, in wood, of medieval wall-paintings, although they are far wider ranging in subject matter. And they are very compulsive. A good comparison with the bench-ends at Altarnun might be the later examples at Braunton and High Bickington, both in Devon. The former includes a carving of St Brannock, carpenters' implements and reticulated tracery, and the latter is exceptionally intricate late Gothic.

*Stanton St John, Oxfordshire. The two kings are one of the unusual split poppyheads, carved in the sixteenth century on bench-ends in the chancel, where there are a number of other carved human and animal heads placed back to back.*

Above left: *Ashwell, Hertfordshire. The end of a stall, in typical poppyhead style, showing a fish, which, symbolically, is the oldest emblem of Christ.*

Above right: *Ivinghoe, Buckinghamshire. A mermaid poppyhead, typically the symbol for pride, lust and deceit, on account of her siren-like effect on human males.*

## Choir stalls and misericords

By the fifteenth century, most churches had a set of wooden stalls on the north and south sides of the chancel, and occasionally – when a screen was present – at the west end, facing the altar. Sometimes, they were put up in double rows, when the back section might be stepped up. Choir stalls tended to be more ornately carved in larger churches or those of monastic origin. Most had a moulded top rail. The vertical sidepieces that separated them into individual seats were, at their most basic, cut away to form simple armrests. At their best, they were equipped with well-formed rests known as elbows. All parts of the stalls might be moulded or decoratively carved, and the work was usually carried out more elaborately than on the bench-ends of the nave.

The poppyhead was favoured as a terminal; figurework, blind tracery, foliage, grotesques, and the likenesses of birds and animals were favoured decorative themes. Some sets of stalls had canopies overhanging the whole run; some had traceried or panelled backs; others were divided into bays, their sides and lower sections seeming to wrap themselves around the sitter; occasionally, the upper sections were pierced, pinnacled and bracketed out. In any of these cases, they might be individually canopied and possessed of much decoration.

If there was an aisle on either side of the choir, any screens that separated this from the chancel were readily used as the back of the choir stalls. Later, stalls were given bench fronts with a bookrest behind the top rail, and a kneeler board, and the front vertical surface was treated with pierced or blind tracery or panelling – depending on the preference of the period. The returns at the ends of the bench front frequently mirrored those at the ends of the stalls; they were intricately carved, and usually terminated in the characteristic poppyhead or winged angel derivative.

Associated with choir stalls are misericords, usually relics of a monastic past.

*Ickleton, Cambridgeshire. An intricately carved poppyhead finial, from the fifteenth century, showing St Michael weighing souls.*

These are hinged projections with carved supports and undersides, whose purpose was to give a little more rest to tired, elderly or infirm monks or clergy than they might otherwise get by just leaning on the arms of the stalls. These 'mercy seats' – named from the Latin *misericordia* – were not intended to be sat on, but to ease the legs of those officiating at the daily services. What makes misericords so appealing a subject for study is the generally more chunky way in which the brackets are carved; the variety of everyday animals, subjects and scenes they depict; the range of bestiary and allegory they included; their frequent irreverence and cheerfulness; and the symbolism designed into them. Perhaps because they are visible only when the bench of the stall is raised, carvers seemed to have been allowed a greater freedom of choice in how they decorated these fittings.

Misericords all follow a similar design. The projection is rounded for maximum comfort; the main carving is on its bracketed underside, and this is then continued into a downward flanking curve that ends on either side in a carving that links with the main theme.

*Ripple, Worcestershire. Some of the fourteen stalls with misericords, made in the fifteenth century; they mostly depict aspects of rural life throughout the year.*

*Ludlow, Shropshire. This misericord, one of thirty-two in the chancel, shows a mermaid with mirror, comb and dolphin supporters; the intention is to warn against female vanity when used to encourage lasciviousness.*

Hereford Cathedral has a fine collection dating from the end of the fourteenth century, showing a wide variety of creatures, real and imaginary, and scenes such as a boar hunt and medieval forms of punishment. Of similar date are those at Chester, and examples showing Old Testament scenes in the cathedral at Worcester. Among the parish churches that have fine sets of misericords, Ludlow in Shropshire is exceptional, having a set dated *c*.1420–50. The twenty-six in the choir stalls at Stratford-upon-Avon (Warwickshire) depict day-to-day scenes and also such fancies as unicorns, mermaids and mermen. There are more to be enjoyed at Great Malvern (Worcestershire), where some have representations of the months of the year. Southwold (Suffolk) has a set that was installed during the fifteenth century.

## Pulpits

Pulpits were introduced into England's churches during the fifteenth century, but it was well into the sixteenth before they became widespread. Most churches had one by the second quarter of the seventeenth century. Because of their assumed importance at the Reformation, there was then a sudden rush to equip all churches

*Lyddington, Rutland. Archbishop William Laud's reforms included a single-altar policy and a return to dignity in church services. So-called 'Laudian rails' were put up to help achieve both; these were erected in 1635 and, unusually, enclose the altar on all four sides.*

and to place the pulpit centrally in a most conspicuous position. Early examples had a hexagonal drum of carved panels, with a top rail and moulded cornice, a bottom rail and a slender stem. The style of carving on the panels indicates the age of the pulpit. From the end of the sixteenth century, an hourglass might be associated with it, encased in a cage made of wrought iron and either joined to the pulpit or held on a bracket attached to a handy pillar. They were intended to regulate the length of the sermon, but it is widely believed that, once the priest got into his stride, they were often simply turned over and the sermon carried on. There is still an original hourglass at Clyffe Pypard (Wiltshire). By the seventeenth century, the pulpit might have a curved stairway with a gracefully turned balustrade. A footstool would have allowed the preacher to see beyond the high-backed pews, and enabled him to be clearly seen and heard by the congregation. The pulpit sometimes had an integral hinged reading desk.

The focal point of the Georgian country church was the two- or three-decker pulpit with carved back piece and hexagonal tester, an acoustic sounding board that was often surrounded by a decorated frieze, which sometimes included drop pendants. Over the next century, these sounding boards gradually increased in size and height to the point where they were sometimes placed at roof level, and they became more highly decorated. They might be carved with foliage and fruit, running vines, sunflowers and doves, and were often gilded, cushioned and hung with velvet. The pulpit was made in oak or deal and was frequently equipped with metal candle-holders. Instantly recognisable are the Jacobean examples, frequently distinguished by their general design, dark colour and patina, and particularly their carved lunettes of decoration. Hardly any part of the surface was left uncarved, although the piece

Below left: *Astley Abbots, Shropshire. The Jacobean pulpit of 1633 has two tiers of panels with characteristic arches filled with carvings of rose bushes and grapes.*

Below right: *Thaxted, Essex. A light, airy interior provides a wonderful setting for this hexagonal, panelled pulpit of c.1680, with its ogee-shaped underside, slender stem and matching staircase.*

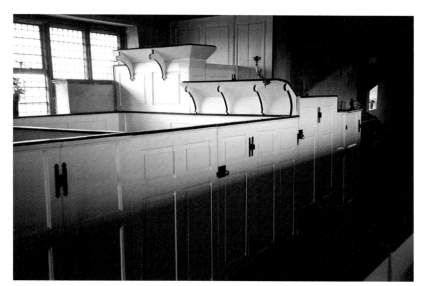

*Fairfield, Kent. The three-decker pulpit, high box pews and square-framed windows with clear glass were all put in when the older church was encased in brick in the eighteenth century.*

was designed rather as a symmetrical whole than as a series of panels. The arches contained a base figure, around which the carvers executed some figurework and angels' heads, but mostly strapwork, fruit and foliage. Even so, the term Jacobean is not precise, as it covers work done late in the Elizabethan era through to the end of the Carolean.

Three-decker pulpits were essential if the priest was to command the attention of worshippers in the galleries, those in the high and horse-box pews, and groups almost hidden away in their especially constructed family pews. There is a fine three-decker pulpit in the wholly eighteenth-century interior at Old Dilton (Wiltshire). The three-decker was arranged on ascending levels: clerk's desk, priest's desk or reading pew, and preaching pulpit. These sections rose almost horizontally, each with its own separate hinged door. In contrast to the recent Jacobean work, the Georgian panelling was mostly plain. In the provinces, it could also be quite rustic.

The priest looked over a room that was tightly packed with woodwork. Above him were the fronts of galleries. Tucked away in a corner was the squire's family pew, raised, carpeted, upholstered, and often with a fireplace. Beneath him was a collection of plainly panelled pews, all fitted with doors that were hinged and locked to keep out the draughts. These pews had bookrests, narrow-ledged seats, and, occasionally, drawers beneath. Galleries were built with their fronts facing the pulpit and might be curved and panelled, with biblical texts painted on the woodwork. The Lord's Prayer, Creed and Ten Commandments were put up in this way, or else they might adorn the panels of an altarpiece. Wooden panels bearing the names of benefactors and local worthies, particularly those involved in charitable bequests or almsgiving, were placed around the walls of the church.

### Lecterns

The purpose of a lectern – more properly the speaker's stand – is as a rest for the church Bible when in use, and they are typically found to the right in the nave when viewed by the congregation. Before the Reformation, they were located in the chancel. The basic form is of a sloping surface, bracketed out from a shaft, with similar brackets at the base. Each of these elements might be carved, moulded, or chased with an infinite variety of decoration, usually in keeping with the basic style of the church. Lecterns are usually free-standing and most commonly made of wood or brass, although they may be of polished stone; and the desk might have a sloping surface on two sides. This type is the most common, and the metal examples can be very ornate. However, birds – particularly the winged eagle that was considered to represent the Christian soul rising and able to soar nearest to heaven – was a commonly carved receptacle for the Bible from the thirteenth century. Indeed, the lectern is often a source of much symbolism. A pelican symbolises the Eucharist, as the female bird was said to sacrifice its own blood to feed its young. There might be dragons at the foot, suggesting that the word above, according to the Bible, could easily subjugate the representations of evil creeping around below.

## Chests

From the earliest times, churches needed to lock away their valuables in some kind of strong box. Feretories or reliquary chests were made to hold relics of saints; poor boxes, dole cupboards and alms boxes were constructed; boxes were built to keep

Bibles away from those who might make off with them; and there were secure depositories for 'holy tithes'. Each has in one way or another been a variation on the church chest, the general receptacle for church plate, vestments, minute books and parish registers. These might be up to 10 feet (3 metres) long. In Saxon times, chests were made of a hollowed-out length of tree, roughly squared off and fitted with a slab of a lid. These are known as dug-out chests or monoxylons; they were usually made of oak and are therefore virtually immovable. Furnished with bands of iron, big locks, and a good hammering of decorative but nonetheless intimidating nails, they were virtually

Left: *Cheddington, Buckinghamshire. A rare example of a seventeenth-century poor box with hasp.*

*Mildenhall, Suffolk. An iron-banded chest with three locks, made in the fourteenth century.*

thief-proof from the earliest times.

When boarded chests, made of planks, and with strap hinges, arrived in the thirteenth century, so too did at least the theoretical possibility of built-in weaknesses. The advantage of this type was that they were lighter and smaller, yet had a more commodious interior and could therefore store a greater amount of material. Large, longer planks were used at the corners so that the chest was raised off the ground. The sides were frequently carved, although at first rather simply. Thereafter, the ornamentation became more intricate, as did the surface plates of any metal locks used. Decorative roundels were carved into the surface, then tracery motifs. The next step was to tongue and groove the planks, dovetail in the corner posts, and then make framed chests.

Medieval chests usually had several locks, so that the keys might variously be held by the priest, the churchwardens, or even a trusted parishioner. In the fifteenth century, the parish chest became mandatory and all keyholders had to be present whenever it was opened. In practice, churches began to accumulate chests, and some had several. The more important might be round-lidded, heavily banded, hasped, and with independent locks. Panelled chests were a development in the late fifteenth century, which was also when linenfold panelling was featured. At the same time, the work of the village carpenter was increasingly enriched by that of a competent wood-carver, who added life to the surfaces. The most ornate, the so-called 'Flemish chests', were imported from continental Europe.

In the seventeenth century the characteristic dark-wood Jacobean chest appeared, and aromatic woods came into use. Walnut, so much easier to carve than old oak, came into fashion; a century later, it was mahogany that pleased the Georgians. There are chests still to be found in our parish churches that are of all types and from all periods from the thirteenth century.

## Organs

The legendary early populariser of the organ was the fourth-century martyr St Catherine of Alexandria, who was introduced into the Christian church in England by returning crusaders in the twelfth century. The inspiration for the instrument is considered to be panpipes, in which each pipe in a run is of different length and produces a single note. By the second century, bellows had been added to this arrangement, to supply the wind. It is also said that Pope Vitalian (reigned 657–672) made church organs popular. The origins may be obscure, but they were favoured by the Benedictines and were recorded as being in use at their religious houses in Abingdon (Oxfordshire), Malmesbury (Wiltshire) and Winchester (Hampshire) by the tenth century. A wind instrument that produces notes by the action of the air from bellows on pipes had been widely

*Brightling, Sussex. In 1820, John 'Mad Jack' Fuller financed this barrel organ, made by W. A. Nicholls, and the gallery in which it stands. It is the largest of its kind in full working order in England and was restored in 1999.*

used in churches since Norman times, using sliders that had to be drawn in order to open and close the pipes to the air. The early organs were portable devices that could be carried around by the player, and inflated by him during use.

The keyboard organ was also invented at about this time, and most larger churches had an organ *in situ* by the end of the thirteenth century. Pipes continued to be added, and, during the fifteenth century, the style of church organ was developed that is still in use today, using keys and pedals. Old organs in country churches may still have pumping handles that were used to fill the bellows with air.

The player sits in a console and has to hand up to five keyboards and another beneath the feet by means of pedals. Particular sounds are selected by stops, which operate a graduated range of organ pipes that have similar tonal quality. The keys and the pedals control a system of valves that force air across the pipes at a steady pressure; the vibration of the air combined with the individual characteristics of each pipe determines the character and the variations of each note. Shorter, smaller pipes admitting smaller amounts of air produce higher notes; lower notes come from larger, longer pipes. The organ is therefore a combined wind and keyboard instrument, usually within an attractive wooden case, constructed so that only the case and the pipes are visible.

Some churches now use the electronic organ, which was introduced in the mid 1930s, and which has no pipes. Harmoniums, a mid-nineteenth-century invention, are sometimes used in place of the conventional pipe organ, and some churches had its forerunner, the seraphine, which was invented in 1833.

The underlying principle behind the organ is simple, but the history of the instrument's development is long, the kit of parts is complicated, and the interrelated reaction between all the components of the modern pipe organ, and their relationship with the player, are technically complex. It is thought that for centuries the organ was exclusively used as a solo instrument, and not as an accompaniment for human voices. Throughout the medieval period, larger churches that had several chapels might also have had several organs.

The Puritans ousted most of the permanent organs that were in England's churches prior to the sixteenth century, and, although the instrument began to be restored to cathedrals and larger churches by the end of the seventeenth century, in villages

it was the local band that provided music for church services. Organs replaced these bands during the eighteenth and nineteenth centuries. Although there are a few early organ cases in existence, most instruments extant are no earlier than Victorian times. There are numerous instances of church organs having been rebuilt over the years. Organs are usually not described in church guide books, and tend to be mentioned only if they are uncharacteristically large or have been played by famous composers.

### Clock jacks

Clock jacks are mechanical human figures that were built to tell the time by hitting a bell at the appropriate moment with either a hammer, or with some implement that was more in keeping with the wielder's

*Wimborne Minster, Dorset. The quarter jack is dressed as a grenadier.*

costume. Thus, the late fifteenth-century soldier in the church at Southwold (Suffolk) – 'Southwold Jack' – holds a sword in one hand and hits his bell with an axe. The seventeenth-century 'Jack-o-the-clock' at Blythburgh, in the same county, also strikes with an axe. Neither one is *in situ*, nor do they perform their original purpose. Clock jacks are rare, and 'quarter jacks' or 'quarter boys', which strike every fifteen minutes, are even more difficult to find. There is one of these at Wimborne Minster (Dorset); it is a large figure, dressed as a soldier, and in command of two bells. A pair of quarter jacks were added, in 1760, to the mid-sixteenth-century tower clock at Rye (Sussex). However, those that now stand each side of the quotation 'For our time is a very shadow that passeth away' are twentieth-century replicas. The clock jack in the church at Minehead (Somerset) is called 'Jack-hammer'.

### Maiden's garlands

Maiden's garlands, also known as 'virgin's crowns', were traditionally composed of black and white paper rosettes on a framework of hazel wood. The custom originated early in the eighteenth century, and had all but died out by the end of it; at Abbotts Ann (Hampshire) it survived. Only spinsters were eligible to have their coffins preceded by maidens clothed in white carrying this symbol of the deceased's purity. The garlands were retained on display in the church, subsequent to the deceased's burial, for as long as no-one disputed the right of claim. There are survivals of maiden's garlands at Minsterley (Shropshire); at Matlock (Derbyshire), where a fine example is preserved in a glass case; at Ashford-in-the-Water in the same county; and at Ilam (Staffordshire).

Right: *Astley Abbots, Shropshire. This maiden's garland, with gloves, is one of several in Shropshire. It is said to have belonged to Hannah Phillips, a young bride who drowned on the eve of her wedding as she crossed the river to prepare the church.*

Below: *Thornham Parva, Suffolk. The painted retable, dating from the 1330s, is over 12 feet (3.7 metres) wide and is the largest surviving medieval altarpiece in England. The figures all have Dominican connections.*

# Churchyards

**The churchyard setting**

The churchyard provides the eye with a setting for the church. If the building itself has a plain exterior, it can be enhanced by the way in which the grounds are kept. One's first impression is largely influenced by this. Ecologists see the churchyard as one of the few places where natural life can develop as it should, and the study of fauna and flora in country churchyards is very rewarding. Others would like to see their contents recorded and photographed, and the ground levelled. One thinks immediately of Cornish churchyards, which, in general, are most attractive. They have two great advantages. They exist in a temperate climate that allows a great variety of subtropical shrubs and other plants to grow. Anywhere else these would be considered to be too exotic and tender. Then there is the intractable granite of which many Cornish churches are made. Since it neither takes readily to carving nor erodes easily, granite provides a perfect, plain and sombre contrast to the excesses of the churchyard flora, thus enhancing its visual value. Particularly along the coastal areas of Cornwall, it is difficult to discern, from any distance, many of the green-grey and brownish granite buildings that nestle amidst dense foliage in steeply banked hollows. St Just-in-Roseland is full of flowering shrubs and trees; Mylor, St Erth and Gulval are much the same.

At Broughton-in-Furness (Cumbria) there is an exceptional display of daffodils in their season. There are many examples of attractive churchyards throughout the Cotswolds. Visitors to the beautiful 'wool' church at Cirencester (Gloucestershire), situated right in the centre of this busy country town, might not realise that there is a churchyard at all. Everyone will have their favourites for attractive churchyards in fine settings. Some worthy contenders include: Ashton-under-Hill (Worcestershire), Astbury (Cheshire), Aylesbury (Buckinghamshire), Blanchland (Northumberland), Bottesford (Leicestershire), Branscombe (Devon), Brockham (Surrey), Cardington (Bedfordshire), Cavendish (Suffolk), Chiddingfold (Surrey), Dedham (Essex), Dereham (Norfolk), Exton (Rutland), Fingest (Buckinghamshire), Fritton (Norfolk),

*Aylesbury, Buckinghamshire. The extensive churchyard in the centre of the town; the thirteenth-century church is built above the remains of an Anglo-Saxon crypt.*

*Kersey, Suffolk. The village street slopes upwards from its ford towards the imposing flint tower of 1481; the fourteenth-century church has a fine porch roof and a medieval screen, and there is an attractive lychgate at the entrance to the churchyard.*

Great Salkeld (Cumbria), Hawkshead (Cumbria), Hopesay (Shropshire), Keswick (Cumbria), Kirkoswald (Cumbria), Leigh (Surrey), Lenham (Kent), Lower Peover (Cheshire), Nether Winchendon (Buckinghamshire), New Buckenham (Norfolk), Oadby (Leicestershire), Oare (Somerset), Painswick (Gloucestershire), Rydal (Cumbria), Snowshill (Gloucestershire) and Taynton (Gloucestershire).

There are some places, too, where the church provides a setting for the churchyard: where it so dominates the skyline that it acts as a backdrop in the distance. This may be by reason of the church's dominant position, in juxtaposition to other buildings, as at Aldbourne (Wiltshire) and Kersey (Suffolk), or at Avebury (Wiltshire), where a deep and wide churchyard separates it from the road. The large Suffolk 'wool' churches are fine examples of this: churches like Lavenham and Long Melford, and Blythburgh, which benefited from the fishing trade. There are many churchyards that provide a vantage point for fine views of the surrounding countryside. Wroughton (Wiltshire), for example, is built on a hill that overlooks the urban sprawl of nearby Swindon, commanding excellent views of the countryside to the north and north-west, and of its industrial neighbour to the north-east. It is always worth looking outwards from a country churchyard to try to get some idea of what the view might have been like when the church, or its predecessor, was built.

Understanding what is around us, and beneath us, in the churchyard is not simply a matter of digesting what is in close proximity, or even in the immediate vicinity, but – particularly if the churchyard is ancient – it must be looked at in relation to the surrounding countryside. In selecting his sites and erecting his buildings, ancient man thought in a way that is unknown to us, and in consequence his intentions are frequently misunderstood. His reasons continue to baffle archaeologists. In trying to visualise what he may have seen, we may gain some understanding of his actions. But as we are unable to feel the external and internal forces and factors which prompted him to venerate certain areas and make them of religious importance, we shall perhaps never unravel many of his mysteries.

There are fine views to be seen from churchyards all over the country, includ-

*Bisham, Berkshire. The River Thames flows past this predominantly flint-built church with its chalky Norman tower; there are good monuments inside.*

ing: Alston (Cumbria), Arley (Worcestershire), Bobbing (Kent), Brampton Ash (Northamptonshire), Bromfield (Cumbria), Delamere (Cheshire), Eaton (Leicestershire), Frindsbury (Kent), Grasmere (Cumbria), Hammerwich (Staffordshire), Herstmonceux (Sussex), Kenley (Shropshire), Kirkby Lonsdale (Cumbria), North Kilworth (Leicestershire), Patrington (Yorkshire), Penn (Buckinghamshire), Prees (Shropshire), Tanworth-in-Arden (Warwickshire), Thornton (Leicestershire), Willingale (Essex) and Woodhead (Derbyshire).

The most pleasant settings are those that merge with their surroundings and do not jar the senses. There are those in which the church, churchyard memorials, buildings and walls are in the same materials, or those that are similar. Bibury (Gloucestershire) is such an example. The most harmonious in the landscape are those built in local stone. They may have long since closed their churchyards for burials, except, perhaps, for interments following cremation. The stone will have mellowed and eroded to the extent that the cursory glance cannot detect work in the individual features spanning perhaps hundreds of years. Churchyards not long closed, or still in active service, will almost certainly have been invaded by foreign marbles. Here and there, one may come across unconventional designs marking individual graves. Concrete cubes, 'marble' circles, rough chunks of stone with inlaid small brasses, and inset photographs are all too frequently found.

In the great span of time, putting up a personal churchyard memorial is a relatively recent innovation. The idea was first in the minds of the rich, simply because they could afford it, and they may have been benefactors of the church; they were important members of the community, leaving behind a reminder of the fact. The Victorians took monumental masonry out of the hands of the local craftsman, standardised designs and displayed them in printed catalogues for universal public consumption, and they set up showrooms. The headstone became available to all, and it is comforting to feel that, by marking the spot of interment with a tangible reminder of the deceased, the memory may linger longer. And, psychologically, it may be equally as comforting to some to know that they will have an established plot on earth for all time. This is the theme that has constantly cropped up in churchyard art. The tradesman is depicted with his tools, as if he may require evidence of his calling on the other side, as at Lewes (Sussex), where there is a fine example from 1747. Writers are often shown with quills and paper; masons have a hammer and chisel. Many were given the benefit of written virtues, which accompany them as some kind of reference.

Individually commemorated burials have both advantages and disadvantages. They give us the opportunity to discover and study memorial design and calligraphy, their fashions and artistic influences. They tell us exactly where certain people are buried, but only if still *in situ*, and this is important to people who may come from far away, seeking an actual site but having no directions beyond the boundary wall. Thousands of weather-stained, lichen-encrusted, eroded tombstones, which were once put up with the best of intentions, now tilt their fractured legends at the sky. Memorials may not necessarily lean because they are exposed to high winds, although some headstones in Cornwall are buttressed for this reason. Trees are living and expanding things, and their roots will eventually break up the soil around nearby monuments, causing subsidence. This will, in turn, tilt headstones and may place stresses on other monuments where there were never intended to be any. As a result, these may begin to collapse. There are many churchyards in which modern headstones have been placed too close to trees, and equally as many that illustrate the foolishness of doing so in the past. They also show how unwise it is to plant adjacent trees and large shrubs after a memorial has been put up. An unsightly churchyard spoils the setting for the church, but what to do with the memorials that cause the problem may be an expensive decision.

The problems of nature are less acute in 'churchyard extensions' but – perhaps because of this – there are more aesthetic considerations. Churchyard extensions are those pieces of land, adjoining established churchyards, which have been secured for further interments close by the church. They should not be confused with municipal cemeteries, which are not discussed in this book. In the extension, the monuments are most likely to be no earlier than the twentieth century, arranged in neat lines, and composed of various 'marbles' with black, white or silver lettering. Apart from the

*Long Sutton, Lincolnshire. The tombstone of a thatcher, showing combs, bats and hooks that were the tools of his trade.*

good order of things and overall uniformity, the most striking difference, as one passes from an old churchyard into the new extension, is likely to be the lack of foliage. The trees, bushes and shrubs which had such important and symbolic meaning to our ancestors, and which gave the churchyard its character, seem to have little place in the neat arrangement of the extension. The occasional rose bush will have been planted, but most of the colour will come from chippings. Individuals – and even this may be of pagan origin – may sometimes plant holly or laurel bushes on single plots. But this does nothing to enhance the setting either of the grounds themselves, or of the church, churchyard and extension as an integral unit.

## Mounting steps

The approach to the churchyard may pass one, two or three ascending steps, the so-called mounting steps or blocks used to help riders get on their horses. The steps were usually placed near the main entrance to the churchyard, or close to the church porch, and were likely to have been set up near to the church by a lord of the manor, primarily for the use of his family. Such steps are invariably hewn out of a single block of stone, and arranged so that they are at right angles to the roadway. It is unlikely that they were ever moved, once put into place, so a set beside the porch in an enclosed churchyard suggests that there was no wall when they were put up. Hence, they will be early examples of their type, as usually evidenced by the considerable degree to which each step has been worn to a deep, smooth curve. In some cases, the middle sections of risers may have all but eroded away. There are nice examples at Altarnun (Cornwall), Bockleton (Worcestershire), Chollerton (Northumberland), Fairfield (Kent), Kirkland (Cumbria), Lowther (Cumbria), Germoe (Cornwall) and Stokesay (Shropshire). There is a double set around the churchyard wall at Broadway (Worcestershire), and four steps by the gate at Ightham (Kent). It was quite common for the vicar to stable his horse in the churchyard.

## Lychgates

The main entrance to many churchyards is beneath a roofed structure called a lychgate. At Troutbeck (Cumbria) there are three, and Stoke Poges (Buckingham-

shire) and Bockleton (Worcestershire) each have two. The name is derived from the Anglo-Saxon word *lich*, meaning corpse or body. The Prayer Book of 1549 required the priest to meet the deceased at the entrance to the churchyard and there conduct the beginning of the burial service. Poorer parishes that could not afford a gate might make do with flat steps at the entrance. There are several examples of these in Cornwall, as at Zennor and Germoe, which also has stone seats for the bearers. The gate at the point of entry into consecrated ground became known as the corpse gate. It provided rest and shelter for the bearers while they were waiting for the priest, and for all who were officiating in the early part of the service. Once the party was ready to move on, the parish bier was fetched from the church, where it was normally stored, and was used to convey the body to the graveside. At Walpole St Peter (Norfolk) there is a portable 'hood' which could be placed over the priest when officiating at the graveside in bad weather.

*Brookland, Kent. A portable grave shelter, made of wood.*

*Bolney, Sussex. The long and narrow coffin stone within the heavily timbered and engineered lychgate with curving braces and wing-swept roof.*

Some lychgates incorporated seats along their length. They were mostly of the bench type and were made of stone, but there are two fine examples made of slate at the entries to the churchyard at St Just-in-Roseland (Cornwall). Other bench seats were made of wood. The corpse or coffin was rested on an oblong wooden or stone support called a coffin stone or corpse table, or less commonly on a three-legged coffin stool. The structure at the entrance to the churchyard at Mylor (Cornwall) has a large granite stone flanked by stepping-stone stiles and stone seats, but the lychgate itself belongs to the twentieth century. A huge, roughly hewn granite boulder serves the purpose at Luxulyan (Cornwall). At Bolney (Sussex) there is an example of a well-made and nicely proportioned coffin stone that is long and narrow.

It is difficult to date lychgates accurately and many are not made of the same materials as the church or the boundary wall. A few remain from the Middle Ages, their oak posts and supports pitted vertically and bleached by the elements to a silver grey. Two of those known to be medieval are Anstey and Ashwell, both in Hertfordshire. That at Boughton Monchelsea (Kent) is dated to 1470 and is supposed to be the oldest extant in Britain, although the lychgate at Limpsfield (Surrey) is also ancient. Most date from the seventeenth and eighteenth centuries and were sometimes made out of the old timbers of the belfry or church roof when these were rebuilt, or when the church was enlarged or restored. One such is at Painswick (Gloucestershire). Many were put up more recently, as memorials to events, groups of people, or even individuals. They may commemorate a vicar who restored the church or added to it by his own artistic endeavour, usually in the nineteenth century. They may recall some local worthy or benefactor, perhaps put up by a spouse or family shortly after the

*Ashwell, Hertfordshire. The delicately timbered medieval lychgate.*

deceased was buried. Lychgates were particularly favoured as memorials to men from the parish who perished in various international conflicts. Queen Victoria's jubilees occasioned a great number of lychgates. Those put up during or since Victorian times frequently have a neat brass plaque on them, bearing the essential details of their dedication. On older ones, there may be religious texts or phrases cut into any plaster work, or carved on horizontal beadwork or bargeboards. Vertical woodwork, if decorated at all, often included continuous floral motifs, and these are also to be found in the spandrels of any windows. Betchworth (Surrey) has a fine structure: wide and high with beautifully decorated bargeboards, and a neat cross cut into the apex. There is a carved lychgate at Battlefield (Shropshire).

Most lychgates comprise a gabled roof of roofing tiles, wooden shingles, horizontal boards or thatch, supported by an arrangement of openwork beams, braces, struts and vertical side members. Arched braces were frequently used in the sides of the structure, whether or not it was otherwise boarded or enclosed, and the whole was executed in varying degrees of workmanship. In longitudinal section, the roof arrangement tended to be a simple king-post, queen-post or open roof-truss type. Some have shaped or carved bargeboarding in the gables, and the woodwork stands on a low wall base of bricks or stone. Before the construction of the canal system, and later the railways, materials used in building the lychgate depended on what was locally available.

The most common types of lychgate have the roof ridge either along the same axis as the passageway beneath, or at right angles to it. In others, two roof ridges cross at right angles, inevitably seen as symbolic, and put up by a parish with more money to spare. The lychgate at Clun (Shropshire) has a four-gabled, tiled roof. That at Fleet (Lincolnshire) is thatched. Sometimes the lychgate was built into a house at the point of entry. Others have rooms or dwellings above them which might have been used by the priest, or as a school room, parish room, library or store. Examples of such buildings are at Long Compton (Warwickshire), where the thatched room over the gate has a chimney and is a half-timbered construction in stone and brick, and Bray (Berkshire), where the room is of brick and timber. Painswick (Gloucestershire) has a plaster and timber building without gates, but with bells carved on the bargeboards. The seventeenth-century lychgate at Wendron (Cornwall) has a granite room above. Slate-hung upper rooms can be seen at Feock, Kenwyn and St Clement, all in the same county. At Ilsington (Devon) the tiled upper room rests on pillars and is larger than the space beneath: it has leaded windows on two sides, a chimney, and a niche containing a statue. The gateways at Hartfield (Sussex) and Penshurst (Kent) are both partly beneath the overhangs of adjacent timber-framed medieval dwellings. That at East Meon (Hampshire) is roofed in stone, and the wholly timber structure at Horton (Staffordshire) was built in 1902.

Occasionally, one comes across a double lychgate with a central support, and some lychgates are considerably wider than the majority. At Bolney (West Sussex) the roof has a wide sweep, like the wings of a bird. It reaches almost to the ground on either side, and the structure has wide, curving braces and is supported by little stone walls. Weston Turville and Chalfont St Giles, both in Buckinghamshire, and Burnsall (North Yorkshire) have double revolving gates on a central post. They are controlled by the action of weights that are suspended to one side on chains over pulleys. The gates at Friston (Sussex) and North Cerney (Gloucestershire) swivel, as do those of the sixteenth century at Hayes (Middlesex). The idea behind the centrally pivoted tapsel gate was that the bearers could negotiate it with ease.

Barsham (Suffolk) has a fine thatched lychgate with timber-framed plasterwork above the lintel, and a carved figure in oak on the centre post. The lychgate at Clifton (Derbyshire), which has little side lights, is famed for its large clock in the gable. At Ightham (Kent) is a double gate, which also has a walkway to one side. At Little Marlow (Buckinghamshire) the double, swinging lychgate is worked by a pulley.

*Weston Turville, Buckinghamshire. A double revolving gate that is controlled by a ball weight and pulley system.*

The beautifully rustic structure at Anstey (Hertfordshire) is tiled and has a little brick room with a massive, studded oak door to one side. The roof is supported by huge posts of oak. The gate at Yateley (Hampshire) is dated 1625, and that at Rostherne (Cheshire) is dated 1640. Staple (Kent) is also seventeenth-century work. There is an early nineteenth-century example at Llangadfan (Powys) and the lychgate at Seale (Surrey) is dated 1863. The lychgate at Overbury (Worcestershire) is a building of note. It has a tiled roof, and the pleasing arrangement of curved braces, supported by a low stone wall, surrounds a large coffin stone which has the proportions of a fine chest tomb.

The distribution of lychgates does not follow any pattern. One of the strangest examples is the combined lychgate and bell tower – a solid, three-stage support for a steeply pitched belfry – which was put up at the entrance to the churchyard at Great Bourton (Oxfordshire) late in the nineteenth century. Interesting lychgates, of later date, include Clifton Hampden (Oxfordshire), built in 1844; Downton (Wiltshire), with its traceried bargeboarding dated 1892; and the Art Nouveau design of six years

*Little Marlow, Buckinghamshire. The double swinging lychgate is operated by a pulley.*

later at Stackpole (Pembrokeshire). Also Victorian is the gate at Bitteswell (Leicestershire), while that at Shere (Surrey) was designed by Lutyens in 1901. Lychgates are sometimes erected as war memorials, as at Plumpton Wall (Cumbria).

## Boundaries and gates

If the churchyard does not have a lychgate, it may be entered by a stile, either a simple wooden or iron gate, or one with some device that admits people, either singly or severally, but keeps out animals. The ball and chain drop-weight type, such as may be seen at Compton Greenfield (Gloucestershire), was designed for that purpose. So, too, were the 'Cornish stiles', one of which can be seen at Zennor (Cornwall). There is a slate stile at Morwenstow in the same county. A tumble-gate allows entry into the churchyard at Chedzoy (Somerset); and Fingest (Buckinghamshire) has two seventeenth-century wishing gates in its boundary wall. Skenfrith (Monmouthshire) has an upright slab set back into the upper part of the wall, and two stone steps below in order to reach it. At Hungerford (Berkshire) there is a five-barred stile.

Churchyard walls are worth investigating. Seale (Surrey) has an old stone wall around a sloping site. The wall at Escomb (Durham) is circular. The upkeep of 'God's acre' was charged to the parish, which, in medieval times, had to enclose it and keep it in good order. They did so with boundary walls which prevented high churchyards from spilling on to surrounding, lower ground, with dry-stone walls, yew hedges and, later, brick walls. The last, as at Farley (Wiltshire), were sometimes put up to match the construction material of the church. Where individuals were responsible for the upkeep of the boundary wall or fence, their initials may appear inscribed on stones or cut into the fence supports. At Herstmonceux (Sussex) each farm in the parish was at some time responsible for the upkeep of a certain length of churchyard fence, which, accordingly, is made up of a number of short runs with double posts. Walls were built not only to contain the ground within, but also to keep out animals. One of the most pleasing forms of walling is the ancient art of herringboning, such as may be seen at Tintagel (Cornwall). The name is derived from the pattern formed when layers of thin stones or bricks are placed diagonally, and the horizontal rows incline alternately to the left and right.

Some churchyard walls mark the extent of the parish boundary and may have in them a stone bearing the initials of a vicar. St Levan (Cornwall) has a stile in the wall

*Wotton, Surrey. Sheep creeps in the wall are a reminder of when livestock was commonly allowed to graze in the churchyard, in order to keep the grass short.*

*Wroxeter, Shropshire. Roman pillars relocated in order to support the churchyard gate.*

and a cross. The most pleasing to the eye are dry-stone walls: layers of flat stones held together not by mortar, but by the pressure of one stone on another and the craftsmanship of the builders. Such walls are usually wider at the base than at the top, where they may be finished with coping stones. More sophisticated examples may have a filling of smaller stones between the outer layers, and may be strengthened by occasional, flat 'through stones'.

Pathways should not be taken for granted. Some are still only worn tracks. Others may be of gravel, pebbles, concrete, tarmac, flagstones or even headstones. Church-yards, particularly in towns, may in modern times have been turned into gardens of remembrance, or they may have one associated with them, as at Madron (Cornwall). Others have been made over to the local authority, either in part or in whole, under deed of covenant, for the purpose of maintaining a municipal precinct garden.

Wrought-iron gates are always worth more than a cursory glance. They usually admit a fair amount of decoration, and even low ones are likely to include an amount of simple scrollwork, but there is nothing outside the church to match the quality of the screens within. This is strange when one considers the fine ironwork that village blacksmiths were fixing to doors as early as the thirteenth century, and the beautiful gates, now centuries old, that mark the entrances to private estates. Certainly, the most intricately made gates are likely to be Georgian. There is a fine pair, dated 1700, at Ashburton (Devon). The gates at Kendal (Cumbria) are surmounted by a riot of bifurcated 'S' scrolls, a motif that also appears on the openwork gateposts. There is a frieze of horizontal 'S' scrolls, which is repeated on the double lock rail below. Each gate has ten verticals, the spaces between, at the foot, being further divided by an arrowhead dog rail. Dog rails were always a feature of openwork gates, irrespective of the material in which they were made. Malpas (Cheshire) has a fine set of gates, made variously throughout the eighteenth century. From the same period are the two gateways with ornamental vases on the posts at Wem (Shropshire) and those at Padstow (Cornwall). The gateway at Stapleford (Nottinghamshire) is Victorian, as are the fine iron gates at Castlemartin (Pembrokeshire). Any lamp holder set over,

215

or close by, the churchyard gate is worthy of inspection as it may prove to be the only remaining Victorian or Edwardian example thereabouts.

## A look around

There are two churches in one churchyard at Swaffham Prior (Cambridgeshire), Evesham (Worcestershire), South Walsham and Reepham (Norfolk), Willingale (Essex) and Alvingham (Lincolnshire). At Trimley (Suffolk) two churchyards, each with a church, adjoin each other. Some churchyards may have an area that is known by another name, perhaps that of a 'lost' village or nearby hamlet which never had a burial ground of its own.

There may seem to be a ditch between the church and the churchyard. This is known as a 'dry area', and in many places it became a necessary excavation in the nineteenth century. By that time, a churchyard that may have been in constant use for around eight hundred years would have risen high above the base of the walls. This could cause damp, and even structural problems. The walls had to be dug out at their base, dried out and given space and time in which to breathe. It is sometimes obvious where this work has been carried out, but the trench has subsequently been allowed to fill in again. There will still be a shallow depression.

It is well worth looking around the churchyard for unexpected objects. There are two standing stones in the churchyard at Rudston (Yorkshire). One of them, undoubtedly of pagan origin, and around which there is the customary superstitious legend, is over 25 feet (7.5 metres) tall, with an unknown length underground. There is a strange arrangement of two mutilated shafts flanking four semicircular stones in pairs in the churchyard at Penrith (Cumbria). A chance find in any churchyard could be a piece of medieval masonry that may never before have been seen so close at hand. In the churchyard at Colyton (Devon) there is the frame of a medieval window. At Iffley (Oxfordshire) there is an ancient font bowl in the grounds. At Stroud (Gloucestershire) is the former top of the spire.

*Covehithe, Suffolk. Too large for its community, the medieval church was partly demolished in the seventeenth century, although the tower was retained as a coastal landmark. A thatched nave was built on to this in 1672, within the ruins of the old church.*

*Brightling, Sussex. The early nineteenth-century pyramid tomb of John 'Mad Jack' Fuller, folly-building politician and philanthropist, who was allegedly placed inside sitting upright wearing a top hat and holding a bottle of claret.*

It is a good idea to walk right around the outside of the church before going in, to see what you can find, both on the ground and in the walls of the building. Often you will see where bits were once built on, or built up to a different height, discernible by the pitch marks of a former roof against a tower wall, or by masonry that has been blocked up at some point in its history. At Dacre (Cumbria) there are four lumps of stone, each shaped and carved to represent a bear in some activity with a cat. Braunstone (Leicestershire) has a carved figure that appears to be a pagan fertility symbol and may well have been the object of worship there before Christianity. Naseby (Northamptonshire) has a large copper ball which was once on top of the spire. What is thought to be a seventh-century stone, but of unknown origin, inscribed *Noti noti*, lies at St Hilary (Cornwall). Several other churchyards in that county contain interesting inscribed stones of almost any age from the fifth century. Examples can be found at Lanivet, Phillack and St Clement. In one corner of the churchyard at Germoe, also in Cornwall, is a roofed seat known as St Germoe's chair. At St Levan (Cornwall) there is a broken rock on which the saint is supposed to have rested when tired from fishing.

A cursory glance around the churchyard will often identify anything that is odd or seemingly out of place. At Brightling (Sussex) there is a pyramid to Mad Jack Fuller; Sharnbrook (Bedfordshire) has an eighteenth-century mausoleum with wrought-iron gates, and there is another at Stone (Staffordshire). Madron (Cornwall) has a mausoleum from the nineteenth century. Bromham (Wiltshire) has a Celtic-style cross to Thomas Moore the poet, and at Dalham (Suffolk) is Sir James Affleck's obelisk. There is another from the eighteenth century at King's Norton (Leicestershire). An eccentric, pyramidal monument in the churchyard at Pinner (Middlesex), topped by a casket lid and open at the base, has an empty coffin shape protruding from each side above the ground. There are also, here and there, detached mausoleums reputed to belong to local saints, such as at Holyhead and Llaneilian (Anglesey). At Patshull

*Semley, Wiltshire. Bronze churchyard memorial to Lieutenant-General D. I. Armstrong (died 1915), shown mounted and wearing a tropical helmet.*

(Staffordshire) stands the stone statue of a man in armour.

In one corner of the grounds at Elkstone (Gloucestershire) is a former priest's house that has fifteenth-century windows. Small stone dwellings of this nature are common and may be seen near to the churchyard boundary wall in many places. There are stone buildings in the churchyard at Downholme (Yorkshire). Thaxted (Essex) has an almshouse within the churchyard, and the nineteenth-century alms-houses run alongside the churchyard of Christ Church, Swindon (Wiltshire). The chancel arch from an earlier church is in the grounds at Distington (Cumbria), and Bodmin (Cornwall) has the ruins of a fourteenth-century chapel. There are parts of a former church, too, at Prestbury (Cheshire). There is an early eighteenth-century gabled house of brick in the churchyard at Diseworth (Leicestershire) and a brick building at Chaddesley Corbett (Worcestershire). The churchyard at Uppingham (Rutland) includes a school, as well as some stonework from an earlier church. The site of an altar in the original church at Hersham (Surrey) is marked by a rectangular commemorative stone in the grounds. There is an early nineteenth-century school building in the churchyard at Wraxall (Somerset).

Occasionally, little huts survive as a reminder of the days when freshly interred bodies were sometimes dug up and delivered to students of anatomy. In areas where there was insufficient money to pay a watchman, a huge stone might be placed on the new graves. It would take several men to move such an object, and so it would stay in position until the corpse was no longer fit for medical purposes. These stones may sometimes be found lying around the churchyard. Watchmen's boxes can be seen at Wanstead (London) and Warblington (Hampshire). At Selborne, in the same county, some of the graves were built with brick walls to discourage body snatching. Henham (Essex) has an iron cage. The most common protection for graves was the stone or iron vault known as a mort-safe. There is still one at Aberfoyle (Stirling, Scotland).

There are a number of dole stones. These are slabs – often the tops of chest tombs situated near the south porch – either made for the purpose of distributing a charity, or set aside for it. Wealthy people sometimes bequeathed a sum of money to the parish so that bread could be bought and distributed among the poor. This took place at the graveside of the benefactor, either on the anniversary of his or her death, or on some other appointed date during the year. There is one that seems to have been purpose-built, decorated only by a cross at either end, at Potterne (Wiltshire). Another is in the churchyard at Dundry (Somerset), and that at Saintbury (Gloucestershire) has an octagonal surface on an octagonal support.

## Detached towers

The largest building in the churchyard, other than the church itself, may be a detached or free-standing tower, belfry or campanile. No bell tower is in a more romantic position than the small thirteenth-century structure, with its slate, pyramidal cap, built into a rock, right on the sea edge at Gunwalloe (Cornwall). A low tower of the same date, but with a gabled roof, is also built into a rock at Lamorran in the same county. Henllan (Denbighshire) is also built on a rock. There is a free-standing bell turret faced with shingles at Combe (Berkshire), a two-stage structure with all-round, lean-to roofs. These form an aisle around the interior arrangement of beamwork. There is a square stage above, and a pyramidal cap.

In marshlands, where the ground was not compact or solid, the weight of a whole tower might cause structural problems. The fabric might break up during settlement, or the tower might collapse. In building towers away from the church, in areas where there might be problems of this type, the builders were at least ensuring that any shift would not endanger the main fabric of the building. It is probable that a number of western towers, irrespective of their location, were not originally planned as an integral part of the church, as they are now, nor were they so erected. Although detached, they were built on the same plane as the nave, which was later extended to meet them. This occurred at Terrington St John (Norfolk). Elsewhere, one may discern awkward joints in the masonry where towers, which now open on to the nave, were once buttressed on their east face – a sign that they were formerly detached.

Although builders feared that the collapse might damage the rest of the church, some substantial detached towers were put up only a few feet from it. Others were erected as far away as 70 feet (21 metres), as in the case of West Walton (Norfolk). At nearby Terrington St Clement the tower just meets with the church at its north-west angle but may be considered as detached, being originally built as such. Also in Norfolk is the detached round tower at Little Snoring, the Norman survivor of a church which is no longer there. A

*Dereham, Norfolk. The detached, four-stage bell tower of 1536, with angle buttresses.*

*Long Sutton, Lincolnshire. The tower has no parapet, but a lead spire and octagonal corner turrets above the belfry stage; internally, much of the church is Norman.*

four-stage structure was put up at Dereham (Norfolk) in the sixteenth century. Tydd St Giles (Cambridgeshire) is another church that seems to have all but banished its tower, a thirteenth-century building with an upper storey of fifteenth-century brick, standing some 50 feet (15 metres) to the south of the main building. At East Bergholt (Suffolk) there is a very rustic-looking, single-storey bell house beside a church that has an incomplete tower. The bell house has a grille of wooden banding above timber boarding on its side, and the whole is topped by a steep, pyramidal roof with a louvred top. There are two detached towers in Suffolk: at Bramfield the circular tower is to the south-west of the church, and at Beccles there is a huge Perpendicular structure with battlements and niches, lying to the south-east of the church.

The steeple at Fleet (Lincolnshire) has a three-stage tower with a stair turret, embattled parapet, and stepped and gabled buttresses. Above is the spire, connected by flying buttresses. It was built in the fourteenth century to the south-west of the church. At Long Sutton, in the same county, a lead spire rises above the thirteenth-century, three-stage, detached tower with its lancet windows and octagonal turrets at the belfry stage.

*East Bergholt, Suffolk. The single-storey bell cage has timber sides and a steep, pyramidal roof with a louvred top.*

There is a detached, wooden turret at Wix (Essex). The fifteenth-century tower at Standon (Hertfordshire) was built away from the church, to the south-east, and was later connected to the chancel by an organ chamber. In Bedfordshire, there is a massive, vaulted, detached tower at Marston Moretaine, built diagonally to the church in the fourteenth century. In the fifteenth century, the four-stage, battlemented tower was put up at Elstow (Bedfordshire). There, a stair turret rises above, there are two two-light bell openings on each face of the belfry stage, and the whole is surmounted by a sharp spike.

The detached tower at Ledbury (Herefordshire) has a spire. Other examples in the same county are the fourteenth-century tower at Richard's Castle, which has a pyramidal roof; a thirteenth-century tower with lancets at Bosbury; and another of the same date at Garway. The last is big and unbuttressed, with a pyramidal roof, and, in the seventeenth century, was connected to the nave by a covered passageway. There is a timber-framed belfry on the detached tower at Holmer, and a timber bell stage on the belfry at Yarpole. Perhaps the best-known of the detached buildings in Herefordshire's churchyards is the belfry at Pembridge. In Gloucestershire, there is a detached thirteenth-century tower with spire at Westbury-on-Severn; and at Berkeley the tower was put up in 1752 on medieval foundations. The tower at Lapworth (Warwickshire) was built in the fourteenth century, attached to the north-east angle of the nave.

The two remaining detached buildings in Wales are the fourteenth-century belfry with its pyramidal cap at Bronllys (Powys) and a tower that was once part of an earlier church but now stands alone at Llangyfelach (Glamorgan). Apart from those already mentioned, Cornwall has a tower that was built on to thirteenth-century masonry to the south of the church at Talland. It also has one of the thirteenth century, with a pyramidal cap of slate, at Feock, and another similar at Gwennap. The belfry at Mylor is made of wood and has a gabled roof, and there is a fifteenth-century tower at Illogan that has lost its church. At Brookland (Kent) there is a magnificent wooden structure that was built in the mid thirteenth century; there is nothing else like it, and it stands close by a church of great interest to the visitor. There is a campanile

*Elstow, Bedfordshire. The four-stage, battlemented, detached tower with its sharp spike and high stair turret was built in the fifteenth century.*

*Brookland, Kent. The octagonal detached wooden belfry has a conical roof in three sections, and dates from the latter part of the thirteenth century.*

on an adjacent hill at Kirkoswald (Cumbria). At Chiseldon (Wiltshire) the tower porch, although not quite separate, has the south clerestory running behind it and is virtually detached.

## Fauna and flora

All churchyards support an amazing amount of wildlife. Some species, like house sparrows, or the swifts that swirl and dip around the tower during the day, and the bats that do so at night, make their homes on or in the church. Bats, usually the pipistrelle, might sometimes be seen hanging from the beams of the roof. An owl may flap away as one enters the churchyard, or remain to scrutinise from a distant gatepost; it might even be seen inside the church, sitting on some lofty tester. A skylark might have its nest amidst the churchyard grasses. Botanists and naturalists might be encountered enthusiastically poking around where the ground is damp or it slopes into a ditch that is partly filled by stagnant water. Artists, too, come to sketch or paint the wild flowers that grow in the grounds. Not only will there be plenty to choose from, but the subjects may often include rare species that are no longer readily found elsewhere in the locality. Sometimes whole groups of artists may be seen at work in large churchyards such as Lavenham (Suffolk).

It is not difficult to understand why the range of fauna and flora is so good, or why there may be species of plants growing in the churchyard that may not be native to the area. Even in rural parts, the churchyard may be the last small patch of ground that has not been cultivated, apart from, perhaps, an annual haymaking. Any seeds dropped by passing birds or carried on the wind may there stand the best chance of re-establishing themselves in the area. Plants known to be native thereabouts, but now no longer widely seen, may still remain in the churchyard, where they stand their best chance of survival. If this is true of the country churchyard, how much more noticeable and important are these factors in the precincts surrounding a town

*Deerhurst, Gloucestershire. Early in the year, snowdrops cover much of the churchyard in this isolated spot next to farmland.*

church, in whose environs pollution may otherwise have exacted a heavy toll.

Perhaps the most beautiful and most primitive form of plant life in the churchyard is likely to be a type of lichen, adhering to stonework or trees. The colour varies, depending on the area, but it is usually in shades of grey, green, yellow and red. Lichen is a slow-growing association of fungus and alga that reproduces when spores drop from one growth to the other, providing that the cells of both come into contact. The resulting crust grows by feeding on the atmosphere, which is how it manages to cover large areas of apparently barren rock or stonework. Its method of feeding means that it is particularly sensitive to air pollution and will not grow

*North Leigh, Oxfordshire. Lichen-encrusted headstones and kerbstones show how clean the air is in the churchyard.*

where there is a high level of sulphur dioxide, such as in towns. But it does not need water to survive and is extremely long-lived. Look for lichen on the walls and roof of any old country church, on monuments and stonework in the churchyard and on the stone walls surrounding it.

Churchyard walls provide shelter for a great deal of nature. Mosses and fungi grow from them, and saxifrage may have taken root in the crevices, along with pellitory – 'herb of the wall', a perennial with green flowers. Look for frogs and toads at the base, where it is likely to be both warm and damp, and do not, on a hot afternoon, be surprised to encounter a grass snake or an adder, basking in the warmth of a broken-down wall. A snake might also be seen on a grassy bank, where the churchyard has been artificially built up to a higher level, for extra burials, and then slopes sharply away.

Churchyards that include mature conifers will usually attract more unusual birds. The little goldcrest is particularly at home there, as are blue tits and greenfinches. Apart from nesting in the trees, some species feed on the berries. Birds such as the tree creeper will nest inside loose bark, while woodpeckers nest within the trunks. If the churchyard includes beech trees, one may see jays, which are particularly fond of beech nuts. Any tall trees, such as elms and oaks, will attract colonies of chattering rooks and crows, and elms – now sadly much depleted – are a great favourite with jackdaws, woodpeckers, kestrels and wood pigeons. Oak trees have a particular religious significance, as the Celtic druids worshipped in their groves. The trees themselves provide food for many species of insects, which, in turn, feed a variety of birds, such as the nuthatch. Among the roots, and in the boles of the larger trees, as well as along the hedges, there may be wood mice, shrews and bank voles, and perhaps hedgehogs and rats. While the smaller mammals forage for insects, grasses and seeds, they will be preyed upon by weasels on the ground, and owls and kestrels from above. Among the smaller trees may be hazel, lime and ash.

Evergreens have long played a significant part in religious ceremonies, and it is not accidental that churchyards are frequently full of them. The red berries produced by several species have symbolic associations with the blood of Christ. Most churchyards have some ivy, and very many seem almost to be held together by it. Like holly, which also appears in churchyards, it may have had some significance in pagan times, when both were used as decoration. Ivy is the all-embracing vine, ubiquitous in early church art. Left to its own devices, it quickly spreads over monuments and walls, entwines itself around trees, and inextricably conjoins with brambles. Within,

*Worth, Sussex. The avenue of trees leading from the sixteenth-century lychgate is known as 'the Ten Apostles'; the church has a semicircular apse and is built on Anglo-Saxon foundations.*

*Newland, Gloucestershire. A wide and spacious church with a graceful fourteenth-century tower, wide aisles and chapels, and Perpendicular windows; nearby is an oak tree that is said to be the largest in England.*

and beneath it, will be insects and grubs in profusion, which will attract the small animals and birds that prey upon them. Brambles, too, have their visitors: butterflies enjoy the soft fruit, as do wasps and other insects, most of which are to the taste of blackbirds.

Gosforth (Cumbria) has a cork tree that was planted in 1833. There are elms at Ross-on-Wye (Herefordshire) and lots of rose bushes at Boughton Monchelsea (Kent). St Newlyn East (Cornwall) has a fig tree growing out of the churchyard wall, and there is a spina Christi tree at Herstmonceux (Sussex). The willow at Ashburton (Devon) is reputed to be descended from one in St Helena; and at Colaton Raleigh (Devon) a colony of bees has lived in a hole in the sandstone tower for as long as anyone can remember. North Luffenham (Rutland) has a walnut tree, and at Sharnford (Leicestershire) there are limes. A cedar grows at Norton (Kent) and Barham (Kent) has beeches. Often the pathway to the churchyard is lined with trees of one type: poplars, limes, laurels and beeches being favourites. The east London churchyard at East Ham was developed as an educational nature reserve.

## The ubiquitous yew

A seemingly essential feature of the churchyard, especially in southern England, but also elsewhere in soil that is chalky or where there is limestone, is *Taxus baccata* – the evergreen native yew tree. In southern areas, there was little choice – the yew being almost the only suitable species. It has a characteristically fluted trunk and gnarled branches, and its dense foliage may engulf large areas of the churchyard. But it may be clipped almost without limit and, as found necessary in the case of many aged examples that have grown dangerously out of shape, will withstand major tree surgery. Some smaller churchyard yews are kept in order by gentle topiary and are frequently clipped to a conical shape. But wherever they are found, yews set the scene in the churchyard. Their height in the foreground or middle distance often balances that of the church, and their characteristic odour pervades the grounds. They seem to be solid and peaceful, the close nature of the foliage providing cool cover on hot sunny days.

225

There are enormous or aged yews all over the south of England. Fine examples exist at Selborne (Hampshire), Wilmington (Sussex) and Crowhurst (Surrey). Many are genuinely eight hundred years old, although church guidebooks often claim an astonishing age for their yews. Certainly some may be older than the nearby church. Pre-Christian use of the site may have included pagan ceremonies in which the foliage of the yew tree played a part. Legend associates the frequency of churchyard yews with evergreens that supposedly gave shelter to the earliest Christian missionaries. Yet they were considered to be sacred before such holy men made their marks, the evergreen foliage being symbolic of everlasting life. In *The Forest Trees of Britain*, published in 1903, the Reverend C. A. Johns conjectured: 'There is a far greater possibility that at the period when crosses were erected in these sacred spots as emblems of victory over death achieved by the Author of our faith, the yew tree was stationed not far off to symbolise, by its durability and slowly altering features, the patient waiting for the resurrection by those who committed the bodies of their friends to the ground in hope.'

Many yew trees were planted by the clergy after the Conquest. Edward I also decreed that this should be done to protect the building from the elements. Yews were usually planted on the south side, one near the main pathway through the churchyard, and another on the way to a secondary entrance. Planting them opposite porches helped to protect the doorways. Medieval longbows and staves were said to have been made from yew wood, although it is doubtful whether much of it came from village churchyards. Large quantities were imported, and the only association the churchyard may have had with yew wood in weaponry was when the grounds were used for archery practice. The suggestion that arrows were made locally from this wood, certainly on any sort of commercial basis, has long been refuted. Yet the yew's incredibly slow rate of growth gives it an elasticity that makes it suitable for all the items mentioned. Villagers would have carried the foliage during Easter processions and spread it over graves. It would have been placed beneath corpses, either on the ground or in the coffin. Yew foliage would never have been found inside the house as, indoors, it was considered to be a harbinger of death.

*Mells, Somerset. The yew alley leading from the north side of the church to open farmland beyond; memorials in the churchyard were designed by Lutyens, who also suggested the planting arrangements.*

The oldest tombs and headstones will often be found under the dense umbrella of foliage created by a spreading churchyard yew. They may have been put there when the tree was just a sapling. Sadly, although its compact foliage and low, spreading habit protected such memorials from the elements, it also hid any secular and unauthorised activity around them. It also helped to encourage neglect – out of sight, out of mind. Tombs and headstones thus hidden are consequently often in a poor state of repair and disarray or may have graffiti on them. Sometimes, this may be quite interesting, for vandalism is by no means a recent innovation. For the researcher into family history, a single churchyard yew might hide a large piece of genealogy.

This venerable plant has not always been seen at its best. In 1854, a *Rural Encyclopaedia* said: 'This tree has usually been seen by the present and last generations of Britons in a state of tortured growth or in an old, declining, or diseased condition... it used to be planted in and near burial grounds in Britain in the same way as the cypress is in other countries, but... it is now seldom employed in that way; and when the auracarias and the many recently introduced pendulous and fastigiate trees become better known, it will probably lose altogether its sepulchral association.' The yew will repay a study of its bird life, for the berries are not poisonous to birds, as the foliage is to cattle. Indeed, a yew hedge was sometimes planted to deter cattle from entering the churchyard.

There is a famous yew tree at Edington (Wiltshire). Most ancient ones have an element of folklore about them. Some are associated with sheltering ghosts at night. At Wroughton (Wiltshire) it is said that a ghost may be raised by walking three times around the tree and pushing a pin into its trunk. The ninety-nine neatly clipped yews at Painswick (Gloucestershire) are world-famous. They were planted at the end of the eighteenth century, and legend insists that it is impossible to grow one hundred. At Broad Clyst (Devon) there are yews all around the churchyard; at Barford (Warwickshire) they line the path to the porch; and at Dunsfold (Surrey) they form a tunnel. Those at Preston (Lancashire) are reputed to have come from the Garden of Gethsemane. Other notable yews can be found at Iffley (Oxfordshire), Helmdon (Northamptonshire), Ulcombe (Kent), Darley Dale (Derbyshire), Tangmere (Sussex) and Stoke Gabriel (Devon).

*Painswick, Gloucestershire. In a churchyard that has some of the county's best tombs there are also these clipped yews, allegedly ninety-nine in number.*

### Medieval and later use

To appreciate how the medieval churchyard developed in a way we might now consider to be improper, we must try to understand how people thought five hundred years to a millennium ago. They were variously subjected to pestilence, plague, hostilities and impermanence. Their life expectancy was hardly half our own. In the early days, their minds were in turmoil, grappling with a need to substitute their fears with their hopes for the all-embracing God, and striving to reach him. In addition, the parish was responsible for the upkeep of the nave, and the priest had to look after the chancel. And so, in the course of time, matters of a secular nature became – for a while at least – inextricably mixed with the more religious. In a way it embodied the true meaning of the community spirit.

In 1287 a Synod of Exeter decreed that secular pleas should not be heard in the churchyard. There is no evidence that this was effective, although churchgoers sometimes petitioned against excessive noise in the churchyard while services were taking place. The main culprit was a common market: vendors and pedlars spread their wares for sale on the tops of table tombs. Horses stood around in the churchyard, and cock fighting took place on consecrated ground. Just as the medieval church was used for all kinds of religious and secular business, people saw the churchyard much as we might now consider the village hall; it was open to almost any event, depending only on its physical dimensions. Naturally, while the churchyard was held in freehold by the priest, it was to his advantage to foster such feelings and activities from which he might supplement his income.

Bells were sometimes cast in the churchyard. With the perils of travel to be considered, and the high cost of transport, it was often more convenient to cast them on site. In this way, bell founders established themselves in new areas. Prayers were said over the bells as they were made. Certain parts of the ceremonies associated with baptism, marriage and burial began in the churchyard, and in some instances concluded there. People frequently passed through on their way to transact business in the church porch: this was considered to be a right and proper place in which to make agreements of a binding nature. Parish notices were also displayed in the porch. As a church might have been used as an armoury or a wool store, depending upon its location, the grounds would often have been visited by tradespeople and merchants associated with these. Town churches, in particular, sometimes served as places of business for guildsmen. They might have been libraries, or places where local children received schooling from the priest. Matters of tithes were resolved

*Long Melford, Suffolk. The Lady Chapel was used as the village school between 1670 and the early nineteenth century; this multiplication table in the east wall is a relic of the later date.*

there, and inquests took place within their walls.

Itinerant merchants set up their stalls beside the church; strolling players, mummers and musicians performed, and miracle plays took place. There were many children's churchyard games, of which fives is probably the best-known survivor. At Martock (Somerset) one can still discern the holes that afforded footholds so that balls could be retrieved from the roof. Archers practised their skills and used the stone boundary walls and even the fabric of the church to sharpen their arrows. Although there were eventually local penalties for those who played sports in the churchyard, the grounds were used for football, single-stick playing and various other contests until the nineteenth century.

Some churchyards were the scenes of skirmishes during the English Civil War, and a number of churches exhibit cannon balls that were recovered from their walls or were found in the churchyard. At Alton (Hampshire) the churchyard was the scene of a full battle, its defenders to a man being forced back to die in the church. Military prisoners were held at Burford (Oxfordshire) when Cromwell's men put down a Levellers' uprising in 1649, and some of the dissenters were executed in the churchyard. The churches of Cirencester, Painswick and Stow-on-the-Wold, all in Gloucestershire, were used as prisons for Royalists during the Civil War. The churchyards so used must have been in a disgraceful state, with soldiers trampling about them and tethering their horses in the grounds, having scant regard for the nature of the place, as at Beetham (Cumbria). Prisoners taken at the Battle of Sedgemoor, in 1685, were locked in the church at Westonzoyland (Somerset).

The medieval churchyard was busy at most times, but for the ordinary person the highlights were the fairs and feast days. The fair was the annual wake or revel, of which the church was usually the main beneficiary. Proceeds helped to provide books, church plate, bell ropes and so on. Everyone was compelled to attend, and, in consequence, the whole event had a good following, probably enhanced by copious amounts of the strong, local ale. This might be brewed in the church house and sold at a price that was fixed by the local abbot. Dancing and games took place, although, theoretically at least, people respected the south side of the grounds, where the majority of graves were to be found, and confined themselves to the north side or open spaces. The result could be a riot of merrymaking, a colourful spectacle that mirrored the brightly painted interior of the church itself.

Animals were always a problem in the churchyard. The first graveyards were not enclosed and so could easily be trampled on and ravaged by cattle and other farm and domestic animals. It was considered important to protect the grounds from destruction and desecration by livestock. There were frequent edicts by lords of the manor or parish overseers seeking to ensure that the owners of animals kept them out of the churchyard. Fines were levied against offenders. Slowly, churchyards came to be enclosed but, while the people of the parish paid for the upkeep of the fencing to keep

*Berwick, Sussex. The marks on the pillar of this South Downs church are said to have been made by medieval archers when sharpening their arrows.*

animals out of the churchyard, the priest sometimes raised money by letting out grazing within. Indeed, the widespread practice of grazing animals in the churchyard persisted throughout Victorian times. Even in the present, one may still encounter a few sheep close-cropping the grass, or meet the occasional tethered goat.

The rector or vicar holds the freehold of the churchyard, but the deceased of the parish have a right to be buried there, subject to available space. The parochial church council has to maintain it, but it is the duty of the churchwardens to see that it is used only for its proper purposes. Churchyards that are closed for burials still remain the responsibility of the parochial church council, although they may abdicate this to some other community body.

### Instruments of correction

The churchyard, by the very nature of its existence, was always presumed to have a beneficial effect on criminals, even if this was only temporary while the fugitive was seeking sanctuary in the church. It was thought that, in that moment at least, they would be recognising the existence of a power for good, which might encourage them to mend their ways. Implements of correction, such as the stocks and whipping posts, were sometimes sited near the church, no doubt so that the unfortunate contained in them might be influenced by the proximity of consecrated ground. Some remain, reminders of a time when people were publicly displayed and abused for minor crimes. A few stocks have now found their way into church porches. There are sets just outside Cornish churchyards, but they are inside at Crantock, and at Feock, where there is a seven-holed set. Small metal ones beyond the boundary wall may be easily missed at Painswick (Gloucestershire). At Market Overton (Rutland) both stocks and whipping post are nearby. St Kew (Cornwall) has a set in the church porch, and Mobberley (Cheshire) has one in the churchyard. A four-holed set is nearby at Marden (Kent), and the whipping post still stands by the churchyard gate at Kingsley (Staffordshire).

*Ashby de la Zouch, Leicestershire. These unique seventeenth-century church finger stocks or finger pillories are simply two planks with grooves cut in them, which could be locked together. They were probably used to discomfit people who either misbehaved in church or did not pay attention to the sermon.*

## Sundials

The sundial seems not to have been developed either architecturally or as a decorative feature between the twelfth and fifteenth centuries. Most extant wall dials are of this period, and they are numerous and, for the most part, uninteresting. They comprise simple scratch dials, as at Westham (Sussex), carved straight on to the exterior stonework of the church, with indifferent spacing between the radiating lines, which also varied in number. At Baydon (Wiltshire) there is one on its side, and another inverted.

Old dials can be found almost anywhere on the south-facing walls of churches, but many are not obvious. A favourite position was above the doorway of the south porch. Others were on buttresses and at the south-west corner of the building. In Cornwall there are many fine examples cut into slate, which inscribed well and tended to last longer. They may include the name of the maker, or they might be dated or include witty thoughts or amusing verses mostly concerned with the passage of time. Their content echoes, perhaps mockingly by way of puns and such like, the sentiments expressed in the epitaphs on the churchyard memorials and tombstones. In this book, much of what is said about lettering forms on churchyard monuments also applies to sundials. There is an ambitious dial, set on little corbels, at Eyam (Derbyshire), which tells world time; and that of 1757 at Tawstock (Devon) also records the hour in various cities.

Slate weathers well, although outside the slate-producing regions most wall dials will have long since lost their gnomons – the projection that casts the shadow. A large, outward-splayed hole where the gnomon once was means that this rusted and dropped out when it wore away the stonework. What may be a faint, rough circle remains, with a central hole, and lines radiating from it, about fifteen degrees apart. It was in the fifteenth century that the day was first divided into twenty-four hours, and mechanical clocks came into general use. Vertical sundials were then adapted more as general timepieces than specific reminders of services, with the number of each hour cut or marked at the end of each line.

There are a good many examples extant from the sixteenth, seventeenth and eighteenth centuries. The great disadvantage of sundials is that they could be relied upon

*Elmley Castle, Worcestershire. The stone-built multiple sundial, dated to 1545, is thought to be the oldest surviving of its type in England.*

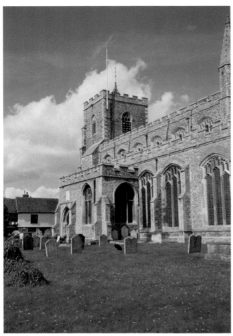

*Clare, Suffolk. The porch, of flint and stone, was built about 1380 and the sundial – with its legend 'Go about your business' – was added in the eighteenth century.*

only during daylight hours when the sun was shining, and they were no use for indicating when the church bells should be rung for mass and vespers in winter. Mechanical clocks and watches were more reliable, and the sundial became more of an ornamental feature in the churchyard, rather than a necessity. The gnomon was placed above a horizontal surface on a free-standing pillar. At Tilston (Cheshire) the sundial is now where the head of the churchyard cross once was. Inigo Jones's design for Chilham (Kent) is an example of a beautiful pedestal dial that is more ornamental than of practical use. There is a heavy, rectangular dial just inside the churchyard at Upton St Leonards (Gloucestershire). At Godshill (Isle of Wight) the sundial is on a cross; and at Wymondham (Leicestershire) it is on the stump of one. Bootle (Cumbria) has a very tall sundial; and at Newbiggin, in the same county, is a medieval dial on a buttress. Christleton (Cheshire) has one on a pillar. At Ightham (Kent) the sundial is dated 1669, and also from the seventeenth century is one on a wooden post at Aldbury (Hertfordshire). The dial with symbolic crossed bones at Zennor (Cornwall) is dated 1737; that at Pilling (Lancashire) was made in 1766; and the dial on the south porch at Clare (Suffolk) was put up in 1790. Another from the eighteenth century is at St Just-in-Penwith (Cornwall). Early nineteenth-century examples can be seen at Tedburn St Mary (Devon) and Seaton Ross (Yorkshire).

*Ellingham, Hampshire. The porch was built substantially of brick in 1720, and the large blue sundial that covers its gable is also reputed to have been put up in the eighteenth century.*

*Tredington, Gloucestershire. The steps, base and slender tapering shaft – some 12 feet (3.7 metres) high – of the churchyard cross were put up in the fourteenth century; the cross on the top is modern.*

## Churchyard crosses

Before the Reformation, every churchyard included a free-standing stone cross. It signified the sanctity of consecrated ground. Many were destroyed by Cromwell's soldiers during the English Civil War. The iconoclasts removed or broke up most of the heads that still bore sculptured images, and defaced or destroyed any whose shafts were similarly adorned. However, the remains of medieval churchyard crosses are still quite common and, although some have been partly restored or rebuilt, most are what was left after the desecration and destruction. In some instances, subsequent levelling of the grounds included the churchyard cross in the overall plan to do away with the tombstones. As a result of all this, one may sometimes find sections of a cross lying together in the churchyard, set in concrete to give some idea of what the original was like, or even built into the fabric of the church. Not all of those still standing may be in their original position, although post-Conquest examples are most likely to be.

For most of the Middle Ages the churchyard cross was the single memorial to almost all who had ever been buried thereabouts. It invariably marked the true centre of the churchyard, at the point to the east of a processional path, midway between the main entrance to the churchyard and the south porch of the church. It was used as a station on days of prayer and thanksgiving. Particularly, these were Rogation Day, Corpus Christi and Palm Sunday. The decorated cross played such an important part on Palm Sunday that it was frequently referred to as the 'Palm Cross'. It also played a part in the secular life of the community, being the point from which public announcements might be made. At Alkborough (Lincolnshire) the smooth, strange shape of the cross shaft is the result of its constant use for honing weapons, scythes and other instruments that had to be given a sharp edge.

The mounted-shaft type of cross predominated, and the remains extant are mainly of this kind. In its complete form, it consisted of steps, base (plinth or socket), shaft, capital (or knop) and head. Crowcombe (Somerset) has a cross with a heavy, foliated knop. What tends to remain, if a restored head has not been added to a new shaft, are steps, base and a short length of the original shaft. There may be between one and six steps made of individual stones, forming a figure, which on plan may be round, square, rectangular, hexagonal or octagonal. The steps diminish in surface area as they rise, and sometimes the treads are continued over the risers as a roll moulding or set-off. This is known as nosing and is not a feature of internal steps. Characteristically in the fourteenth century, the riser of one step in each set might admit carved panels on each of its faces, but rarely was such decoration lavished on more than one tier. There is a good fourteenth-century cross at North Cerney (Gloucestershire) and

233

*Ashleworth, Gloucestershire. The fourteenth-century churchyard lantern cross with figurework in the head, now located on the village green.*

one from the fifteenth century at Tattershall (Lincolnshire).

The foot of the shaft was received in a socket or plinth, some of which are comparatively tall. These either follow the shape of the steps or are square, occasionally with chamfered, vertical edges. They are more likely to have decoration, ranging from plain trefoils in the thirteenth century to panelled quatrefoils and heraldry during the fourteenth century. The majority of shafts are square on plan and taper upwards. They often have chamfered edges terminating in typical stops. Most are plain, but some have figurework or minor carving along their length, the latter more often at the point of contact with the base. A niche, or recess, occasionally canopied, was sometimes built into one side of the shaft or socket. This might hold a sculpture, a monstrance or the pyx on ceremonial occasions. An example of this is at Great Malvern (Worcestershire). The monstrance was a sacred, ornate container with glass sides in which was placed the consecrated wafer or Host. The pyx was an enclosed, ornamental box or casket, usually circular and made of precious metal, in which the wafers were stored before being consecrated. This was usually kept in an aumbry, or cupboard, in the wall of the chancel. In normal use, the pyx was subject to high ritual, being traditionally placed on the altar beneath a tabernacle or canopy; sometimes it was suspended, in which case it might take the form of a veiled dove.

There is a complete, although restored, medieval cross of the gabled type at Ampney Crucis (Gloucestershire), and another at Somersby (Lincolnshire). The fourteenth-century cross at Tyberton (Herefordshire) is also gabled, with the figure of Christ on the cross on one side, and the Virgin and Child on the other. Cross shafts known to have been made in the fourteenth century include one with a lantern head and niches at Ashleworth (Gloucestershire); Bishop's Lydeard (Somerset), which has figurework; Higham Ferrers (Northamptonshire), where there is an amount of floral decoration and other minor decorative motifs; Ross-on-Wye (Herefordshire); and Blakemere in the same county. Other interesting medieval churchyard crosses include those at St Mawgan-in-Pydar (Cornwall), Chewton Mendip (Somerset), Cricklade and Bremhill (Wiltshire), North Hinksey (Oxfordshire), Croxton (Cambridgeshire) and Ightfield (Shropshire),which has quatrefoils at the base and figures on the angles. At Highley (Shropshire) the shaft has cable moulding and figurework.

The fifteenth-century cross at Iron Acton (Gloucestershire), despite having been badly mutilated, is worthy of note. At Castle Hedingham (Essex) the cross is of the twelfth century, although restored. The cross at Ombersley (Worcestershire) was put up in the fifteenth century but has been attended to at various times. It has a medieval base of four worn steps, set on a circular plinth. The upper step has quatrefoils, the head is from the seventeenth century, and it has the addition of an eighteenth-century ball finial. At Rampisham (Dorset) there is sixteenth-century figurework in tableaux on the base. The medieval shaft at Iffley (Oxfordshire) received a new top in the nineteenth century. Later crosses of note may be seen at Sulham (Berkshire) and St Peter, Bournemouth (Dorset).

## Burials

During their occupation of Britain the Romans raised single, inscribed tombstones over their dead and even, occasionally, made stone coffins. Tradition continued the Norman precedent of beginning burials at one side of the grounds, working across and then starting again at the beginning. Consequently, in the course of time, people were buried one on top of the other. The bodies of some who died while away from home might be rendered down and only the bones returned for burial. Throughout the Middle Ages, most people were interred in only a shroud, tied head and foot. The body was taken to the graveside on the parish bier and placed straight into the ground. A sprig of rosemary for remembrance (also symbolically used at weddings) was sometimes put in the grave, or yew foliage as a symbol of immortality.

Churchyard burials during the twelfth and thirteenth centuries were sometimes made in rectangular stone coffins, let into the ground to their upper edges and covered with stone slabs. The usual, early method was to hollow out a single block of stone so that one indentation fitted the head, and another the body. Such receptacles were usually wider at one end than the other and might have had a drain hole in the bottom. The ledgers that covered them were thick, and either rectangular or coffin-shaped in cross plan, and flat or gently coped. They included no inscription and, apart from an incised Latin or floriated cross, were plain. Priests, knights and others with a trade of note within the community might also have a subsidiary carving in low relief, indicating the nature of their calling. A knight, for example, might be remembered by an heraldic shield. Gradually the basic cross became more floral, assuming leaf-form decoration, which developed as naturalistic foliage. The next step was to cut a crude outline of the deceased, the forerunner of the fully developed effigy within the church. When the flat coffin slab became the elevated ledger of the chest tomb, its potential as a surface for embellishment was not realised, such being confined to its vertical faces. Later, coffin slabs were sometimes put up in conjunction with headstones and footstones. However, individual churchyard monuments seem to have declined in popularity by the fourteenth century. There may have been wide-spread disillusionment, and disbelief in the possibility of the resurrection, following catastrophes such as the Black Death.

*Lady St Mary, Wareham, Dorset. This thirteenth-century coffin, made of Purbeck stone, was dug up in the churchyard in the eighteenth century.*

By law, between 1667 and 1814, the shroud had to be made of wool, in an attempt to help a declining wool trade that had for so long financed the building of magnificent churches. There was an indifferent response to the original Act, and it was amended in 1679. This new Act required that a certificate be produced for every burial, before the service took place. Even so, it was 1696 before this was rigorously enforced.

People could not buy plots as they can today, and the closest many got to interment in a coffin was temporary residence in the one that belonged to the parish. Consequently, no one could feel that they actually owned any part of the churchyard. As true religious feeling declined within the church, so too did respect towards those buried in the grounds. Bodies continued to be placed one above the other, and the ground level of many churchyards rose to the top of any surrounding wall, or even higher. Sextons removed the bones from previous burials in order to make way for new ones. They sometimes collected the bones in crypts or charnel houses, or buried them together in a communal trench. Grave-diggers stole the fixtures from the coffins for resale. As the graveyards became so overcrowded, private individuals opened up plots and crammed in bodies at an alarming rate. They commanded good prices for what must have been fairly indecent burials. All of this rapidly caused some very acute problems. Records from early in the nineteenth century frequently mention the stench that emanated from graveyards as a result of so much decaying flesh, so shallowly buried.

## Headstones

The headstones of churchyard graves are the counterparts of the wall tablets within the church, although they are in no way as well preserved, nor do they give as much information. They became popular after the Reformation, and by the end of the sixteenth century the increasing number of people who could afford to buy burial plots also decided that their last resting place on earth should be marked in some way. Between c.1700 and 1850 some remarkable monumental masonry was created, where materials allowed the craftsmen to work skilfully. The best tombs and headstones are Georgian. Headstones were made in local stone to begin with, and, later, artificial stone, slate, polished 'marbles' and cast iron were used. Where local stone was used because it was plentiful, the material might be the same as that used to build the church, and obtained from the same quarry. Iron grave markers appear in areas where there was always little freestone, such as Sussex and Kent, and iron smelting had gone on from the earliest times. Everywhere else, iron was, for hundreds of years, the easiest to hand. Transportation of stone was always a costly business, even by waterway, before the railways opened up the country and made it much more practicable. It was laborious, time-consuming and hazardous, and therefore headstones were sometimes reused. Examples of these can be seen at Heptonstall (Yorkshire). But when transport communications improved, the business of the local mason, using locally quarried stone, declined. Shiny white marbles came into fashion; people took to them as something of a novelty, and firms of monumental masons increased in popularity.

Inscriptions were traditionally carved into a vertical surface of the headstone, although some might be affixed on metal or terracotta plates. An older headstone, in which there was no further personal interest, was sometimes re-cut with the details of another person, and used to mark a more recent interment. The style of inscriptions, and that of the headstones generally, varies considerably between areas. Groups of headstones in a particular district often show the unmistakable hand of a single sculptor. A signature may occasionally reveal the identity of a craftsman from long ago. Especially in the more rural areas, local craftsmen were almost entirely responsible for this work until late in the nineteenth century, a time when tombstones were being given comparatively little ornamentation or decoration.

All headstones are subject to weathering. The softer stones may well have originally taken the best carving but are now in the poorest condition. Air pollution and industrial grime have turned others from a grubby brown to a sooty black. The more porous the original material, the less likely it is to have withstood the elements, leaving a stone that has been badly eroded.

Most headstones are single, although some double plots may be identified by stones that are twice the normal width, each with two shaped heads. Just as materials and standards of lettering varied, so too the size and shape of headstones developed regional characteristics. In some areas they always remained small, perhaps no more than 2 to 3 feet (600 to 900 mm) tall, like the early medieval ones, or even less. Individual churchyards show their own preferences for both size and the shape of the head. Whichever sort of headstone is found, the inscription may commemorate one or two people, or even whole families. Early ones were thick in relation to their height. They increased in size and diminished in thickness. Some headstones in the exposed far west had to be buttressed against the prevailing winds. Graves may also have smaller footstones, usually giving only initials and date. Care should be taken not to confuse these with small or early headstones. Other graves may be enclosed in bedheads or graveboards.

At the beginning of the seventeenth century there was little decoration on headstones. They were fairly small and thick, and were mostly made of stone, although some of the common shapes were still being made in wood. The heads were flat, except where a scroll formed the shoulders and perhaps flanked a winged angel's head, symbolic of the departing soul. Early seventeenth-century angels had lean features. Their wings, the shape of handlebar moustaches, tended to stick awkwardly out of their heads in the place of ears. There are thousands of examples of sad, lone angels, crudely cut on seventeenth- and eighteenth-century tombstones by rural craftsmen. But the influence of Classical art was to change their lean appearance into healthy, well-fed cherubs, trumpeting their victory over death, and winging into the hereafter with a smile and a tune.

The general carving, as well as the lettering, was decisive, bold and crude, with little attention to layout. Roman capital letters were commonly used, but there was also some lower-case work, and letters with tails ended in loops or hooks. If the word at the end of the line could not be completed because of lack of space, it might be abbreviated awkwardly, carried on to the next line, or finished by squashing it

*Kempley, Gloucestershire. Eighteenth-century, lichen-encrusted headstones with their deeply carved and shaped, classically symbolic heads and sides, in a daffodil-laced churchyard.*

*Petersfield, Hampshire. The tombstone to John Small (died 1826); he was a maker of cricket balls and bats, a playing member of the Hambledon Club, scorer of the first-recorded century in a first-class cricket match, and allegedly the eighteenth century's finest batsman.*

in above. The letters were uneven: neither straight up and down, nor sloping in the same direction as each other. Words were run together without spacing, and only the width of the stone imposed any constraint on the mason's layout. If the text had a border, any word that could not be contained within it at the end of a line might continue over the border into what we would call the margin. It all seems to have got worse before it got better, or perhaps it was just poor, local standards of lettering that produced inscriptions with insertions above the line, and words at right angles to the rest of the text or crammed in at the end of the line in tiny characters. In the seventeenth century, early attempts were also made at italic forms of lettering and these were more effective when done on slate. In other instances, a potentially strong line might be marred by the soft or brittle texture of the material into which it was cut.

By the middle of the seventeenth century, the top of the stone was being shaped to admit an angel's head in the hood. Alternatively, the shoulders were so carved that they curved around a head placed in each corner or spandrel, retaining the scroll concept from the centre of the headstone to the outer edges. The text was sometimes cut into a cartouche shape, which was then becoming popular for internal monuments. It might be surmounted by a skull or an urn. The influence of Classical art was adding decorative motifs such as swags, garlands, fruit and flowers. The calligraphic style of lettering quickly became popular and was applied with some interesting effects. This was especially well done in the slate-producing areas, for the italic swirls looked particularly impressive when cut sharply into the dark, impermeable background of slate. The faces of angels, as well as their wings, also took on a calligraphic style. Lettering generally became smaller, more controlled and decorative. By the latter half of the century, the headstone resembled a plaque surrounded by all manner of Classical designs: pilasters, columns and even pediments. Shangton and Swithland, both in Leicestershire, have particularly attractive collections of seventeenth-century headstones.

In the matter of decorative quality and lettering, one can only generalise. In some rural areas at the beginning of the eighteenth century, the quality of this work was barely any better than half a century before. In addition, the Classical influences, which elsewhere were being put to considerable use when the century began, were slower in showing. Different styles of lettering were coming into fashion at the start of the century, which was to become remarkable for the great variety of forms and styles achieved by masons, sculptors and engravers. They used and adapted ancient designs, incised and in relief, but rarely in juxtaposition on the same headstone. Commonly, the tails of key letters were continued into scrolls, and individual words of importance were given additional embellishment. The witty or droll remarks by way of epitaphs gradually gave way to short, stereotyped phrases such as 'at rest' and 'at peace'. Most decoration was cut into the upper part of the headstone, and in some cases this occupied the largest portion of the stone's surface. Whole biblical scenes might be carved there. These were often interspersed with, or surmounted by, winged heads of angels or cherubs. Skulls, too, remained popular.

The increased desire for individually commemorated graves provided a greater need for the skills of the local mason, and work by specific families of masons in particular areas became more frequent and therefore more obvious. There was an increase in individuality, as regards the type of ornamentation, within the framework of prevailing taste. So, too, an element of individuality began to pervade the styles of lettering. There was some contraction of words, but layout was generally improved. Before the letters were decoratively done they were, for a while, extremely clear and simple.

Angels discovered bodies and drifted across headstones, blowing their trumpets; and, with the fashion for Classical drapery at its height, some became very voluptuous indeed. By the late eighteenth century, they were taking their places as the centrepieces of tableaux, amidst shells, urns, drapery and symbolism. Angels' features grew more cherubic, and feathery wings sprouted from their shoulders. The urn predominated as a favoured motif, usually cut into the head of the stone, and associated with swags, fruit and flowers. Some beautiful examples were carved in slate, with the decoration, even of pedimented obelisks, done in relief with symmetrical design and lettering. What was elsewhere sculpted out of freestone was beautifully engraved in the slate regions. It is there that the great variety of lettering can still be seen at its best. At Narborough (Leicestershire) there is a good collection of tall eighteenth- and nineteenth-century headstones made out of Swithland slate, decorated with Classical motifs in relief. The Wealden iron industry produced grave slabs in that material, such as are to be found at Cowden (Kent). At Madeley (Shropshire) there are nineteenth-century cast-iron tombs. A series of pretty terracotta plaques appeared on headstones in Sussex, and there, as well as in Kent, one finds a number

*Aylsham, Norfolk. Landscape gardener Humphry Repton died in 1818; his memorial, allegedly written by himself and enclosed in a rose garden of his own design, stands against the south wall of the chancel.*

239

*Breedon-on-the-Hill, Leicestershire. A flat tombstone of the late eighteenth century, showing various styles of the calligrapher's art.*

of strangely headed stones overloaded with skulls. Some foreign 'marbles' were imported, and composite stones became popular. Most old churchyards that have not been cleared can provide examples of eighteenth-century headstones. There are some attractive ones at Hambledon and Hayling Island (Hampshire), Cley-next-the-Sea and Blakeney (Norfolk), Narborough (Leicestershire), Inglesham (Wiltshire) and Shilton (Oxfordshire).

Religious feeling in the nineteenth century dictated that not only should everyone have a separate plot but each should be decently commemorated by a headstone or some other memorial. It had been relatively easy to move aside old bones and insert new coffins, until the ground was so overcrowded that it was impractical to continue. But headstones were another problem altogether. They did not allow cramming or facilitate surreptitious clearances; they were permanent, as far as the Victorians were concerned, and emphasised the ownership, sanctity and privacy of the grave plot.

This they achieved from the mid nineteenth century with kerbs, cast-iron rails and all manner of fences and boundary markers. The work of the local man, with his regional peculiarities of style and rustic lettering, gave way to the standard typefaces and designs advertised in the catalogues of the larger firms of monumental masons. These typefaces were as variable as the materials used: deeply and perfectly cut, some were leaded or shaded, and might have three-dimensional effects. The craftsmen experimented widely with their own styles of lettering, and headstones of this period often include many different kinds within the same piece of text, and even slight alternatives for individual letters within the same line. The two most popular styles of headstones were the depressed, pointed type based loosely on the lancet, and the symbolic triple head, which represented the Holy Trinity. A line of small motifs invariably followed the shape of the head, which was otherwise fairly plain except, perhaps, for the Classical-style urn. Fruit and flowers were always popular and these, as well as figurework, became more naturalistic. Inscriptions became all important again after a dull period, and they were often surrounded by simple, but formal, items of Classical architecture. There were obelisks and casket-shaped monuments, much statuary and the ubiquitous free-standing cross, many of all these in white marble. Some of this came from Italy, although there were a number of inferior 'marbles'. There was a particular vogue in the churchyards for Cornish and Scottish granite.

Epitaphs are those words of wit and wisdom, poignancy and sadness, in rhyme or prose, which people have long directed should go on their own memorials. They often reflect on the life of the deceased, the manner of death, and contain an accompaniment for the afterlife. While a good many are unique, and there are some gems among them, a great number are universal in spirit, if not almost word for word. Epitaphs comprise a whole field of study in themselves and considerable books have been devoted to the subject.

### Graveboards

An alternative to the headstone, especially in the south-east, where there was not much decent local freestone, was the wooden graveboard. These covered the grave lengthways. They were long, horizontal planks supported at either end by low, wooden uprights that might themselves be terminated in poppyhead finials. Some had chamfered upper edges along their length, on which an inscription could be cut. More frequently, the horizontal surface was painted white and lettered in black. Graveboards may be difficult to find: being made of wood, albeit oak or teak, they eventually rotted with age. However, even outside, wooden memorials usually outlast local interest in the person they are commemorating. They were less expensive and could more easily be removed and disposed of, if necessary. Another advantage of this type of memorial was that it could be designed to be removed easily when the grass was being cut, to be replaced when the mowing was done. The current practice of putting plots so close together, side by side, makes it difficult to use even a pair of shears between the tombstones, once they have been erected, and impossible to work with a mower.

In those churchyards that still have them, the graveboards are more usually located in the most inconspicuous parts. Those who could afford it soon preferred stone tombs and memorials, even if they had to import the materials into their area. The distribution of types of memorial within the churchyard is evidence of a definite class structure. Those who could afford only a wooden board between two uprights, when a choice was available, and painted instead of being carved, were tucked into out-of-the-way corners of the grounds. The legends on most old graveboards are no longer decipherable. Their use was particularly widespread in Surrey, Kent and around the Chilterns. Some nineteenth-century examples that can still be read are in the churchyards at Burstow and Mickleham (Surrey).

### Chest tombs

Chest tombs, or table tombs, originated from the wooden shrines that were erected around the remains of local saints, although the concept was not developed in community use for several centuries. Someone who was able to finance a fine raised tomb would be unlikely to place it outside when the altar tomb, the internal equivalent, provided a psychologically more comfortable alternative. Inside, it was also more likely to remain in good condition, and in the same place. The hollow chest arrangement above graves in the churchyard was a side effect of the altar tomb concept of a rectangular box, designed to form the high base for a recumbent effigy. In the churchyard, the effigy was always omitted, and the only likenesses of the deceased might have been the few portrait busts carved on the ends of some chests in the eighteenth century. Even these were more by way of symmetrical decoration, when the ends of many chest tombs were being dealt with in a similar way to the surfaces

*Tewkesbury Abbey, Gloucestershire. Clipped yews are a feature of the county's churchyards, and usually, as here, line walkways; here, too, there are some fine chest tombs.*

of headstones. The tops of chest tombs always remained above the level of grass and weeds, and they were certain to stand out from even a forest of headstones. Yet, as they are hollow, they are liable to collapse through the action of stress, soil erosion, age and the encroachment of tree roots. Care should be taken when standing next to chest tombs and monuments that have derived from them, and which now appear to be in an unsafe condition, for the slabs that make them up are extremely heavy. Many are covered in lichen, which is not to their detriment, although it may have made the inscriptions unreadable. Ivy and creeper might have scrambled over them and obliterated any wording or decoration that was once on the surfaces of older monuments. The most that can be said in favour of such flora is that it looks pretty and provides a habitat for churchyard wildlife.

Early chest tombs were rectangular stone boxes with little, if any, decoration and no inscription. In the fourteenth century the sides, like those of other items of church furniture such as fonts, were worked into a resemblance of window tracery. Cusped quatrefoils and shields epitomised the spirit of the fifteenth century and appeared on both sides. Then, and in the following century, the chest was surmounted by a thick stone slab that was either chamfered or moulded at the edges. The base of the chest rested on a simple plinth. Prosperous people could afford fine tombs, and the full flowering of the art can be seen to best advantage at Tewkesbury Abbey (Gloucestershire), which is the town's parish church. The great 'wool' churches of East Anglia in particular, and those of the Cotswolds to a lesser degree, attest to the generosity of the wealthy in the service of their God, and in the expectation of prayers for their own souls. In these areas there are plenty of extremely fine chest tombs, in keeping with the benefactions made by the persons they commemorate. Even so, the era of the ornate chest tomb was short-lived. Locally, the designers were frequently families of masons who worked within a fairly small area. Good chest tombs in an otherwise indifferent churchyard, perhaps surrounding a church of no apparent wealth, usually indicated the last resting place of well-to-do families – gentry, wealthy farmers, landowners and key community tradespeople – perhaps

242

interred during one of the periods when religion was less fashionable. Older, plainer chest tombs of the financially secure, but less rich, local families may well be found scattered throughout those parts of the churchyard that were in current use for burials at the time they were erected. Later, the tombs of this level of occupant tended to form family groups.

The chest tomb became fairly frequent and widespread early in the seventeenth century. It was restrained in execution but reached its zenith with the Georgians. Early ones are most likely to be near the south door of the church. An odd, but similar, monument is the carved slate slab on a brick base in the churchyard at St Enodoc (Cornwall). It is dated 1687 and is remarkable for its rustic, incised figurework. The heavy ledger slab of a narrow seventeenth-century chest tomb may well have served as a dole stone for the distribution of bread to the poor of the parish, or for some other charity.

The proportions of the basic rectangle were standardised during the seventeenth century to an equal width and height, and a length equal to the sum of both – the common 'double cube' arrangement. Plain panelling was sometimes done on all vertical surfaces, and in the eighteenth century these were often curved. The monument typically had a base and plinth, and the hitherto flat ledger might be capped with either a curved lid or one that was casket-shaped. Some of these were heavy in both design and execution, pyramidal or obelisk-shaped, and topped by a finial. There are a number of these – in effect large caskets – scattered around Cotswold churchyards. Elsewhere, a variation on the casket lid was the double gable arrangement.

The early eighteenth-century chest tomb still had a heavy ledger slab, cut away on the underside to meet the top of the tomb below. There were table tombs which, as the name suggests, comprised a flat slab, with or without inscription or ornamentation on its surface, supported by a pillar at each corner, resting on a flat base. The edges of both the slab and the base might be moulded or chamfered, and the pillars plain or fluted. From the mid seventeenth century until well into the eighteenth, a popular, flamboyant Cotswold variation on the basic shape, mainly by way of decoration, was the lyre-shape design to the ends. In this, the upper edge of the tomb was

*Boldre, Hampshire. The chest tomb of William Gilpin – born in 1724, and rector here from 1777 until his death in 1804 – who wrote and illustrated works on the scenery of Britain and was foremost in promoting the cult of the picturesque.*

*Westdean, East Sussex. The little tower, with its oddly shaped Sussex cap, is supported on Norman arches; there are some interesting chest tombs in the grounds.*

continued outwards on each side as shoulders. These formed acanthus leaves that curved inwards as they plunged downwards, ending in a loose coil that resembled the volute of an Ionic capital, although a rather more elongated one. The spaces between were filled with Classical motifs: fruit and flowers, heads, and symbols of death, eternity and triumph. With the Georgians came the fashion for Baroque-style chest tombs with turned balusters at the angles. Good examples of these from the seventeenth and eighteenth centuries are at Chaddleworth (Berkshire), Painswick, Stroud, Daglingworth, Winson, Harescombe, Broadwell and Duntisbourne Rouse (all in Gloucestershire), Herstmonceux (Sussex), Chard (Somerset) and Christleton (Cheshire). In country areas that were not particularly wealthy, the chest tomb of the eighteenth century was likely to have been conservatively decorated in relief, with an urn at the centre, flanked by swags, fruit and flowers, and corner drapes. Inscriptions were most usually done on the sides and were sometimes carved in oval plaques with decorated frames. Where there are two such inscriptions on either side of the chest,

*St Botolph, Bishopsgate, London. The extravagant casket memorial to Sir Williams Rawlins (died 1838), upholsterer, founder of an insurance company, and Sheriff of the City of London.*

*Burford, Oxfordshire. The churchyard has a fine collection of seventeenth- and eighteenth-century roll-top and bale tombs decorated with symbolic carvings.*

they commemorate different members of the same family. Even the simplest chests commonly had their corners worked into pilasters or balusters.

Some of these monuments were protected by iron grilles or sets of taller railings. During the eighteenth century local blacksmiths installed much very good ironwork in village churchyards. In Victorian times the craft became something of an art and, while the railings around the tomb might be reduced in height, the variety of shapes and appendages increased. Fleurs-de-lis, vine scrolls and strawberry-leaf designs were popular. There are fine examples at St Illtyd (Monmouthshire) and Madeley (Shropshire). Work on the five surfaces of the chest was still restrained, but now the corners might be inset by square colonnettes with caps and bases. Classical motifs continued to predominate, heavily mixed with figurework. Perhaps the likeness of the deceased, or the tools of his trade, appeared on the ends of tombs. In the nineteenth century pedestal tombs with urns as finials developed into obelisk shapes on high bases.

After something of a lull, late nineteenth-century families revived the popularity of the chest tomb. Tombs of close relations may often be found grouped together in the churchyard. Most of these monuments record little more than the basic essentials and are not outstanding. The majority of nineteenth-century churchyard monuments are generally heavy, and often depressing. Gothic Revival tombs were overpowering. There were many three-dimensional representations of the Classical motifs, with central urn design, or something similar. The ledger of the chest might be used as the base for this kind of free-standing sculpture and, in some instances, the whole may be surmounted by a canopy on corner pillars.

## Bale tombs

Bale tombs are an east Cotswold variation on the basic chest tomb. The name is derived from the design and appearance of the semi-cylindrical stone that runs the length of the ledger slab on top of the tomb, in much the same position as one may encounter a recumbent effigy inside the church. Such stones are carved with deep grooves at regular intervals along their length. The grooves usually run from the base of one side, straight over the curving surface, to the base of the other. On some the grooves run diagonally. It is widely assumed that these are meant to represent

*Dymock, Gloucestershire. 'Tea-caddy' tombs were popular in the eighteenth century and were so-called because of their resemblance to the containers for what was then an expensive product used by fashionable society.*

corded bales of cloth, and that the tomb is therefore of a person connected with the wool trade. However, this is not always the case. It has also been suggested that they may be symbolic of the corpse, wrapped in a shroud of wool – a legal requirement when the industry was suffering hard times. The ends of the 'bale' usually took the form of a skull set in a scallop or shell, and the positioning of this symbol of death may give the real clue to exactly what the 'bale' represents. The decoration on the tomb underneath was as for other chest tombs of the period. Bale tombs can be seen in many Gloucestershire and Oxfordshire churchyards; there are good examples at Stow-on-the-Wold, Fairford and Bibury in Gloucestershire, and at Asthall, Swinbrook, Burford and Letcombe Regis in Oxfordshire.

### Tea-caddy tombs

Another Cotswold variation on the chest tomb, dating from the eighteenth century, is the tea-caddy tomb; eccentric tombs elsewhere may resemble it in basic shape even if they were constructed at a different time. The tea-caddy is tall in relation to its ground area, as if the chest has been set at ninety degrees to its normal position. It may be rectangular, circular or square on plan and is sometimes tapered or topped by a 'lid' with some kind of finial. The latter might be a ball, an urn, or some similar device. The amazing churchyard at Painswick (Gloucestershire) has several among its treasures. Others may be found at, for example, Withington (Gloucestershire) and Kington St Michael (Wiltshire).

When it comes to variations on churchyard memorial furniture based around the chest-tomb concept, there is no doubt that the Cotswolds excel. However, churchyard memorials are always rewarding wherever they are found. The general quality of the stonework tells much about local materials and the economic status of the parish at datable times in its history; and the tenor of the wording and the styles of lettering are strong reflections of its social history.

# Further reading

The following is a selection of general books on church art and architecture.

Anderson, W. *The Rise of Gothic*. Hutchinson, 1985.
Bailey, B. *Churchyards of England and Wales*. Hale, 1987.
Beaulah, K., and van Lemmen, Hans. *Church Tiles of the Nineteenth Century*. Shire, second edition, 2001.
Bellamy, R. *Spirit in Stone*. Pentland Press, 2001.
Betjeman, J. (editor). *Collins Pocket Guide to English Parish Churches*. Collins, 1968.
Betjeman, J. *Pictorial History of English Architecture*. Penguin, 1974.
Betjeman, J., and Kerr, N. *John Betjeman's Guide to English Parish Churches*. Harper Collins, 1993.
Blatch, M. *Parish Churches of England in Colour*. Blandford, 1974.
Bottomley, F. *The Church Explorer's Guide*. Kaye & Ward, 1978.
Bradley, C. *Churches*. Watts, 1994.
Braun, H. *Introduction to English Medieval Architecture*. Faber, 1951.
Braun, H. *Parish Churches: Their Architectural Development in England*. Faber, 1970.
Brown, R. J. *The English Village Church*. Hale, 1998.
Burgess, F. *English Churchyard Memorials*. Lutterworth Press, 1963.
Butler, L. A. S., and Morris, R. K. *The Anglo-Saxon Church*. CBA, 1986.
Cave, C. J. P. *Roof Bosses in Medieval Churches*. Oxford University Press, 1948.
Chamberlin, E. R. *The English Parish Church*. Hodder & Stoughton, 1993.
Child, M. *Discovering Church Architecture*. Shire, 1976; reprinted 2004.
Child, M. *English Church Architecture: A Visual Guide*. Batsford, 1981.
Clapham, A. *English Romanesque Architecture*. Oxford University Press, 1934.
Clarke, B., and Betjeman, J. *English Churches*. Studio Vista, 1964.
Clifton-Taylor, A. *English Parish Churches as Works of Art*. Batsford, 1975.
Clowney, P. *Exploring Churches*. Lion, 1993.
Cook, G. H. *The English Medieval Parish Church*. Phoenix, 1954.
Cook, G. H. *Medieval Chantries and Chantry Chapels*. Phoenix, 1947.
Cox, J. C. *English Church Fittings and Furniture*. Batsford, 1933.
Cox, J. C. *The English Parish Church*. EP Publishing, 1914 (facsimile.)
Cox, J. C., and Ford, C. B. *Parish Churches of England*. Batsford, 1935.
Crossley, F. H. *English Church Craftsmanship*. Batsford, 1941.
Crossley, F. H. *English Church Design 1040–1540*. Batsford, 1945.
Crossley, F. H. *English Church Monuments*. Batsford, 1921.
Crossley, F. H. *English Church Woodwork and Furniture*. Batsford, 1918.
Cunnington, P. *How Old Is That Church?* Blandford, 1990.
Delderfield, E. R. *Church Furniture*. David & Charles, 1966.
Dirsztay, P. *Church Furnishings*. Routledge & Kegan Paul, 1978.
Esdaile, K. A. *English Church Monuments 1510–1840*. Batsford, 1946.
Fewins, C. *The Church Explorer's Handbook*. The Open Churches Trust/Canterbury Press, 2005.
Fisher, E. A. *Anglo-Saxon Towers*. David & Charles, 1969.
Fisher, E. A. *Greater Anglo-Saxon Churches*. Faber, 1962.
Friar, S. *Companion to the English Parish Church*. Sutton, 1996.
Fryer, A. C. *Wooden Monumental Effigies in England and Wales*. Stock, 1924.
Harbison, R. *The Shell Guide to English Parish Churches*. Andre Deutsch, 1993.
Harries, J., and Hicks, C. *Discovering Stained Glass*. Shire, third edition 1996; reprinted 2006.

Hayman, R. *Church Misericords and Bench Ends*. Shire, 1989; reprinted 2005.

Henderson, C. *Cornish Church Guide*. Bradford Barton, 1964.

Howard, F. G. *Medieval Styles of the English Parish Church*. Batsford, 1936.

Howell, P., and Sutton, I. *Faber Guide to Victorian Churches*. Faber, 1988.

Howkins, C. *Discovering Church Furniture*. Shire, second edition 1980.

Hutton, G., and Smith, E. *English Parish Churches*. Thames & Hudson, 1952.

Jenkins, S. *England's Thousand Best Churches*. Allen Lane Penguin 1999.

Jones, L. E. *The Beauty of English Churches*. Constable, 1978.

Jones, L. E. *County Guide to English Churches*. Countryside, 1992.

Jones, L. E. *Enjoying Historic Churches*. Baker, 1964.

Jones, L. E. *Guide to Some Interesting Old English Churches*. Baker, 1965.

Jones, L. E. *What to See in a Country Church*. Phoenix, 1960.

Jordan, O. *Jordan's Guide to English Churches.* King's England Press, 2000.

Kemp, B. *Church Monuments*. Shire, 1985; reprinted 1997.

Kemp, B. *English Church Monuments*. Batsford, 1981.

Laird, M. *English Misericords*. Murray, 1986.

Lees, H. *Hallowed Ground*. Picton, 1996.

Maude, T. *Guided by a Stonemason*. St Martin's Press, 1997.

Needham, A. *How to Study an Old Church*. Batsford, 1957.

Norfolk County Council. *Guidelines for New Uses for Redundant Churches*. Norfolk County Council, 1978.

Norman, E. R. *The House of God: Church Architecture, Style and History*. Thames & Hudson, 1990.

Nye, T. M. *Parish Church Architecture*. Batsford, 1965.

Pearson, L. F. *Discovering Famous Graves*. Shire, second edition 2004.

Pevsner, N. *Buildings of England* series. Penguin.

Platt, C. *Parish Churches of Medieval England*. Secker & Warburg, 1981.

Pounds, N. *Church Fonts*. Shire, 1995.

Powell, K. *Church Builders of the Twentieth Century*. Academy Editions, 1997.

Randall, G. *The English Parish Church*. Batsford, 1982.

Robinson, J. M. *Treasures of English Parish Churches*. Vintage/Ebury, 1995.

Rouse, E. C. *Medieval Wall Paintings*. Shire, fourth edition 1991; reprinted 2004.

Short, E. *Post War Church Building*. Hollis & Carter, 1947.

Sinden, D. *The English Country Church*. Sidgwick & Jackson, 1988.

Smith, E., and Cook, O. *British Churches*. Dutton Vista, 1964.

Thompson, A. H. *Historical Growth of the English Parish Church*. Cambridge University Press, 1911.

Tracy, C. *English Gothic Choir Stalls 1200–1400*. Boydell, 1990.

Upton, D. *Holy Things and Profane*. Yale University Press, 1997.

Whiffen, M. *Stuart and Georgian Churches*. Batsford, 1947.

Wright, Geoffrey N. *Discovering Epitaphs*. Shire, second edition 1996, reprinted 2004.

# Gazetteer

This list gives a representative selection of each period of church architecture in the respective counties. The key refers to the period of the principal interest in each church. Most frequently this is the fabric in general, although it may sometimes be an exceptional part of the church (such as, for example, a Saxon tower or a decoratively vaulted Early English chancel) which is particularly significant, and which exemplifies the period as a whole.

Abbreviations: D = Decorated. EE = Early English. N = Norman. P = Perpendicular. R = Renaissance and Classical. S = Saxon. Tr = Transitional. V = Victorian.

**Bedfordshire**. Barton-le-Clay (EE). Biggleswade (P). Bletsoe (D). Caddington (S/N). Chalgrave (EE/D). Clapham (S). Dean (EE/D). Eaton Bray (EE). Elstow (N). Felmersham (EE). Luton: St Mary (P). Marston Moretaine (D/P). Milton Bryan (N). Odell (P). Sandy (D). Stagsden (EE/D). Stevington (S). Streatley (D). Sundon (EE/D). Swineshead (D). Toddington (P). Turvey (N). Willington (P). Woburn (V). Wymington (D).

**Berkshire**. Avington (N). Bisham (N). Hamstead Marshall (R). Lambourn (N/P). Newbury (P). Shottesbrooke (D). Upton (N). Warfield (D). Wickham (S/V).

**Buckinghamshire**. Bledlow (EE). Chenies (P). Chetwode (EE). Dorney (R). Fenny Stratford (R). Fingest (N). Gayhurst (R). Haddenham (P). Hanslope (P). Hillesden (P). Ivinghoe (EE). Leckhampstead (Tr). Lillingstone Lovell (N/D). Little Kimble (D). Little Missenden (S). Maids Moreton (P/R). Milton Keynes (D). Newton Longville (Tr). Olney (D). Stewkley (N). Stoke Poges (S/N/EE). Stone (N). Waddesdon (Tr). Willen (R). Wing (S).

**Cambridgeshire**. Alconbury (EE). Balsham (P). Barnack (S). Barrington (EE). Bottisham (D). Buckden (P). Burwell (P). Bury (EE). Castor (N). Cherry Hinton (EE). Chesterton (EE). Conington (P). Elsworth (D). Elton (D). Foxton (EE). Fulbourn (D). Grantchester (D). Great Paxton (S). Great Staughton (EE). Haddenham (EE). Harlton (D). Haslingfield (D). Hemingford Grey (N/EE). Ickleton (N). Isleham (D). Keyston (N). Kirtling (N). Landwade (D). Leighton Bromswold (R). Leverington (D). Little Gidding (R). March (P). Oakington (EE). Old Weston (D). Over (D). Ramsey (N). St Neots (P). Soham (Tr/D). Sutton (D). Trumpington (D). Walsoken (N/EE). Warboys (N). Willingham (D). Wisbech (N). Wittering (S). Yaxley (D/P).

**Cheshire**. Acton (P). Astbury (P). Birtles (V). Bunbury (D/P). Chester: St John (N/EE). Congleton (R). Great Budworth (P). Lower Peover (D/P). Macclesfield (V). Nantwich (D/P). Nether Peover (R). Prestbury (N). Stockport (V). Warrington (D). Winwick (P). Witton (P). Wybunbury (P).

**Cornwall**. Altarnun (N/P). Antony (EE/D). Blisland (N). Bodmin (P). Breage (P). Budock (EE). Callington (P). Crantock (N/EE). Cury (N). Duloe (EE). Egloskerry (N). Falmouth (R). Fowey (D). Germoe (N). Gorran (P). Gunwalloe (N/P). Helston (R). Kilkhampton (N). Ladock (EE). Landewednack (N). Lanreath (P). Lanteglos-by-Fowey (D). Launceston (D/P). Lelant (N). Lostwithiel (D). Morwenstow (N). Mullion (N). Mylor (N/P). Padstow (EE). Penzance (V). Probus (P). St Austell (P). St Breward (N/P). St Buryan (P). St Cleer (P). St Clement (EE/D). St Endellion (S/N). St Enodoc (N/EE). St Ewe (D). St Germans (N). St Ive (D). St Ives (P). St Just-in-Penwith (P). St Mawgan-in-Pydar (EE). St Mellion (D). St Neot (D/P). Talland (EE). Tintagel (N). Veryan (N/D). Zennor (N).

**Cumbria**. Bewcastle (S). Brampton (R). Bridekirk (N/EE). Brigham (D). Brougham (P). Kirkby Lonsdale (N). Kirklinton (N). Lanercost (EE). St Bees (N/EE). Torpenhow (R). Wreay (V).

**Derbyshire**. Ashbourne (EE). Ashover (N). Ault Hucknall (N). Bakewell (S). Carsington (R). Derby: All Saints (P). Eckington (N/R). Ellaston (R). Melbourne (N). Morley (D). Norbury (D). Pleasley (N). Repton (S). Sandiacre (D). Steetley (N). Tideswell (D). Whitwell (N). Wirksworth (S). Youlgreave (N).

**Devon**. Alwington (P). Ashburton (P). Ashprington (P). Ashton (P). Aveton Gifford (EE). Axmouth (N). Babbacombe (V). Bere Ferrers (D/P). Branscombe (N/EE). Braunton (N/EE). Brentor (EE). Bridford (P). Broad Clyst (P). Chittlehampton (P). Colyton (P). Cornworthy (R). Crediton (P). Cruwys Morchard (D/P). Cullompton (P). Harberton (P). Hartland (P). Higher Bickington (R). Holbeton (V). Honeychurch (N). Ipplepen (D/P). Kentisbeare (P). Lapford (P). Manaton (D/P). Molland (R). Ottery St Mary (EE/D). Parracombe (R). Plymtree (P). Sutcombe (P). Swimbridge (P). Tawstock (D). Teignmouth (V). Tiverton (P). Totnes (P). Widecombe in the Moor (P). Wolborough (P). Yealmpton (V).

**Dorset**. Abbotsbury (R). Affpuddle (EE). Beaminster (P). Bere Regis (N). Blandford Forum (R). Bridport (P). Cattistock (V). Cerne Abbas (EE/P). Chalbury (R). Charlton Marshall (R). Charminster (N/P). Church Knowle (EE). Cranborne (P). Dorchester: St Peter (P). Frampton (R). Ibberton (D). Iwerne Minster (Tr). Kingston (V). Lyme Regis (N). Melbury Bubb (S). Moreton (R). Piddletrenthide (P). Portland (R). Powerstock (N). Puddletown (R). Sandford Orcas (EE). Shillingstone (N). Studland (N). Trent (D). Wareham: St Martin (S). Whitchurch Canonicorum (Tr). Whitcombe (EE). Wimborne Minster (N). Winterborne Tomson (N). Winterbourne Steepleton (S). Worth Matravers (N). Yetminster (S).

**Durham**. Aycliffe (S/N). Barnard Castle (Tr). Billingham (S). Brancepeth (R). Darlington (EE/D). Easington (N/EE). Egglescliffe (P). Escomb (S). Gainford (EE). Hartlepool: St Hilda (EE). Haughton-le-Skerne (N). Heighington (N/EE). Jarrow (S/N). Lanchester (Tr/EE). Monkwearmouth (S). Norton (S). Pittington (N). Seaham (S). Sedgefield (R). South Church (EE). Staindrop (S/N/EE). Stockton-on-Tees: St Thomas (R). Sunderland: Holy Trinity (R). West Boldon (EE). Whickham (N/Tr).

**Essex**. Berden (EE). Blackmore (N/D). Bocking (P). Bradwell-on-Sea (S). Brightlingsea (EE/P). Castle Hedingham (Tr). Chelmsford (P). Chipping Ongar (N). Coggeshall (P). Colchester: Holy Trinity (S). Copford (Tr). Dedham (P). Earl's Colne (D). East Horndon (P). Fryerning (P). Great Bromley (D). Great Leighs (N). Great Sampford (D). Greensted (S). Hadleigh (N). High Ongar (N). Ingatestone (P). Ingrave (R). Lambourne End (R). Lawford (D). Layer Marney (P). Little Dunmow (Tr). Little Maplestead (D). Maldon: All Saints (D). Margaretting (P). Pentlow (N). Rainham (N). Rivenhall (V). Saffron Walden (P). Stebbing (D). Thaxted (D/P). Tilty (D). Waltham Abbey (N). West Mersea (S).

**Gloucestershire**. Almondsbury (EE). Ampney Crucis (S/N). Ampney St Mary (N). Berkeley (EE). Beverston (EE). Bibury (S/N). Bishop's Cleeve (N). Bitton (D/P). Buckland (EE). Chedworth (P). Chipping Campden (P). Cirencester (D/P). Cold Aston (P). Daglingworth (S). Daylesford (V). Deerhurst (S). Duntisbourne Rouse (S/N). Elkstone (N). Fairford (P). Great Washbourne (N). Hailes (N). Highnam (V). Kempley (N). Lechlade (P). Leonard Stanley (N). Little Barrington (N). Minchinhampton (D). Newland (EE/D). North Cerney (N). Northleach (P). Oddington (EE). Ozleworth (N). Painswick (R). Somerford Keynes (S). South Cerney (Tr). Stanton (N). Tetbury (R). Thornbury (P). Upleadon (N). Winchcombe (P). Windrush (N). Wotton-under-Edge (EE). Yate (P).

**Hampshire**. Ashmansworth (N). Avington (R). Boarhunt (S). Boldre (EE). Bramley (Tr). Breamore (S). Corhampton (S). Crondall (N). East Meon (N). Easton (N). Hale (R). Hambledon (S/N/EE). Headbourne Worthy (S). Hinton Ampner (S). Hound (EE). Lyndhurst (V). Minstead (R). Petersfield (N). Portchester (N). Ringwood (EE). Selborne (N). Sherborne St John (P). Sopley (EE). South Hayling (D). Southwick (R). Titchfield (S). Warblington (EE). Winchester: St John (Tr); St Peter (Tr). Winchfield (N).

**Herefordshire**. Abbey Dore (N/EE). Aconbury (P). Bosbury (Tr). Brinsop (D). Castle Frome (N). Eardisley (N). Eaton Bishop (D). Ewyas Harold (EE). Garway (N). Hoarwithy (V). Holme Lacy (D). Kilpeck (N). Kingsland (D). Ledbury (N/D). Leominster (N/D). Madley (D). Moccas (N). Monnington on Wye (R). Much Marcle (EE). Orleton (EE). Pembridge (D). Shobdon (R). Tyberton (R). Weobley (D). Weston-under-Penyard (N). Whitbourne (D).

**Hertfordshire**. Abbots Langley (N/D). Anstey (EE/D). Ardeley (P). Ashwell (D). Ayot St Lawrence (R). Ayot St Peter (V). Bishop's Stortford: St Michael (P). Broxbourne (P). Cheshunt (P). Chipping Barnet (P). East Barnet (N). Flamstead (D). Great Amwell (N). Great Offley (EE). Great Wymondley (N). Hemel Hempstead (N). Hitchin (D/P). Monken Hadley

(P/V). Redbourn (N/D). St Albans: St Michael (S/N). St Paul's Walden (D/R). Sandridge (N). South Mimms (P). Totteridge (R/V). Weston (N).

**Kent**. Adisham (EE). Aldington (P). Ashford (P). Barfreston (N). Biddenden (D/P). Birchington (D). Brabourne (N). Charing (D/P). Chartham (D/V). Chiddingstone (R). Cliffe (D). Cobham (EE/R). Cooling (EE/D). Cranbrook (P). Darenth (Tr). Eastry (EE). Elham (EE). Fairfield (R). Faversham (D). Hythe (EE). Ightham (D/P). Ivychurch (D). Kemsing (N). Lenham (EE). Littlebourne (EE). Lullingstone (R). Lydd (D). Maidstone (P). Mereworth (R). Minster-in-Sheppey (S). Minster-in-Thanet (S). New Romney (N/D). Newington (D/P). Northfleet (D). Otford (N). Patrixbourne (N). Penshurst (EE/D). Queenborough (D). St Margaret's at Cliffe (N). St Nicholas at Wade (N). Sandwich (N). Upper Hardres (N/P). Seal (R). Stone (EE). Swanscombe (S). Tenterden (EE/P). Westwell (EE). Wye (R).

**Lancashire**. Barton-upon-Irwell (V). Billinge (R). Great Mitton (EE). Halsall (D). Lancaster (P). Pendlebury (V). Prestwich (D). Rochdale (EE). Sefton (D/P). Slaidburn (R). Standish (P). Whalley (S/EE/P).

**Leicestershire**. Bottesford (D). Breedon-on-the-Hill (S). Claybrooke Parva (D). Gaddesby (D). King's Norton (R). Lubenham (N). Market Harborough (D). Melton Mowbray (D). Stapleford (R). Staunton Harold (R). Stoke Golding (D). Twycross (D).

**Lincolnshire**. Addlethorpe (P). Algarkirk (EE). Alkborough (S). Barton-on-Humber (S/N). Boston (D/P). Bottesford (EE). Brant Broughton (D). Burgh le Marsh (D). Caythorpe (D). Claypole (EE). Corringham (N). Donington (D). Ewerby (D). Folkingham (P). Freiston (N). Gainsborough (R). Gedney (EE/D). Grantham: St Wulfram (N/D). Haltham (EE). Hannah (R). Harlaxton (EE). Heckington (D). Holbeach (D). Hough-on-the-Hill (S). Kirkstead (EE). Kirton-in-Holland (P). Langton-by-Spilsby (R). Long Sutton (N/EE). Louth (D/P). Marston (EE). Middle Rasen (N). Moulton (Tr/P). Navenby (EE). Old Clee (N). Old Leake (D/P). Pickworth (D). Spalding (P). Stamford: All Saints (EE). Stoke Rochford (N). Stow (S/N). Stragglethorpe (S/N). Swaton (EE/D). Tattershall (P). Tealby (N/P). Walesby (EE). Well (R). Weston (N). Whaplode (Tr).

**London: the City of London**. All Hallows Barking (P/R), All Hallows London Wall (R), St Andrew Holborn (R), St Andrew Undershaft (P), St Anne and St Agnes, Gresham Street (R), St Bartholomew-the-Great, Smithfield (N), St Bartholomew-the-Less (P/R), St Benet Paul's Wharf (R), St Botolph Aldersgate (P/R), St Botolph Aldgate (R), St Botolph Bishopsgate (R), St Bride, Fleet Street (R), St Clement Eastcheap (R), St Giles Cripplegate (P), St Helen Bishopsgate (D/P/R), St James Garlickhithe (R), St Katharine Cree (P/R), St Lawrence Jewry (R), St Margaret Lothbury (R), St Margaret Pattens (R), St Martin Ludgate (R), St Mary Abchurch (D/R), St Mary-le-Bow, Cheapside (R), St Mary Woolnoth (R), St Michael Cornhill (R), St Peter upon Cornhill (R), St Sepulchre, Holborn Viaduct (P/V), St Stephen Walbrook (R), St Vedast, Foster Lane (N), Temple Church (N).

**London: Inner**. Bermondsey: St Olave (EE/P). Bethnal Green: St Matthew (R). Bloomsbury: St George (R). Brixton: St Matthew (R). Camberwell: St George (V), St Giles (V). Camden Town: St Michael (V). Charlton: St Luke (R). Chelsea: All Saints (P), Holy Trinity (V), St Luke (R). Clerkenwell: St James (R). Deptford: St Paul (R). East Ham: St Mary Magdalene (N). Greenwich: St Alphege (R). Hackney: St John (V). Hendon: St Mary (N). Holborn: St Giles-in-the-Fields (R). Kensington: St Mary Abbots (V). Kilburn: St Augustine (V). Limehouse: St Anne (R). Marylebone: All Saints (V), All Souls, Langham Place (R), St Mary (R), St Peter (R). Pimlico: St James the Less (V). Shoreditch: St Leonard (R). Southwark: St Magnus (R), St Mary Overie (Southwark Cathedral) (EE/V). Spitalfields: Christ Church (R). St Pancras: St Mary Magdalene (V), St Pancras (R). Stepney: St Dunstan and All Saints (S/EE), St George-in-the-East (R). Vauxhall: St Peter (V). Walworth: St Peter (R). West Norwood: St Luke (R). Westminster: St Clement Danes (R), St James, Piccadilly (R), St John, Smith Square (R), St Martin-in-the-Fields (R/V), St Mary-le-Strand (R), St Paul, Covent Garden (R).

**Middlesex.** Cowley (D). Cranford (P/R). Enfield (P). Friern Barnet (N). Greenford (R). Harrow-on-the-Hill (N/EE/D). Hayes (P). Isleworth (V). Sunbury-on-Thames (R). Whitchurch (R).

**Norfolk**. Attleborough (D). Aylsham (D). Barton Turf (P). Beeston (D). Bessingham (S). Binham (N). Burnham Deepdale (S). Burnham Norton (S/N/P). Castle Acre (EE/P). Castle Rising (N). Cawston (P). Cley-next-the-Sea (D). Cromer (P). Dereham (EE/D). Elsing (D). Glandford (V). Gooderstone (D/P). Great Dunham (N). Great Walsingham (EE/D). Great Yarmouth (Tr). Haddiscoe (S). Hales (N). Happisburgh (P). Hunstanton (R). King's Lynn: St Nicholas (P). Little Snoring (N). Ludham (D). Necton (P). North Creake (P). North Elmham (EE/P). North Walsham (P). Northwold (EE). Norwich: St Peter Mancroft (P). Oxborough (R). Potter Heigham (N). Rougham (N). Salle (P). Salthouse (P). Snettisham (D). South Creake (P). South Lopham (N). Swaffham (D/P). Terrington St Clement (P). Tilney All Saints (N/P). Trunch (N/P). Walpole St Peter (P). West Walton (EE). Weybourne (S). Winterton (P). Worstead (P). Wymondham (N).

**Northamptonshire**. Aldwincle (P). Aynho (R). Brixworth (S). Cottesbrooke (R). Crick (D). Earls Barton (S). Easton-on-the-Hill (P). Finedon (D). Fotheringhay (P). Great Brington (EE). Higham Ferrers (D). Kettering (P). King's Sutton (D/P). Kingsthorpe (N). Lowick (P). Middleton Cheney (D). Northampton: St Peter (N). Oundle (D/P). Passenham (R). Polebrook (Tr). Raunds (EE/D). Rothwell (Tr/EE). Rushden (P). Strixton (EE). Titchmarsh (P). Warmington (EE/D). Whiston (P). Woodford (N/EE).

**Northumberland**. Alnwick (P). Bamburgh (EE). Berwick-upon-Tweed: Holy Trinity (R). Bolam (S). Bywell (S). Corbridge (S). Doddington (EE). Edlingham (N). Haltwhistle (EE). Heddon-on-the-Wall (N). Hexham (S/EE). Newcastle upon Tyne: All Saints (R); St Thomas (R). Norham (N). Ovingham (S/EE). Seaton Delaval (N). Warden (S/N). Warkworth (N).

**Nottinghamshire**. Blidworth (R). Blyth (N). Bunny (D/P). Carlton in Lindrick (S/N). Clifton (N). Clumber (V). East Markham (P). Hawton (D). Laneham (N). Newark-on-Trent: St Mary (D/P). Normanton on Soar (EE). Ossington (R). Plumtree (N/EE). South Collingham (N). South Scarle (N). Woodborough (D). Worksop (N).

**Oxfordshire**. Abingdon: St Helen (EE), St Nicholas (N). Adderbury (D). Asthall (Tr). Bampton (Tr/EE). Blewbury (N/P). Bloxham (D/P). Broughton (D). Burford (N). Buscot (Tr). Caversfield (S). Checkendon (N). Chinnor (D). Chipping Norton (D/P). Chislehampton (R). Cholsey (N/EE). Church Hanborough (N). Cogges (D). Compton Beauchamp (EE). Crowmarsh Gifford (N). Cuddesdon (Tr). Dorchester-on-Thames (Tr/D). Ewelme (P). Faringdon (Tr/EE). Goring (N). Great Haseley (Tr/D). Great Milton (D). Great Rollright (N). Hanwell (D). Henley-on-Thames (P). Horley (N). Iffley (N). Islip (R). Kidlington (EE/D). Langford (Tr). Lewknor (R). Minster Lovell (P). North Leigh (S). North Moreton (D). Oxford: St Michael (S). Rycote (R). Shipton-under-Wychwood (EE). Shorthampton (EE). Shrivenham (R). South Newington (N/EE). Sparsholt (D). Stanton Harcourt (EE). Steventon (D). Sutton Courtenay (N/EE). Swinbrook (D/P). Thame (EE/D/P). Uffington (EE). Wallingford: St Leonard (N), St Peter (R). Widford (N/EE). Witney (EE/D). Yarnton (P).

**Rutland**. Ashwell (D). Brooke (N). Clipsham (N). Cottesmere (N/EE). Edith Weston (N). Empingham (EE/D). Exton (D). Greetham (EE/D). Hambleton (N/EE). Ketton (N/D). Langham (EE/D/P). Little Casterton (EE). Lyddington (P). Manton (EE). Market Overton (D). Morcott (N). Normanton (R). North Luffenham (EE/D). Oakham (D). Preston (N). South Luffenham (EE). Stoke Dry (EE/D). Stretton (N/EE). Teigh (R). Tickencote (N). Tixover (N). Upper Hambleton (D). Uppingham (D). Whissendine (D/P). Wing (N).

**Shropshire**. Acton Burnell (EE). Bromfield (EE). Burford (P). Church Stretton (D). Claverley (N). Cleobury Mortimer (N). Clun (N). Cold Weston (N). Ellesmere (P). Heath Chapel (N). Langley (P). Llanyblodwel (V). Ludlow (D/P). Lydbury North (EE). Melverley (D). Minsterley (R). Shifnal (N). Shrewsbury: St Mary (Tr/EE). Tong (P). Worfield (D).

**Somerset**. Axbridge (P). Batcombe (P). Bishop's Lydeard (P). Brent Knoll (P). Bridgwater (D). Bruton (P). Brympton d'Evercy (D/P). Cameley (N). Chewton Mendip (P). Clevedon (Tr). Compton Martin (N). Crewkerne (P). Croscombe (R). Culbone (S/N/D). Curry Rivel (P). Doulting (D). Dundry (P). Dunster (D/P). East Brent (D/P). Evercreech (P). Glastonbury (P). Goathurst (D/P). High Ham (P). Huish Episcopi (D/P). Ilminster (P). Isle Abbotts (D/P). Kingsbury Episcopi (D). Kingston St Mary (D). Leigh upon Mendip (P). Lullington (N). Martock (P). Mells (P). Muchelney (P). North Cadbury (P). North Petherton (P). Oare (R).

Queen Camel (D). Selworthy (P). Shepton Mallet (EE). Somerton (EE/D). Stogumber (P). Stogursey (N). Stoke sub Hamdon (N). Swell (P). Taunton: St Mary (P). Trull (P). Wedmore (P). Wells: St Cuthbert (P). Westonzoyland (P). Wrington (D/P). Yatton (P). Yeovil (P).

**Staffordshire.** Alstonefield (N). Ashley (V). Audley (D). Barton-under-Needwood (P). Broughton (R). Cheadle (V). Checkley (D). Clifton Campville (D). Denstone (V). Eccleshall (EE). Hoar Cross (V). Ingestre (R). Penkridge (D). Stafford: St Chad (N); St Mary (D). Tamworth (D). Tutbury (N).

**Suffolk.** Acton (EE). Beccles (P). Blythburgh (P). Boxted (R). Bramfield (D). Bungay (P). Bury St Edmunds: St Mary (P). Cavendish (D). Clare (P). Denston (P). Earl Stonham (P). Euston (R). Eye (P). Framlingham (P). Fressingfield (D). Hadleigh (P). Hessett (P). Icklingham (D). Kersey (D). Lavenham (D/P). Long Melford (P). Lowestoft (P). Mildenhall (D). Needham Market (P). Polstead (N). Rattlesden (P). Stoke-by-Nayland (D). Stowmarket (D). Sudbury (P). Thornham Parva (S/N). Ufford (N/P). Wingfield (P). Woodbridge (P). Woolpit (D/P).

**Surrey.** Albury (S/N). Beddington (P). Carshalton (R). Chiddingfold (EE). Compton (N). Crowhurst (N). Croydon: St Michael and All Angels (V). Dunsfold (EE/D). Esher (R). Gatton (V). Great Bookham (D). Hascombe (V). Lingfield (P). Morden (R). Ockham (EE). Pyrford (N). St Martha on the Hill (N). Shere (N). Stoke d'Abernon (N/EE). West Horsley (S/N).

**Sussex.** Amberley (N). Apuldram (EE). Arundel (D/P). Ashburnham (P). Battle (Tr). Bishopstone (S/N). Bosham (S/EE). Burpham (Tr/P). Buxted (D). Clayton (S/N). Climping (N/EE). Coombes (N). Cuckfield (P). Didling (EE). Eastbourne (Tr). Etchingham (D). Friston (N). Glynde (R). Hardham (N). Heathfield (D). Herstmonceux (D/P). Lullington (EE). Mayfield (N). New Shoreham (Tr). Old Shoreham (N). Pagham (Tr). Pevensey (EE). Playden (N). Poynings (P). Pulborough (P). Rodmell (EE). Rye (N/EE). Sompting (S). South Harting (EE). South Malling (R). Steyning (N). Tangmere (EE). West Hoathly (EE/D). West Itchenor (EE). Winchelsea (D/P). Wisborough Green (EE). Wiston (D). Worth (S/N).

**Warwickshire.** Astley (D). Baddesley Clinton (R). Berkswell (N). Bilton (D). Birmingham: St Paul (R). Coleshill (P). Dunchurch (D). Hampton Lucy (R). King's Norton (P). Knowle (P). Lapworth (P). Lower Brailes (D). Lower Shuckburgh (V). Northfield (EE). Stoneleigh (N). Stratford-upon-Avon (EE/D/P). Tysoe (D). Wappenbury (EE). Warwick: St Mary (P). Wootton Wawen (S). Yardley (P).

**Wiltshire.** Alton Barnes (S). Amesbury (EE/D). Avebury (S). Bishops Cannings (EE). Bishopstone (near Salisbury) (D). Bradford-on-Avon: St Lawrence (S). Broad Hinton (EE). Codford St Peter (S). Corsham (N). Cricklade: St Sampson (EE/D/P). Devizes: St John (N); St Mary (N). Downton (D). Edington (D/P). Farley (R). Great Bedwyn (Tr/P). Hardenhuish (R). Hullavington (N). Inglesham (S/EE). Lacock (D/P). Lydiard Tregoze (R). Malmesbury (N). Marlborough: St Peter (R). Mere (P). Mildenhall (R). Netheravon (EE). Potterne (EE). Preshute (N). Purton (EE/P). Salisbury: St Thomas (P). Stanton Fitzwarren (N). Stapleford (N). Steeple Ashton (P). Swindon: St Mark (V). Tisbury (N). Trowbridge (P). Wilton (V).

**Worcestershire.** Astley (N). Beckford (N). Bewdley (R). Bockleton (N/EE). Bredon (N). Bretforton (Tr). Broadway (N/Tr). Bromsgrove (EE). Chaddesley Corbett (Tr). Dormston (P). Earl's Croome (N). Eckington (EE/D). Evesham: All Saints (P); St Lawrence (P). Feckenham (EE). Great Witley (N). Halesowen (N/P). Hanley Castle (R). Hartlebury (V). Holt (N). Kidderminster (P). Kinnersley (D). Martley (N/P). Pedmore (N). Pirton (N). Rochford (N). Rock (N). Shrawley (N). Stourbridge: St Thomas (R). Worcester: All Saints (R).

**Yorkshire.** Adel (N). Arksey (N). Barton-le-Street (N). Bedale (EE). Beeford (P). Beverley: St Mary (P). Bingley (V). Birkin (N). Cawood (EE). Cottingham (P). Coxwold (P/R). Ecclesfield (P). Fewston (N). Fishlake (Tr). Goodmanham (N). Grosmont (EE). Hedon (P). Hemingbrough (N/EE/P). Kirkburn (N). Knaresborough (D). Lastingham (N). Ledsham (S). Masham (P). North Newbald (N). Northallerton (EE). Patrington (D). Raskelf (V). Ravenfield (R). Riccall (EE). Rossington (N). Rotherham (P). Scarborough (V). Skipton (P). Studley Royal (V). Tadcaster (P). Thirsk (P). Thorpe Salvin (N). Tickhill (N). Wadworth (D). Wawne (P). Whitby (R).

# Index of churches

*Page numbers in italic refer to illustrations.*

# Index of persons

# General index